CREATIVE PHOTO EDITING

14 LESSONS TO TRANSFORM PHOTOS INTO ART

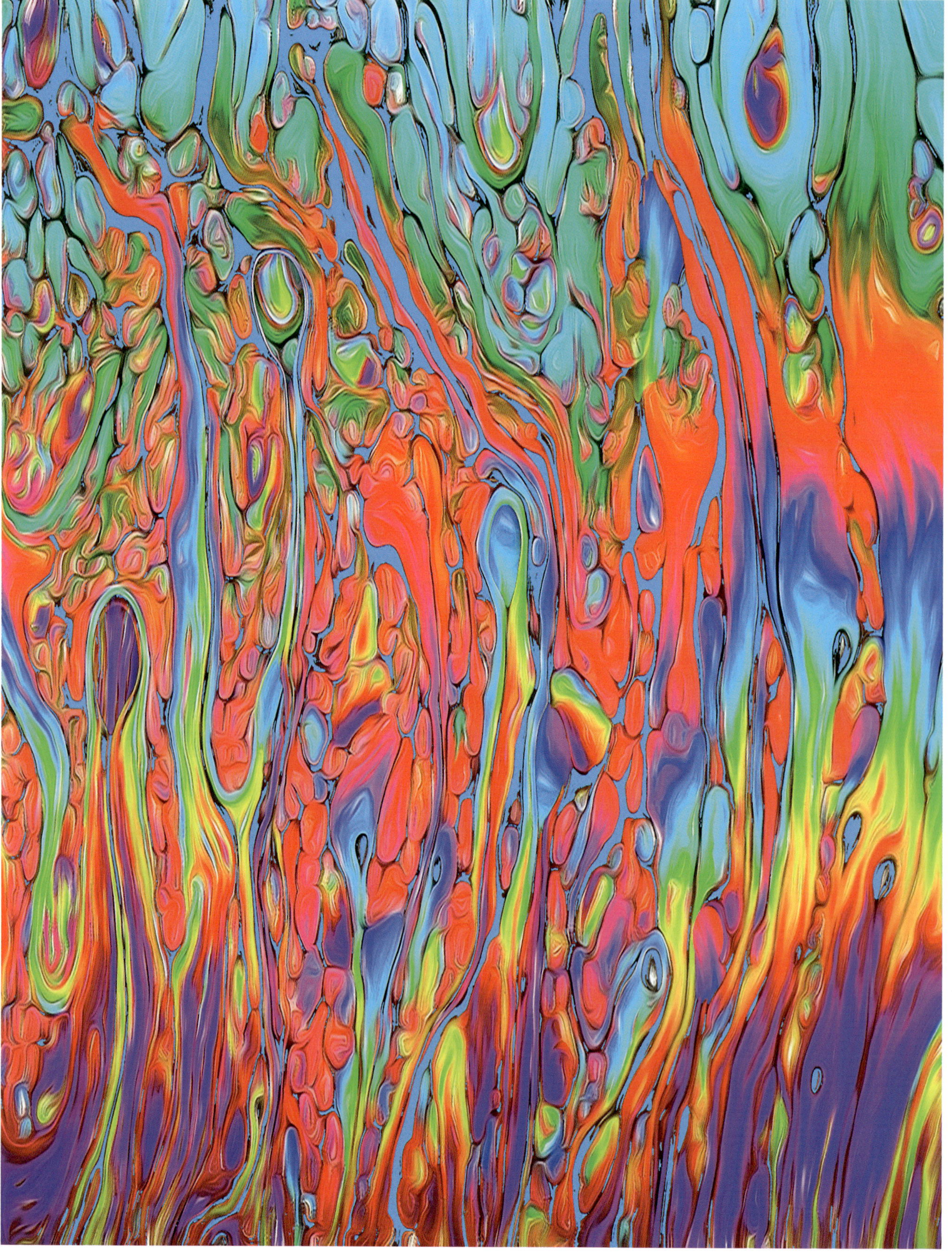

John Humphrey

CREATIVE PHOTO EDITING

14 LESSONS TO TRANSFORM PHOTOS INTO ART

THE CROWOOD PRESS

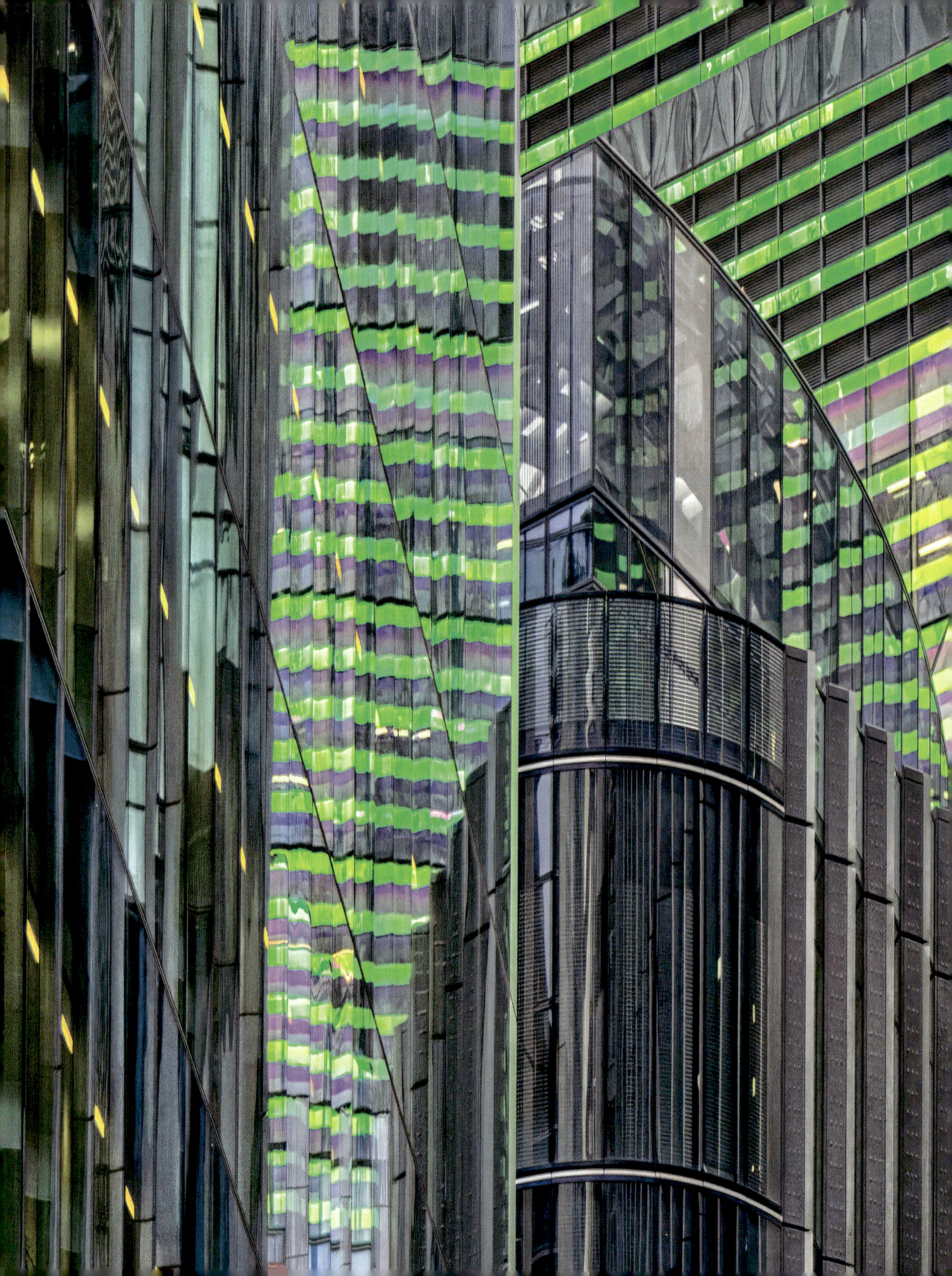

CONTENTS

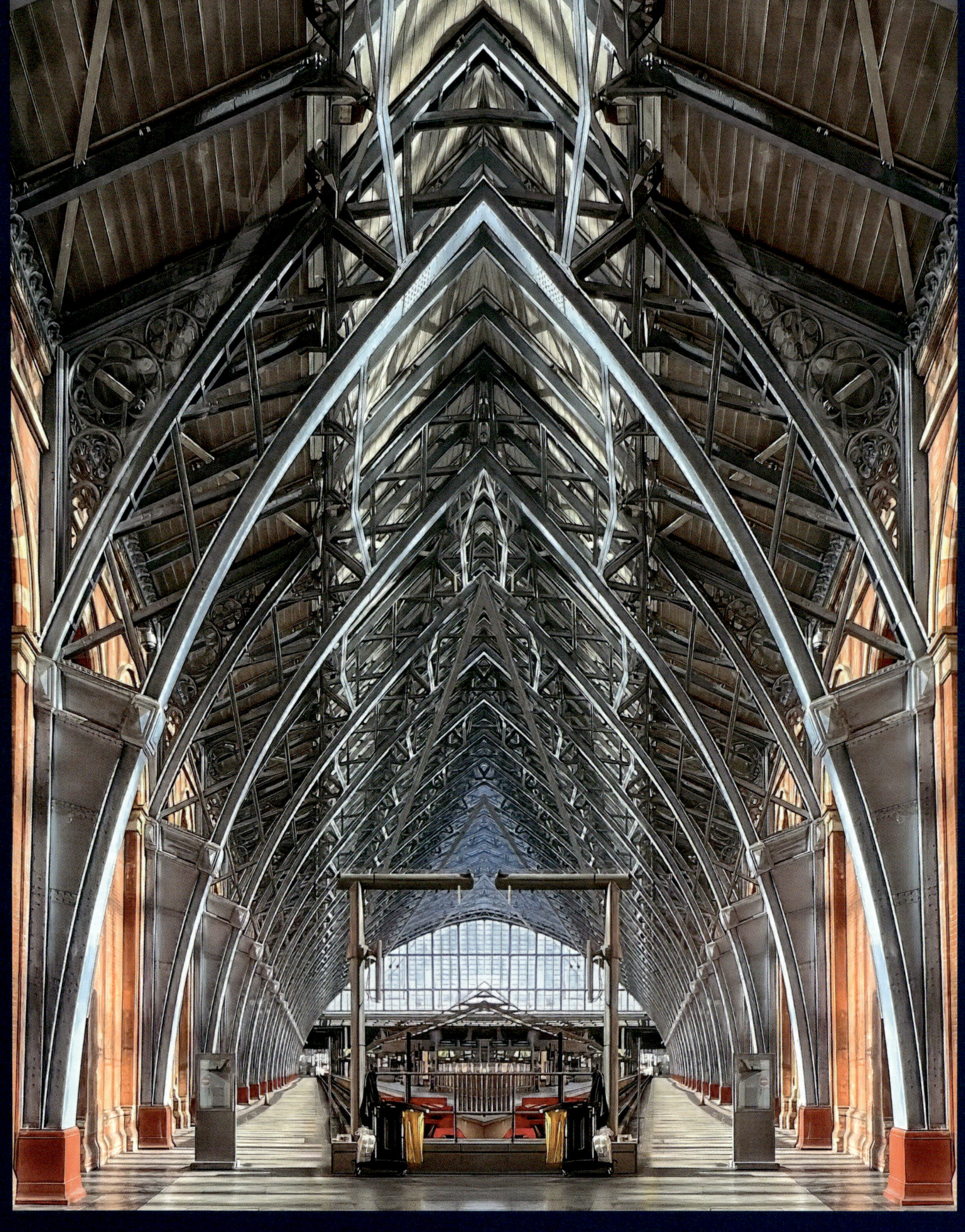

INTRODUCTION

The Internet informs us that five billion photographs are taken every day – 57,000 per second! This huge number is driven by the inclusion of cameras in smartphones, with phone pictures accounting for more than 90% of all of those taken. Many of these pictures are taken to record holidays, special occasions and families. They might be shared briefly with friends, often by showing them on the phone screen. Some find their way to social media where they may be appreciated or ignored.

This book is designed to show that these pictures could have another life. Armed with some techniques that can be used at the time of taking, or by making digital adjustments, we can take a relatively ordinary photograph and transform it into a striking artwork.

Photography is a unique and universal form of art. It does not require expensive equipment or formal training. It enables us to recapture the creativity we had as children. Now that most photography has become digital, we can afford to experiment and to develop our own style.

I have aimed to set out in fourteen 'Lessons' some approaches to producing pictures from photographs that are distinctive and personal. The Lessons set out the steps to produce the illustrated examples. However, they are not the end of the story. Once you find an approach that works for you, do add variations of your own. You will find beauty in the mundane and turn ordinary into extraordinary. I wish you well on that creative journey.

John Humphrey

FACING PAGE
Fig 0.3 **A section of London's St Pancras Station, mirrored as described in Lesson 11 to create a symmetrical image.**

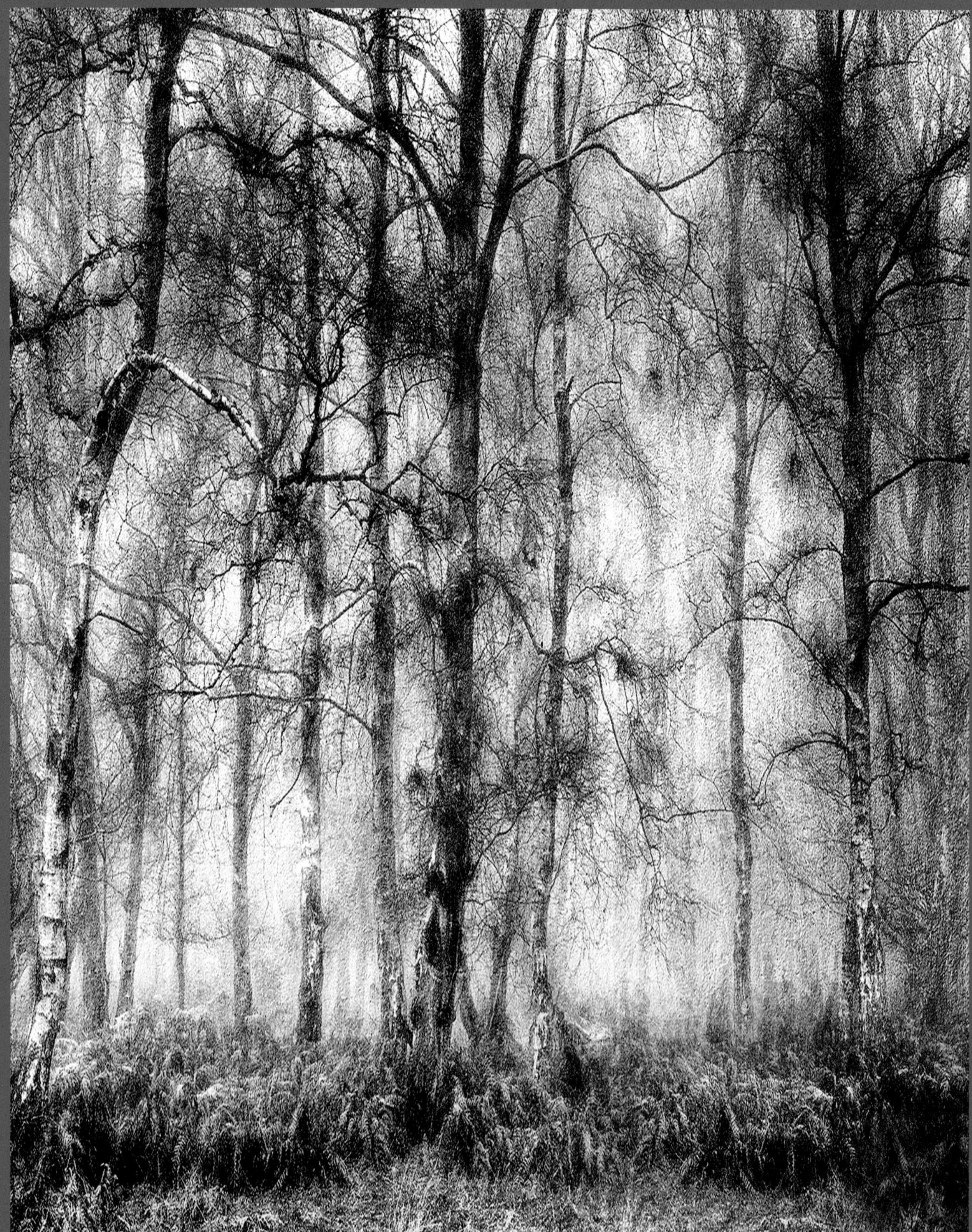

GETTING STARTED

The journey of a thousand miles begins with the first step
LAO TZU

Photography projects can feel daunting. Camera settings seem ever more complicated, with impenetrable menus and submenus. Image-processing software offers thousands of options with mystifying terms. Before pictures can be saved, decisions must be made about their resolution, aspect ratio and file format. And then there is 'impostor syndrome', in which we question whether our pictures are any good anyway.

I urge you to press on regardless. Mistakes in digital photography are easy to undo, and nothing will be broken. Transforming photographs is creatively liberating and shows that we can all be artists. The Lessons in this book offer ideas and techniques to get things underway. I hope that some of them will prompt further experimenting and will help with the development of your own personal style.

FACING PAGE
Fig 0.4 **A wintry wood scene converted to black and white as in Lesson 1 to emphasise the feeling of coldness, and with noise texture added as described in Lesson 3.**

STARTING PICTURES

It is often said that, if you are going to make digital changes to a picture, you must have a good picture to start with. Don't believe it! One of the pleasures of the photography transformations described in this book is that they can often rescue pictures that simply didn't work first time round. There are several reasons for thinking that a photograph is not up to scratch:

- The composition doesn't work.
- Focus is in the wrong place.
- The image is too dark or too light.
- The camera or the subject moved.
- Image resolution is too low.
- The picture is boring.

However, somewhere in these failed pictures there is likely to be an opportunity for creative manipulation. One of the pleasures of finding transformation techniques that suit your personal style is to revisit the hundreds of pictures sitting neglected on your hard disk, and to realise that they can have a new life.

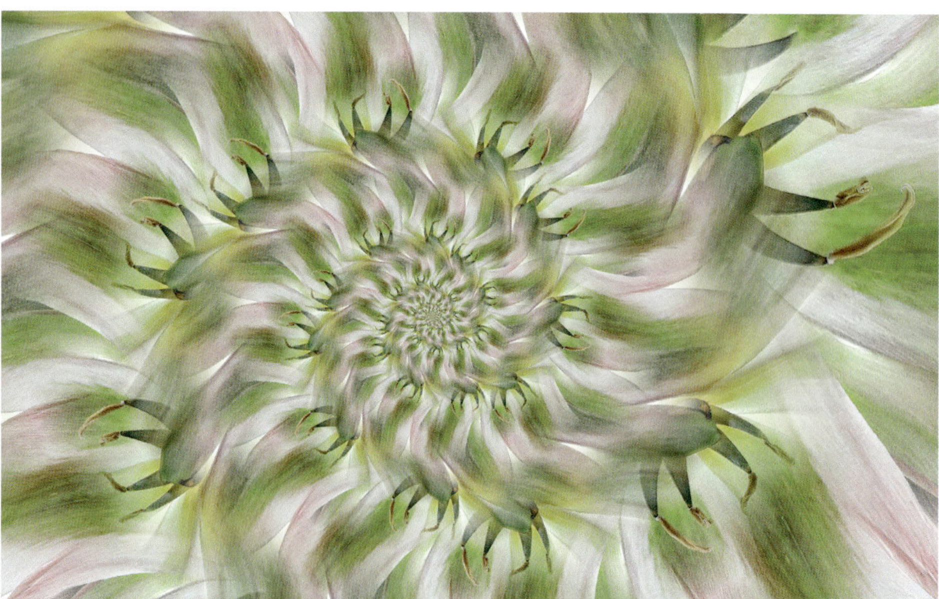

Fig 0.5 **The starting picture was of a tulip past its best, but the colour and texture were well suited to conversion to a continuous spiral using the Droste treatment described in Lesson 14.**

Of course, not every picture conceals a hidden masterpiece. But the flaws noted above might well be capable of correction and may even present some advantages and opportunities.

Composition can often be corrected by cropping in to a more balanced section of the picture. Concern that this might result in an image that has too low a resolution is understandable but might be resolved by upsizing the picture, possibly using software specially designed for the purpose. This is considered in Lesson 13. It is also possible that a lower resolution might be advantageous if the intention is to apply artistic software filters to the image. Many of the techniques set out in this book are more effective with low-resolution images. Composition problems can be a result of lines that should be vertical or horizontal being on a slope, the most common example being a sloping horizon. This is usually straightforward to correct in software, albeit with a little loss of the edges of the picture.

Focus is less of a challenge than it once was now that virtually all cameras incorporate autofocusing, and cameras with small sensors – such as smartphone cameras – have a wide depth of field, which results in most of the scene being in focus. However, it is still possible that the autofocus has picked the wrong part of the image, and the desirable part is blurry. Again, software, often using artificial intelligence, might come to the rescue. This won't work miracles, so an out-of-focus section that nevertheless has promising shapes and colours could be worth treating with software filters, maybe to convert into an abstract.

Over- and underexposure resulting in loss of detail in the highlights or shadows might again be capable of rescue in software. This is particularly the case for dark shadows which, by adjustment in the levels or curves settings in software, may reveal surprising levels of detail. Loss of detail in light areas, described as burned-out highlights, can be more difficult to resolve and is one reason for taking pictures in RAW format. RAW is the

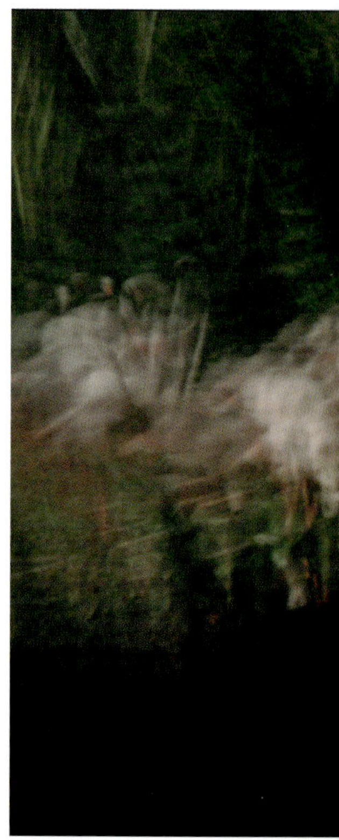

file format that contains unprocessed image data from a digital camera and, in a RAW editor, offers the best chance of retrieving the full subject detail. If all else fails, can the exposure limitations be turned to advantage? Maybe the overexposed picture has potential as a high-key or minimalist image, and the underexposed picture could be dark, atmospheric and moody.

Movement of the camera or subject is a familiar experience. If the camera is handheld, as is usually the case, then there is almost sure to be some blurring from camera shake. For most pictures this is not noticeable because either the shutter speed is sufficiently fast to minimise any blur, or because anti-shake control in the camera reduces the effect. As with the focus challenge, it is possible to make some level of correction in software. Failing that, it is possible that the movement blur has pictorial potential that can be exploited to artistic advantage, as in Figure 0.6.

Image resolution is an interesting challenge and is discussed in several of the Lessons. Low resolution might be the result of the camera being set for recording low-res pictures, probably to enable more pictures to be saved on the SIM card, or so that pictures can be readily transferred by Wi-Fi or email. It will also result from images being cropped to remove unwanted areas. Once again, software might bring the resolution up to the desired size for printing or projecting, but possibly without the desired sharp clarity. However, high resolution is often not needed for artistic, particularly abstract, pictures. And if the intention is to apply digital filters, the low resolution might well be an advantage.

Boring pictures abound! Our own photographs generally don't bore us. They take us back to memorable events or beautiful places. But they will not have the same appeal to others, and we may need a critical friend, or perhaps a camera-club judge, to give an objective opinion. The purpose of this book is to re-examine those pictures for their artistic potential.

Fig 0.6 **The picture of flamingos at night was unacceptable because of motion blur resulting from movement of the birds and the camera. However, a cropped and adjusted area delivered an impressionistic image of the scene.**

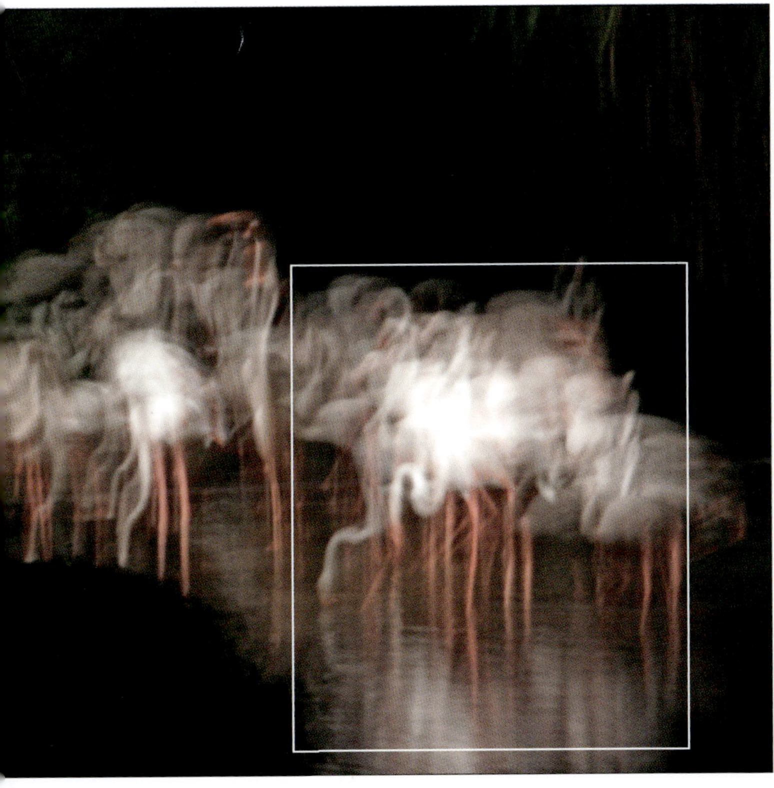

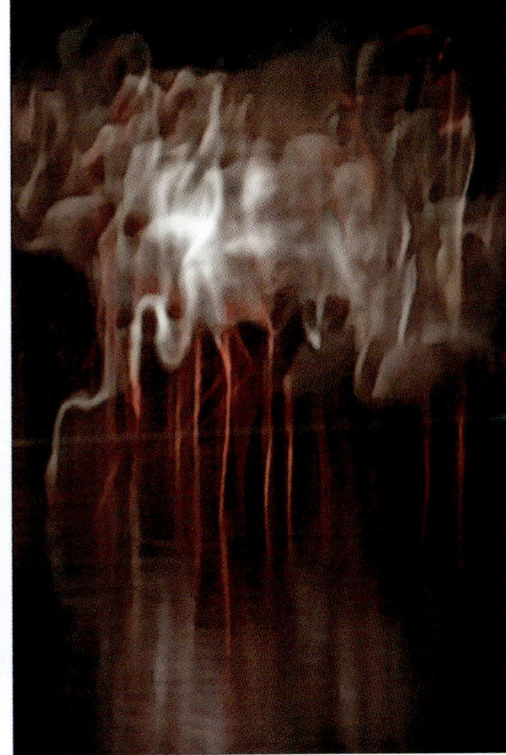

SOFTWARE

The 1990s saw the emergence of photo-editing software to accompany the launch of consumer digital cameras. Photoshop 1.0 was followed by CorelDRAW and PaintShop Pro. In the 2000s, the use of digital photography overtook film, and the software developed rapidly. Programs now include Adobe Lightroom, Photoshop Elements, GIMP, Capture One Pro, Luminar AI, DxO PhotoLab, ON1 Photo RAW and PhotoScape X. To add further choice (and complication), there is also a range of supplementary imaging software for specific tasks. These can be stand-alone programs or plug-ins that can be accessed from the mainstream software. They include the Nik Collection, Topaz Photo AI, Retouch4me, Alien Skin Eye Candy, the AKVIS suite and Luminar Neo.

It would be unrealistic to present the steps to a particular transformation using every available software package. So the convention in this book will be based on Photoshop, the most widely used imaging program. However, the tools in Photoshop that are described here are available in most photo software. For software other than Photoshop, it is worth checking out the way to access them.

Setup

The opening page of much software, Photoshop included, can at first look bewilderingly complicated. The usual default is to have the toolbar visible on the left, selected panels on the right, the main menu at the top and the options bar underneath the main menu.

The **toolbar** is generally a fixed vertical strip and gives tools for selection, cropping, retouching and so on. Some tools have sub-tools that can be accessed by right-clicking.

The **panels** can be chosen to suit and include Color, Brush settings and Gradients. In Figure 0.7 the top panel is the Layers panel and underneath is the History panel. These panels can be moved, resized or grouped.

The **menu** bar at the very top of the screen contains drop-down menus like File, Edit, Image, Layer, Select, Filter, View, Window and Help.

The **options** bar displays options for the currently selected tool, such as the brush size for the Brush tool.

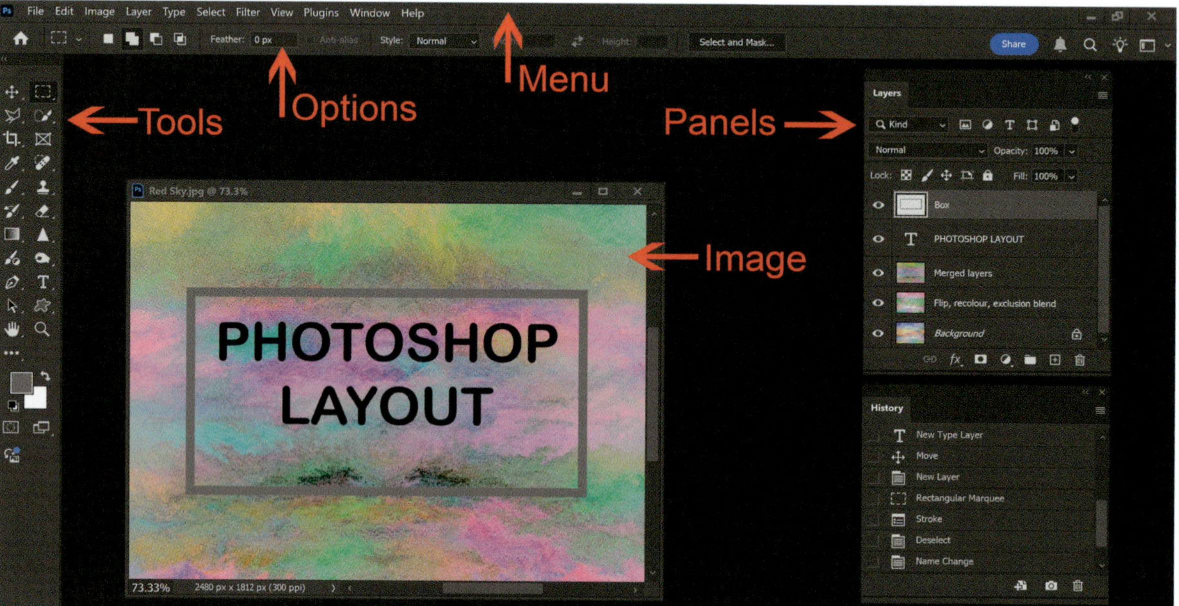

Fig 0.7 **The basic Photoshop screen showing the terminology used in this book, with panels open for Layers and History.**

KEY TOOLS

Despite the variety of software available for image manipulation, certain tools and settings are common to most packages and are used in these Lessons. They are summarised here and described in more detail for each transformation.

Histogram

The histogram is a graphical representation of the tonal values in an image. It shows the brightness levels (tones) of the image and is a key tool for understanding and adjusting the exposure and contrast of a photo. The horizontal axis represents the tonal range divided into 256 levels. The vertical axis represents the number of pixels at each tonal value. In Photoshop it is accessed through Levels (Image > Adjustments > Levels) or Curves (Image > Adjustments > Curves). The histogram can be adjusted by moving the sliders in these tools; for example, moving the middle slider in Levels to the left lightens the overall image.

Filters

Filters are the tools used to apply special effects or modify images for creativity or correction. They can add textures, blur an image in a range of ways, sharpen edges or produce artistic effects. Filters are shown as drop-down options from the Filter menu, and they can be applied to an entire layer or a selection of the picture.

Layers

Layers are a key feature of creative photo-editing software. They enable images to be constructed and edited non-destructively. Layers are like transparent sheets stacked on top of each other, each with different elements of the image. The contents of a layer can be adjusted independently without affecting other layers. Crucially, the way in which layers combine with each other can be managed, for example by changing the opacity of a layer, or by using layer blend modes. Blend modes are described within the relevant Lessons.

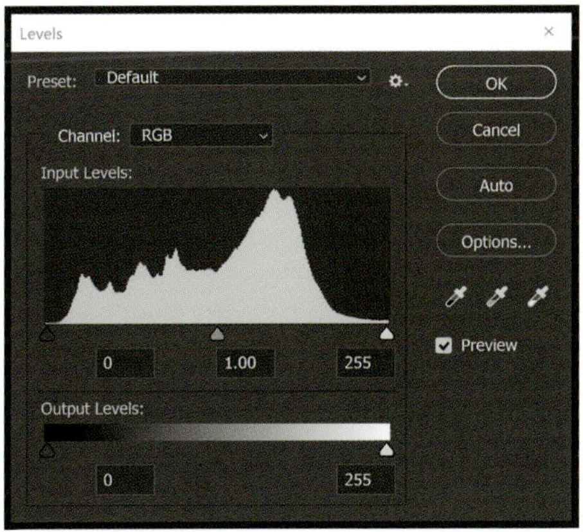

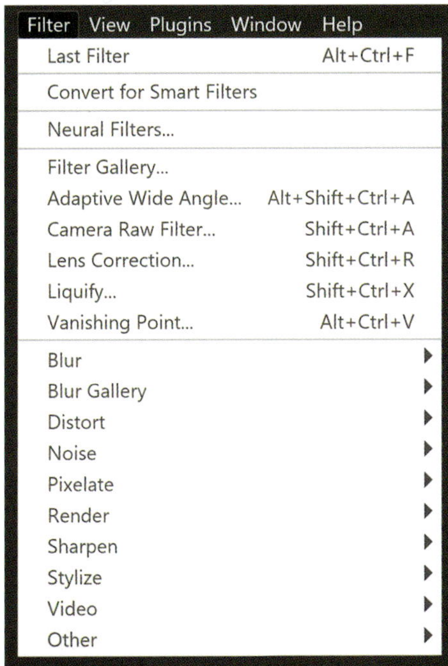

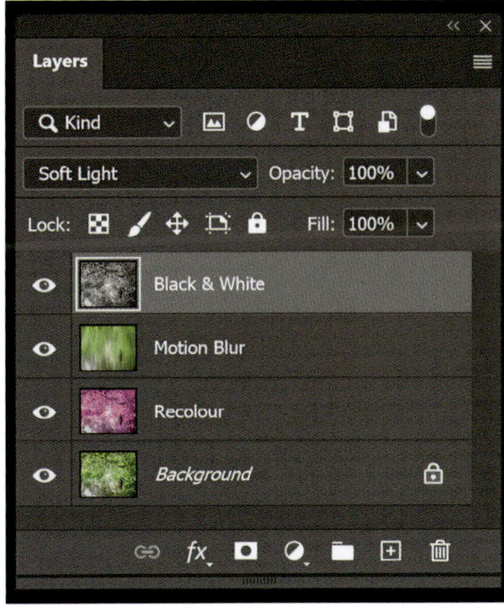

TOP RIGHT
Fig 0.8 **The Levels histogram showing a gradation of tones from black to white.**

MIDDLE RIGHT
Fig 0.9 **The main Filter menu in Photoshop. Each of the lower options offers a further drop-down menu of alternatives.**

RIGHT
Fig 0.10 **A Photoshop Layers panel showing a starting picture that has been progressively recoloured, blurred and converted to black and white. The top layer has been blended with the blurred layer using the soft light blend mode.**

Hue and Saturation

Artistic transformation of photographs often involves adjustments to the image colour and saturation. In Photoshop the tool is in the image adjustments set (Image > Adjustments > Hue/ Saturation). This offers three sliders. The top slider changes the colour distribution of the picture and can alter all the image colours, or a single colour selected in the drop-down menu. Sometimes it is not clear which named colour is the one to be changed, in which case clicking on the colour will reset the selection to that exact hue. It is worth noting that dragging this slider fully either right or left will convert colours to their complementary colours. This tool can also be used for toning the image by clicking the Colorize box and using the slider to pick the tone colour. The middle slider changes saturation. Sliding right increases saturation and sliding left decreases it. The bottom slider makes the image darker or lighter in a similar way to the middle slider in the Levels setting.

Selections

It is often necessary to make image transformations to only one part of a picture. To achieve this, a selection must be made. Only the content within the selection will then be affected by image adjustments. Photoshop automates the process for some selections and has dedicated tools for selecting skies and for selecting the main subject in a picture. These are options under the Select drop-down menu. For manual control of the process, selection tools are grouped in three sets towards the top of the Photoshop toolbar. Right-click on any selection box to see the options. Key selection tools are:

Rectangular and elliptical marquee tools. Click and drag to make the selection. Hold Shift while dragging to constrain proportions (perfect squares or circles) and hold Alt or Option to draw from the centre outward.

Lasso Tools. These are freehand selections. The Polygonal Lasso creates straight-edged selections, and the Magnetic Lasso automatically snaps to edges in the image.

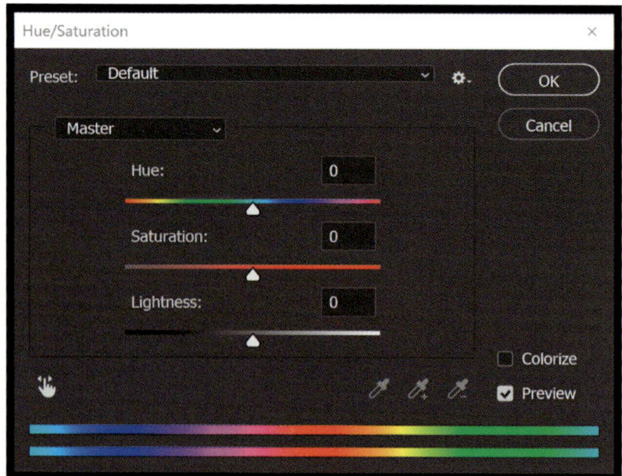

Fig 0.11 **Photoshop's hue and saturation controls. Sliders allow for independent control of image colour, saturation and lightness. With the preview box ticked, the effect of the adjustments can be viewed as they are made.**

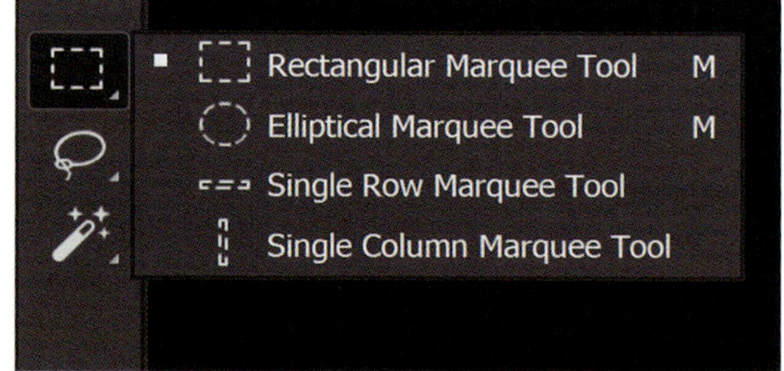

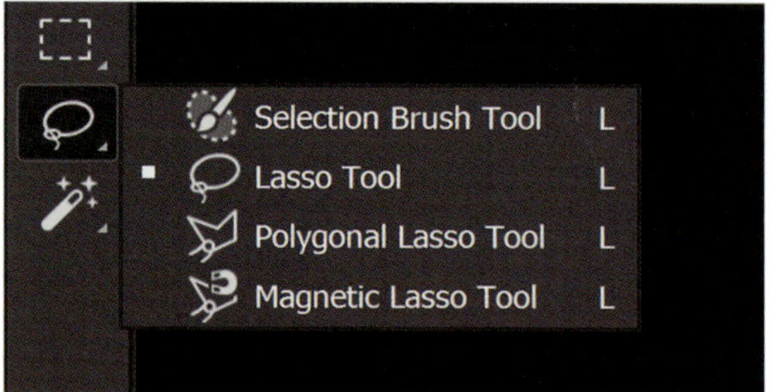

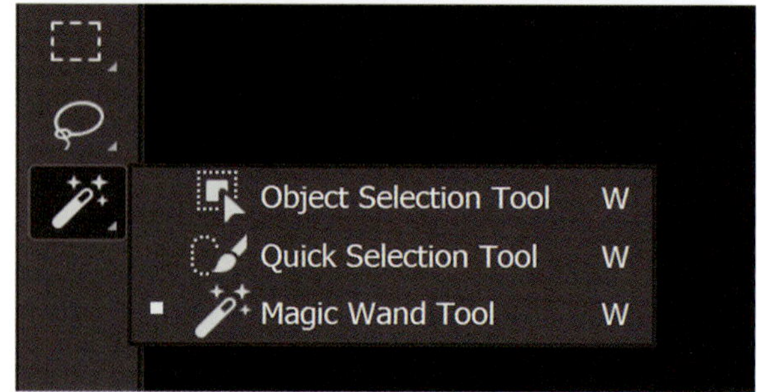

Fig 0.12 **The main image-selection options in Photoshop. Each of the three main boxes offer drop-down selections, giving eleven tools in total. The letters M, L and W beside the tools show the keyboard shortcuts.**

Quick Selection Tool. When brushed over an area to be selected, this tool detects edges automatically.

Magic Wand Tool. This selects areas of similar colour. The Tolerance setting in the Options bar controls how much colour variation is selected.

The **Select and Mask** box appears in the Options bar when a selection tool is active. This allows the selection to be fine-tuned and, for example, enables the selection edges to be feathered. This is often important to hide the selection edges once the image adjustments have been made.

A **View Mode** such as Overlay and On Black can be chosen to see the selection clearly.

KEYBOARD SHORTCUTS

In this book, the route to the various tools and techniques is described using the Photoshop menu system since this shows the location of each control option. However, for regular use of tools it is worth becoming familiar with keyboard shortcuts that bypass the menus. There are hundreds of such shortcuts, so for particular tasks it is worth an internet search to see if a quick keyboard route is available. Table 1 shows the shortcuts for the main tools described in the Lessons.

This of course is not a comprehensive guide to every aspect of photography software. However, it introduces the main tools used in the transformations in this book and will be a starting point in exploring the endless byways of modern imaging programs. Keep exploring and experimenting to find the steps that lead to your own personal style.

Table 1
Photoshop Keyboard Shortcuts

Effect	Windows	Mac
Free transform (for selections or layers above the background)	Control + T	Command + T
Increase/decrease brush size	] [	] [
Increase/decrease brush hardness	} {	} {
Default (black/white) foreground/background colours	D	D
Switch foreground/background colours	X	X
Invert (negative)	Control + I	Command + I
Levels	Control + L	Command + L
Curves	Control + M	Command + M
Hue/saturation	Control + U	Command + U
New layer via copy	Control + J	Command + J
Merge visible while retaining original layers	Alt + Merge Visible	Option + Merge Visible
Change tool opacity	1-0	1-0
View and open layer mask	Alt + click on mask	Option + click on mask

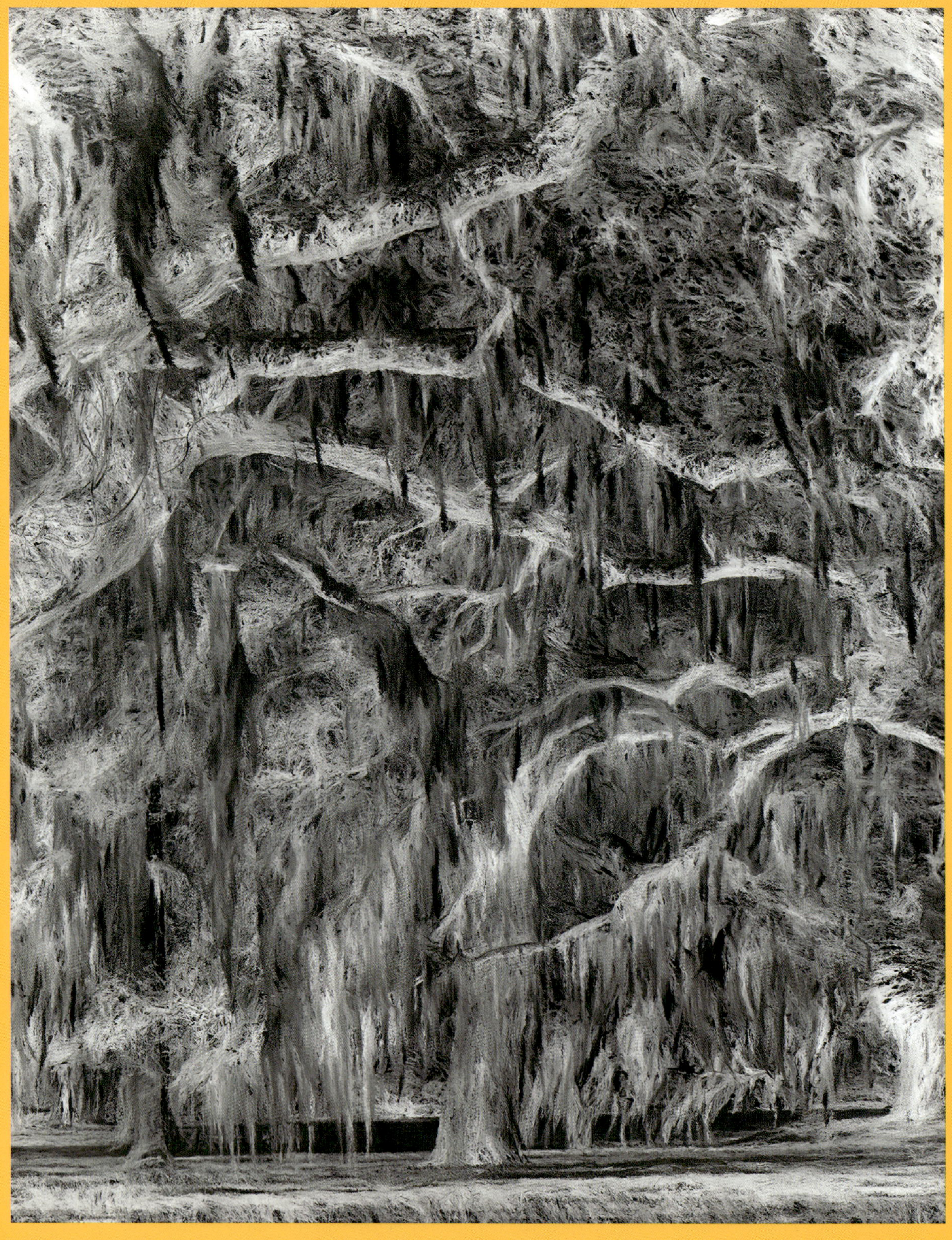

Fig 1.1 **A photograph of trees in the Carolinas draped in Spanish moss. To add impact, the photograph was converted first to black and white and then to its negative. This converts the pale moss to black and gives the overall image an infrared appearance.**

LESSON 1

BLACK AND WHITE

A monochrome picture is one that has only one colour or hue. There will be light and dark tones (tints and shades) of that hue as it progresses from white to black. The hue can be any colour, but much monochrome photography has no colour at all, producing black and white pictures with a simple tonal range from white, through greys to black.

The history of photography has mostly been based on black and white images, with popular colour photography only emerging in the 1970s. As a result, black and white pictures can have an old-fashioned look. However, black and white photography is now recognised as a creative medium in its own right and is gaining in popularity. The absence of colour encourages close focus on the subject and will often create a sense of mood or drama.

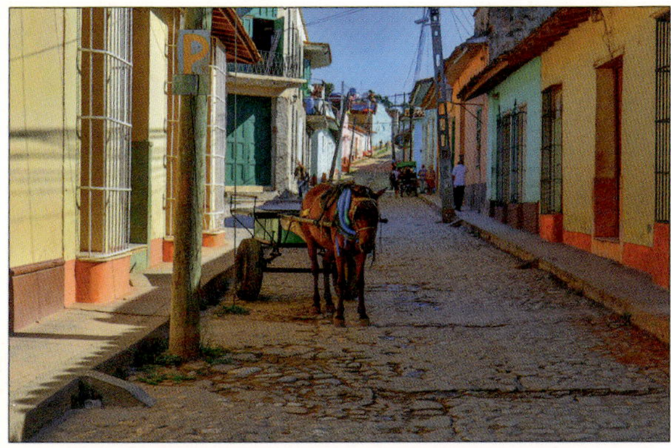

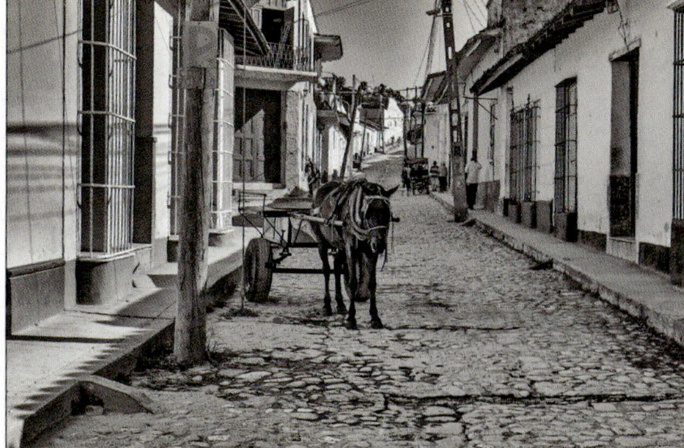

Fig 1.2 **A picture from the colourful town of Trinidad in Cuba. Conversion to black and white presents a much more graphic image and emphasises the shapes and textures.**

COMPOSITION FOR BLACK AND WHITE

Taking photographs with monochrome in mind presents a particular challenge. This is that we are viewing the subject in colour and the separation of different elements of the scene might depend on their colour contrast. However, if those elements have the same tone, they will look the same in monochrome.

To deliver effective black and white pictures, here are a few points to consider:

1. Look for a wide variety of tones. The range of shades of light and dark will govern the balance of the final picture.
2. Aim to avoid high-contrast lighting such as bright sunlight (a challenge in most photography). The extreme contrast between shadows and highlights is likely to look excessively harsh in black and white.
3. For compositional balance, look for a smooth progression across the tones.
4. Look for detail in the shadows and highlights. These are important elements of a monochrome picture but should not appear as unattractive blocks of black or white.
5. If available, make the most of texture in the subjects. Texture, for example in animal fur or in foliage, can look beautiful without colour.

However, sometimes compositional rules are there to be broken. Ansel Adams said, 'The so-called rules of photographic composition are, in my opinion, invalid, irrelevant, immaterial.' So don't let rules or guidelines stifle your creativity.

Fig 1.3 **Vibrant colours, as in these red, blue and green circles, look the same when converted to black and white because they have similar tone density.**

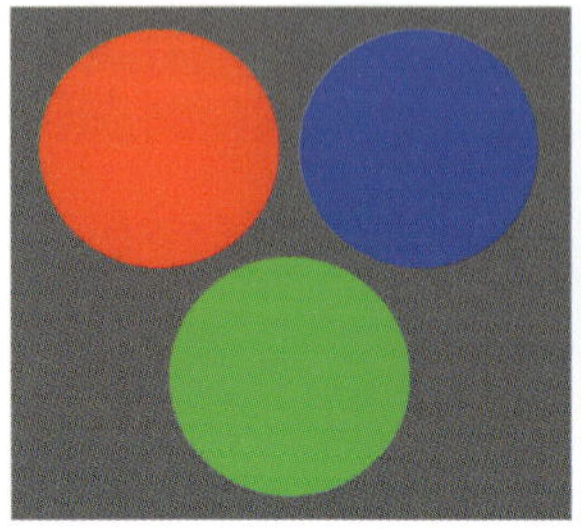

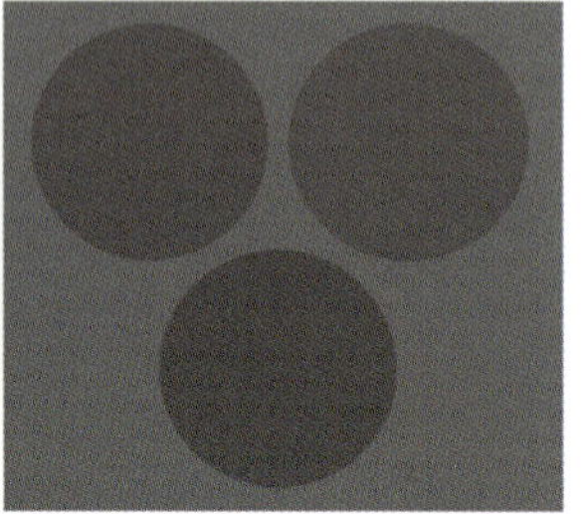

BLACK AND WHITE SUBJECTS

Black and white photography is often used to portray harsh reality, for example in war reporting and some street and urban photography, where colour might be too 'pretty' for the nature of the subject.

It might at first seem that flowers are unlikely candidates for conversion to black and white since colour is a part of their appeal. In practice the texture and structure of flowers can often be better appreciated in the absence of colour.

Portraits are often well suited to monochrome treatment and, with the sepia toning explained in Lesson 2, will echo the vintage appearance of monochrome pictures from the nineteenth century.

Architectural structures can be natural candidates for monochrome treatment. Black and white emphasises the lines and shapes in buildings and eliminates the distractions of colour.

One particular application for monochrome pictures is to emphasise the atmosphere and mood in pictures taken in poor weather such as mist, rain and snow. These can represent excellent photographic opportunities. The absence of colour highlights the feeling of cold and damp.

Fig 1.4 **The harsh reality of a scene of graffiti and abandoned waste is better represented by removing colour.**

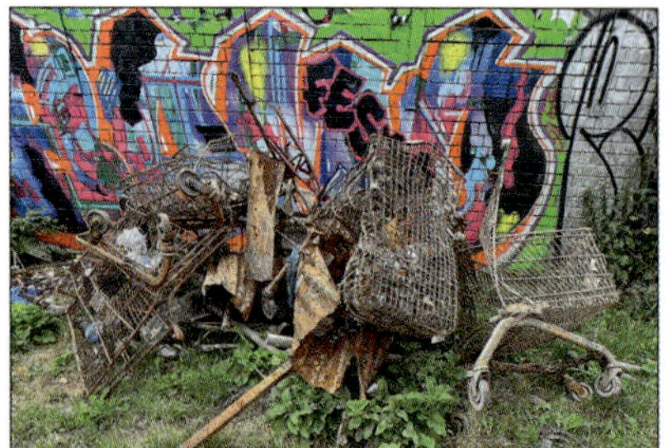

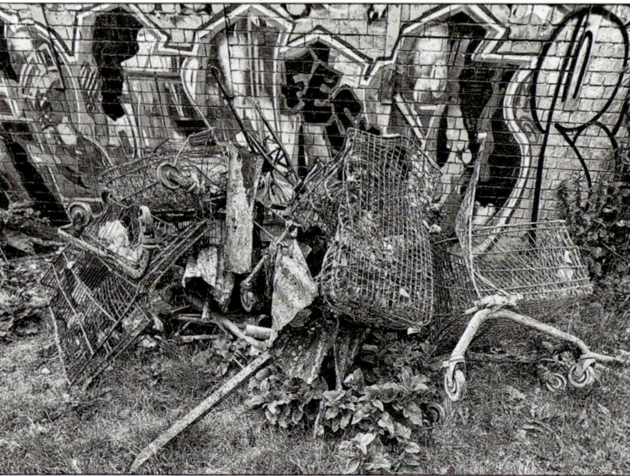

Fig 1.5 **The original photograph of this peony flower is not reliant on colour for its impact, but has a wide range of tones and textures that are well suited to black and white conversion.**

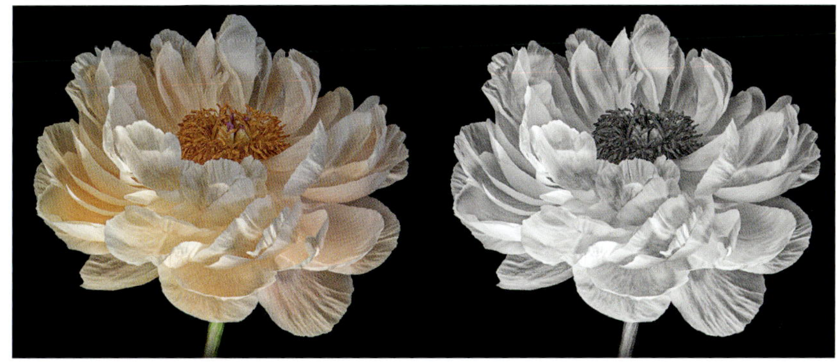

Fig 1.6 **Conversion of a portrait to black and white can emphasise the character of the subject and remove the distractions of colour. Tinting the picture to sepia, as described in Lesson 2, gives the impression of old-style portraiture.**

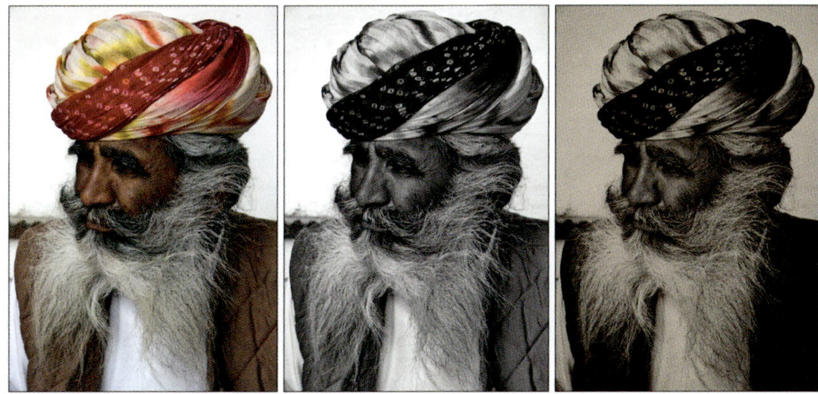

Fig 1.7 **Architectural subjects are well suited to black and white treatment. In this picture, the buildings of the City of London can be more easily appreciated without the distractions of colour.**

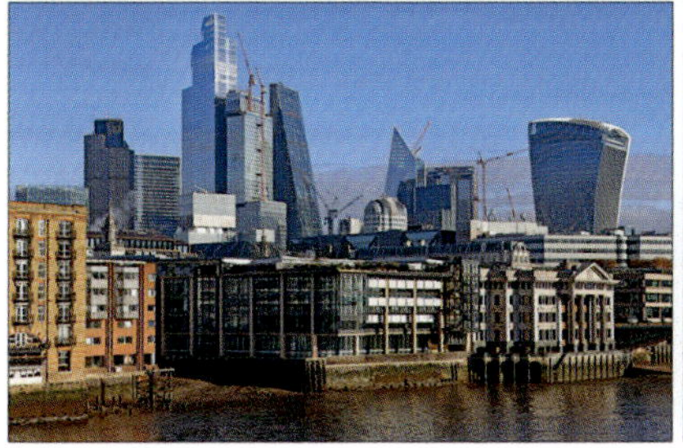

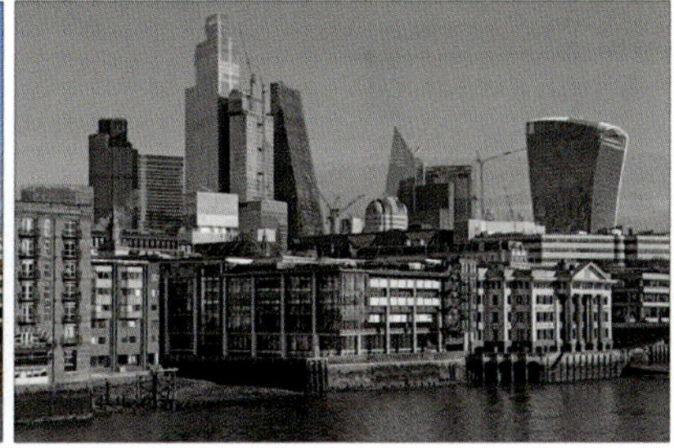

Fig 1.8 **The mood of cold-weather pictures, in this case a photograph of trees taken during a snowstorm, can be captured by conversion to black and white. Image contrast has been reduced as described later to further emphasise the feeling of coldness.**

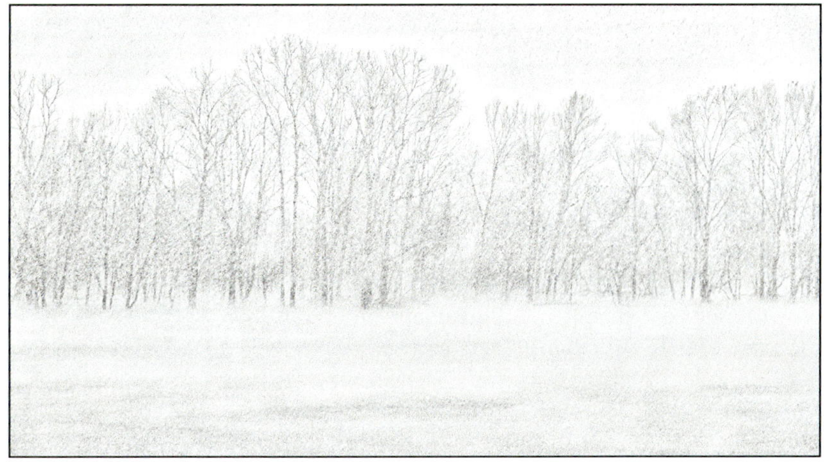

MONOCHROME TECHNIQUES

There are many routes to producing photographs without colour. One option is to return to 'wet chemistry' and use a film camera with black and white film. It is also possible to purchase digital cameras that will take only black and white pictures. These cameras do not have the filter systems required for colour and can produce extremely high-quality results. Other cameras often have a settings option that enables the scene to be viewed and recorded in black and white.

Since most digital cameras produce colour pictures, some treatment is required to convert the image to monochrome.

THE DIGITAL METHODS

There are many ways to remove colour from photographs in software. Some of the Photoshop techniques are described below, though similar tools are available in most digital photo programs. It is worth noting that there are specialist packages specifically designed for mono pictures, for example Nik Silver Efex, which gives great control over the final appearance and previews a range of possible adjustments.

Grayscale

In the Mode setting in Photoshop (Image > Mode > Grayscale) the picture can be converted to black and white with shades of grey. Since conversion to grayscale is a one-way journey, it is wise to also save the colour original for use in the future.

Desaturating

A very simple way to remove colour is to desaturate the picture (Image > Adjustments > Hue/Saturation; drag the middle saturation slider over to the left). This is quick and easy but doesn't allow for any fine adjustment.

Black & White Setting

The Black & White setting in Photoshop (Image > Adjustments > Black & White) is, not surprisingly, designed to produce black and white pictures. Unlike the desaturation method, it offers considerable control over the final result. Six sliders are presented, each with a colour label. These enable adjustment of the tonal distribution of the desaturated result. If, for example, the slider labelled Reds is moved to the right, the red colours in the starting picture will give a lighter result in the monochrome version (or darker if moved left). If you are unsure which colour is to be adjusted, the cursor can be clicked in the picture and dragged left or right to make the change. The Black & White adjustment settings can also be used to add tones to a picture as described in Lesson 2.

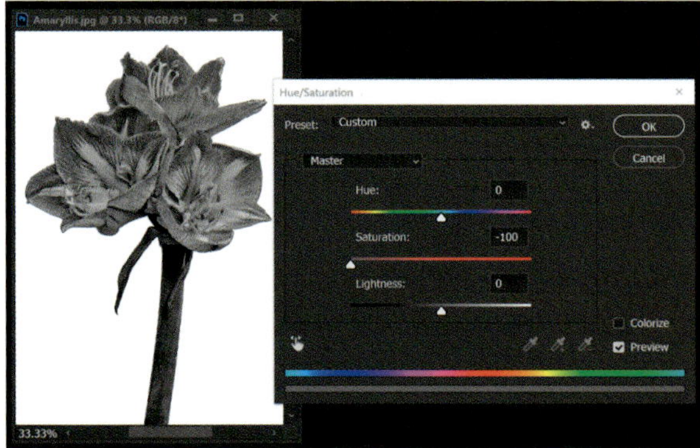

Fig 1.9 **Conversion of a picture of an amaryllis flower by removing saturation in the Photoshop settings. The saturation slider in Hue/Saturation has been moved fully to the left.**

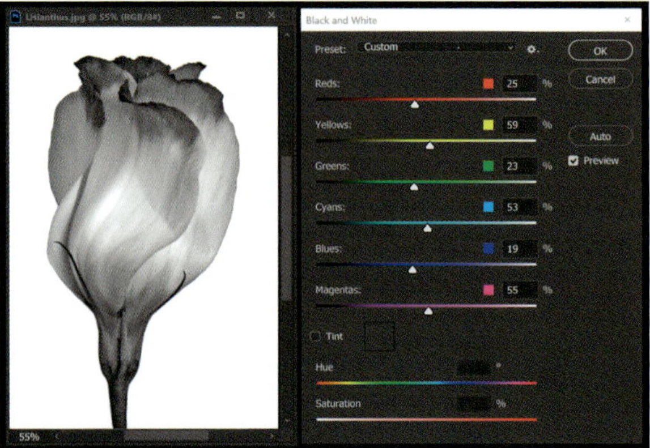

Fig 1.10 **The Black & White tool in Photoshop, used to remove colour from a picture of a lisianthus flower. The colour sliders are used to change the black and white intensity contributed by each of the colours in the original picture.**

Gradient Map Adjustment Layer

Photoshop's Gradient Map Adjustment Layer (Layer > New Adjustment Layer > Gradient Map) allows for control of the conversion process, as well as the split toning described in Lesson 2. When this is opened, a gradient will be applied to the image. This will be a gradient from the foreground to the background colour. Since the default colours are black and white, this will result in a black and white picture. If this doesn't happen, reset the foreground and background by clicking on them and locating black or white in the Color Picker. Click on the displayed gradient and the Gradient Editor will open. The black and white end points of the displayed gradient can now be moved to change the contrast of the picture, or the midpoint slider can be moved left or right to lighten or darken the midtones.

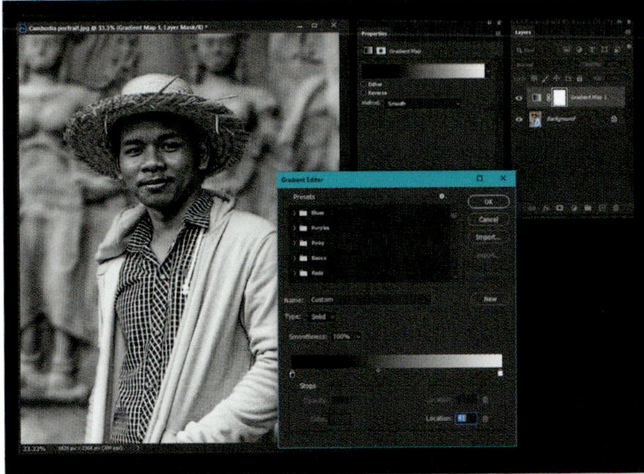

Fig 1.11 **Opening the Gradient Editor in Photoshop's Gradient Map Adjustment Layer allows full control of the conversion to black and white, and enables contrast adjustment of the final image.**

CHANGING CONTRAST

Changing image contrast adjusts the difference between the darkest and lightest tones. This can dramatically change the nature and the impact of a black and white picture. A simple adjustment can be found in Photoshop's Brightness/Contrast setting (Image > Adjustments > Brightness/ Contrast). A slider allows contrast to be reduced or increased. Another slider changes brightness by making all tones darker or lighter. More extreme adjustments to contrast can be made in the Gradient Editor described above by dragging the ends of the image gradient towards the centre.

Fig 1.12 **A stone archway showing low contrast and high contrast treatments.**

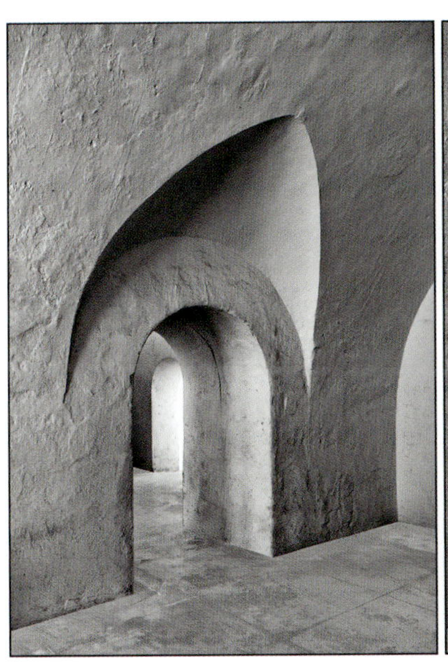

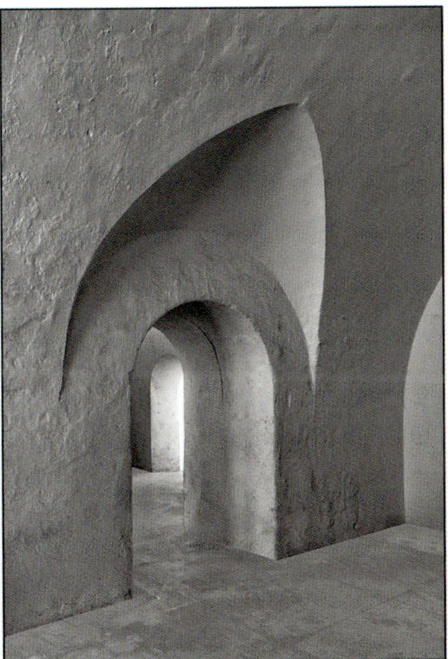

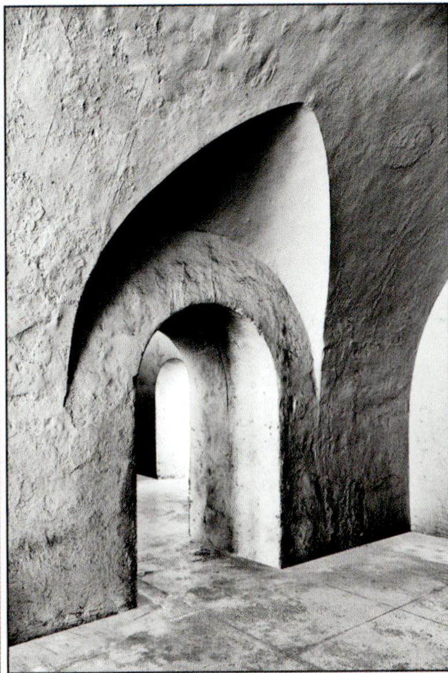

THRESHOLD ADJUSTMENT

The most dramatic contrast effect is to present the picture with black and white tones only, no shades of grey. In Photoshop's Threshold setting (Image > Adjustments > Threshold), the level setting allows adjustment of the tonal point in the original image above which only black will be presented, and below which only white. A level of 1 produces an entirely white image and 255, the maximum, entirely black.

Fig 1.13 **A sweet-pea flower converted to black and white by desaturating to preserve the range of tones, compared with conversion via Photoshop's Threshold setting to give a picture with only pure black and pure white.**

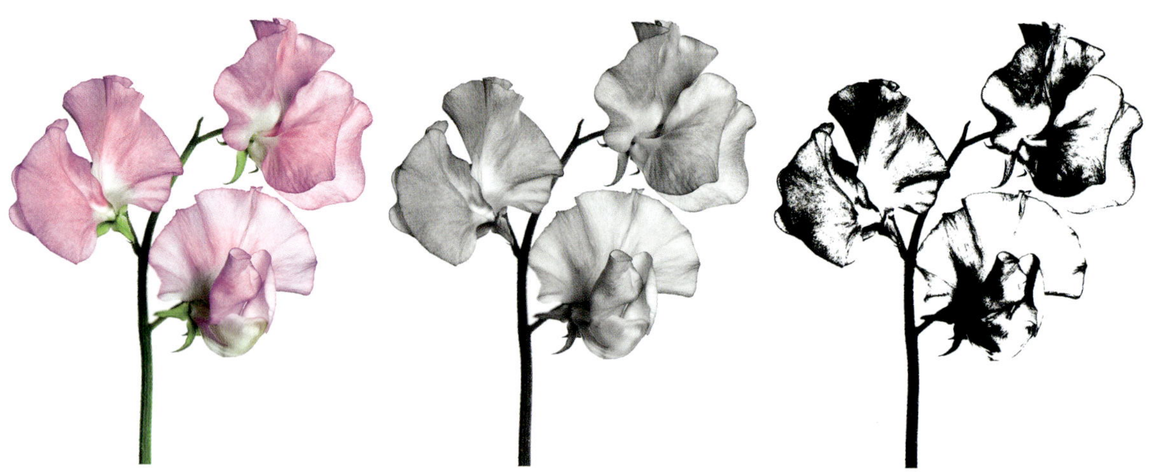

BLACK AND WHITE - KEYS

REMOVING colour from a picture encourages focus on the subject and its composition, and can add a sense of mood or drama.

COLOUR is a relatively recent introduction in the history of photography, so black and white pictures can have a nostalgic old-fashioned appearance.

MANY subjects are suited to presentation in black and white, for example street, portrait and architecture.

IT IS possible for cameras to be dedicated to black and white photography, for example by using black and white film or sensors without colour filters, but it is more usual to convert digital colour pictures to monochrome using software.

THERE ARE many routes to black and white conversion, some allowing for sophisticated adjustment of factors such as brightness and contrast.

FACING PAGE
Fig 1.14 **A freesia flower converted to black and white to emphasise the range of tones and textures, and to allow the composition to be more easily appreciated.**

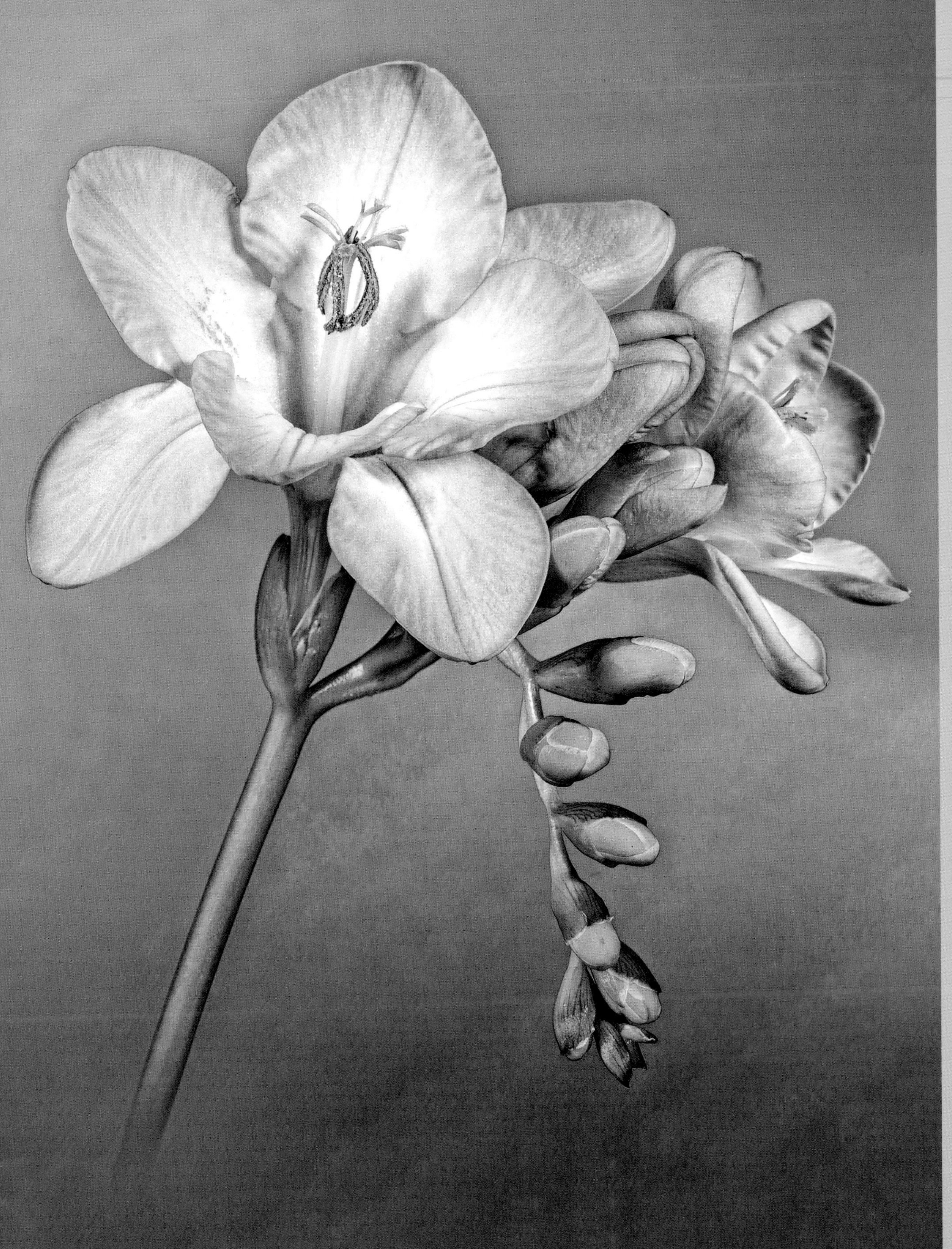

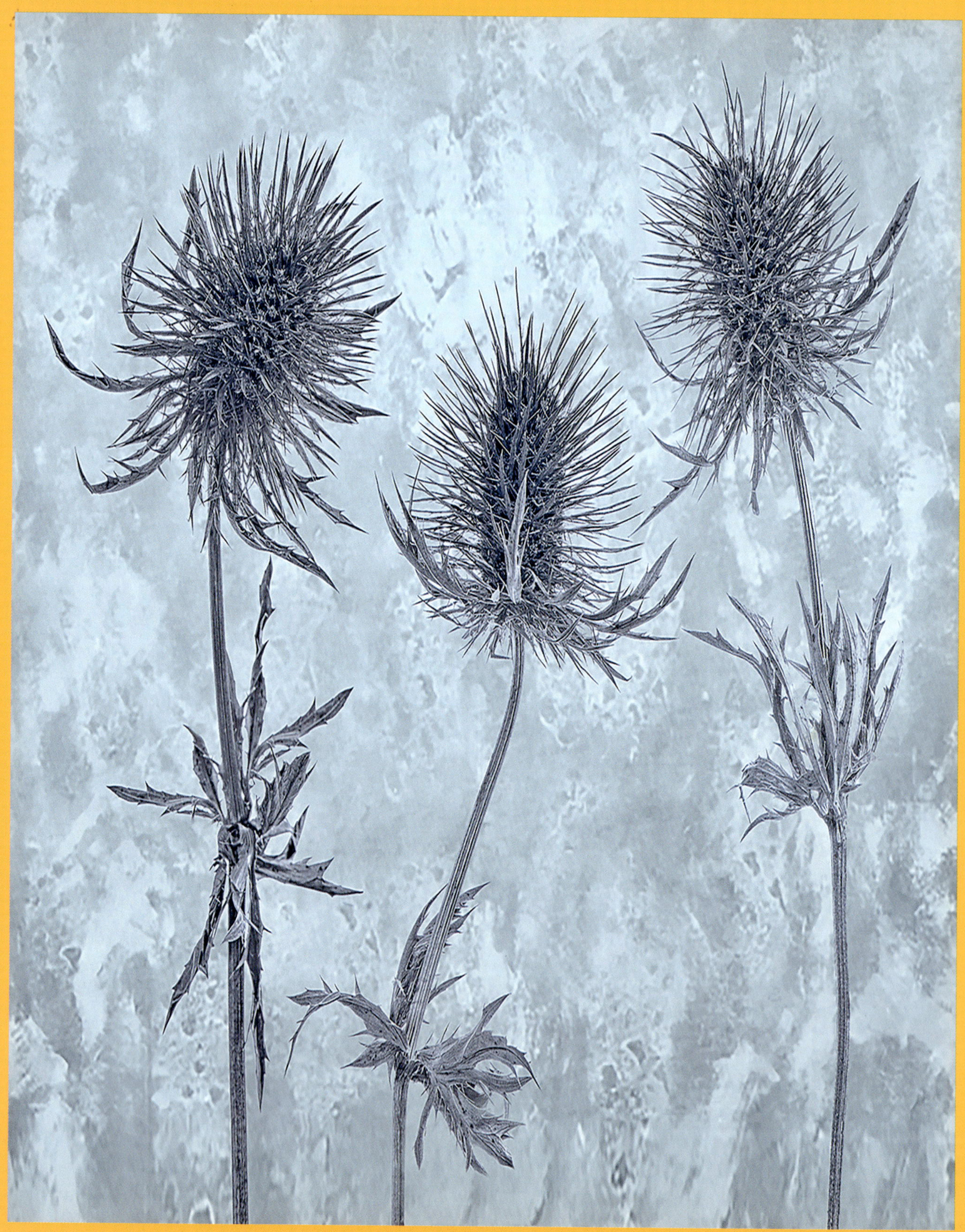

Fig 2.1 **An arrangement of eryngium flower stems toned with a Delft-blue colour.**

LESSON 2

TONING

Lesson 1 covered one aspect of removing colours from a picture to produce monochrome images, namely conversion to black and white. In this case the tone of the image progresses from white to black through shades of grey. However, the intermediate hue does not have to be colourless and if a colour is used along the gradient, the resulting toned picture can take on a very different appearance.

In early photographic prints it is common to see monochrome pictures with a reddish-brown tone, usually referred to as sepia. This was used because it was relatively easy to apply during the 'wet chemistry' processing of black and white film. For the portrait photography of the nineteenth century, it had the merit of converting the rather cold black and white pictures to images with a soft warmth. This is probably the earliest example of artistic photographic image manipulation. With the emergence of digital processing, it became possible to use any colour in a toned photograph. Blue toning can contribute a gentle softness, as in the eryngiums in Figure 2.1 or, with a sharper blue, a feeling of coldness.

In practice, any colour at all can be selected for toning and, together with adjustments to saturation, will deliver a limitless range of new pictures.

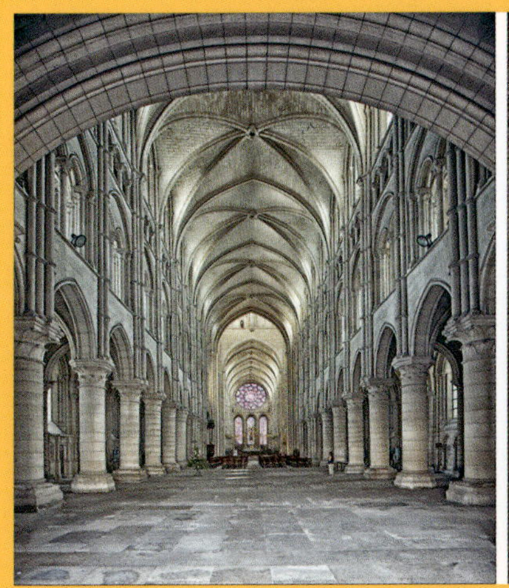

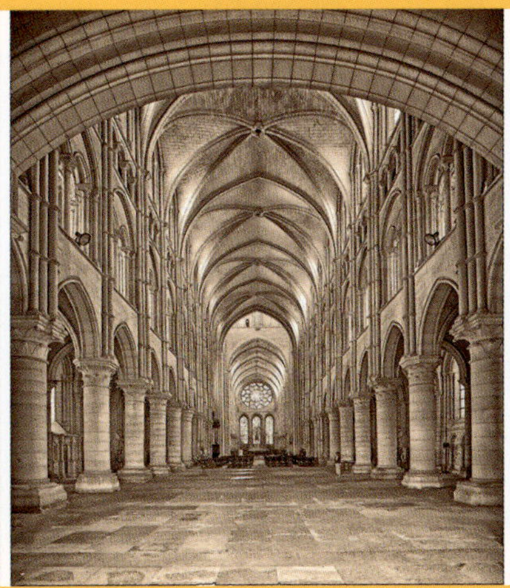

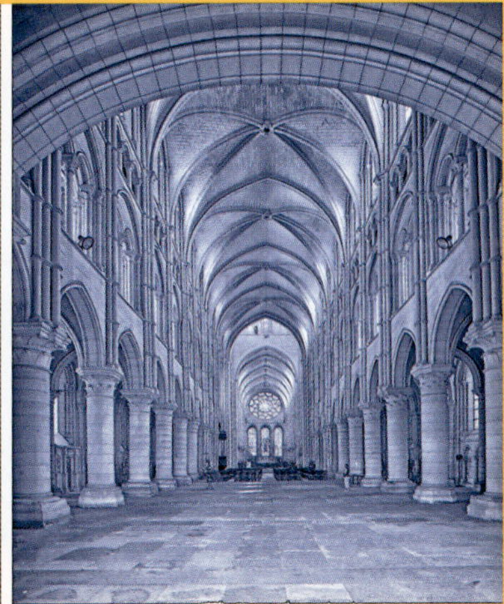

Fig 2.2 **A colour image of Laon Cathedral compared with classic sepia colouring to impart warmth, and a blue tone giving a feeling of austerity and coldness.**

TONING TECHNIQUES

As always in digital processing, there is no shortage of routes to creating toned photographs. The techniques for black and white conversion presented in Lesson 1 usually also have an option for adding a colour tone. For example, the Black & White setting (Image > Adjustments > Black & White) includes a Tint box which, when ticked, activates hue and saturation sliders to allow any tone colour to be applied and adjusted. Alternatively, clicking on the colour box opens Photoshop's Color Picker, within which any colour can selected.

In Photoshop's hue and saturation settings (Image > Adjustments > Hue/Saturation) there is a box marked Colorize. When selected, this enables the sliders to view and select a full range of hues and to control the levels of saturation and lightness. This can also be achieved non-destructively through the Hue/Saturation Adjustment Layer (Layer > New Adjustment Layer > Hue/Saturation) where there are also sliders for hue, saturation and lightness.

An especially valuable application of image toning is to combine the coloured original picture with a toned version. This adds a hint of the toned colour and, whilst the original colours remain, the resulting image has a new mood. Effective applications of this are to add warmer, autumnal tones to woodland scenes, or colder tones to wintry landscapes. A controllable way to achieve this is to make two layers of the starting picture in Photoshop (Layer > Duplicate Layer) and to tone the top layer using one of the techniques described above. Then reduce the opacity of that layer using the Opacity slider in the Layers panel. The slider can be manually adjusted to give the desired appearance, but typically an opacity of around 50% will produce an effective blend of the two layers.

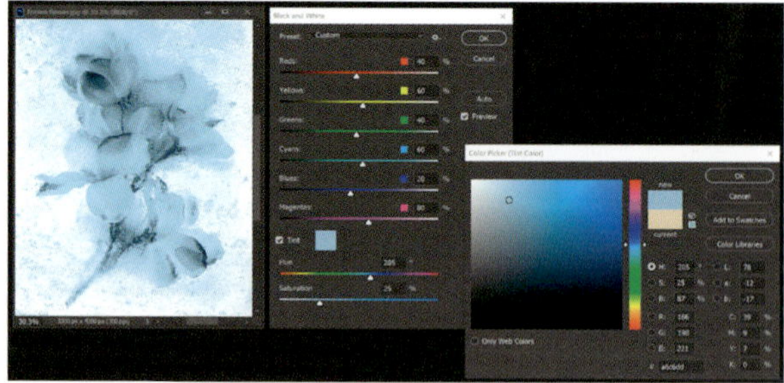

Fig 2.3 **Photoshop's Black & White setting with the Tint box ticked and a light blue colour selected in the Color Picker to tone a picture of a frozen flower.**

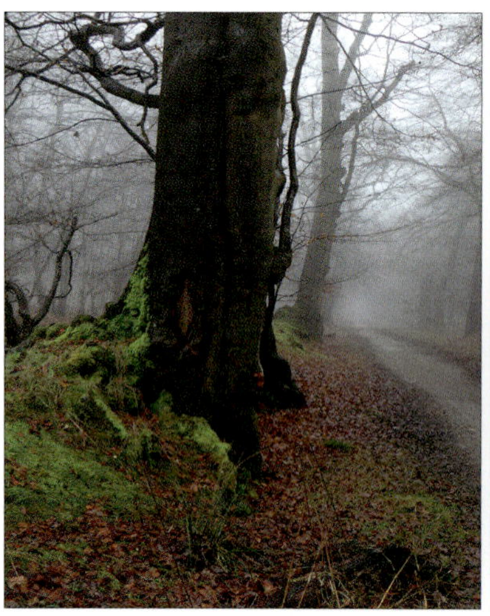

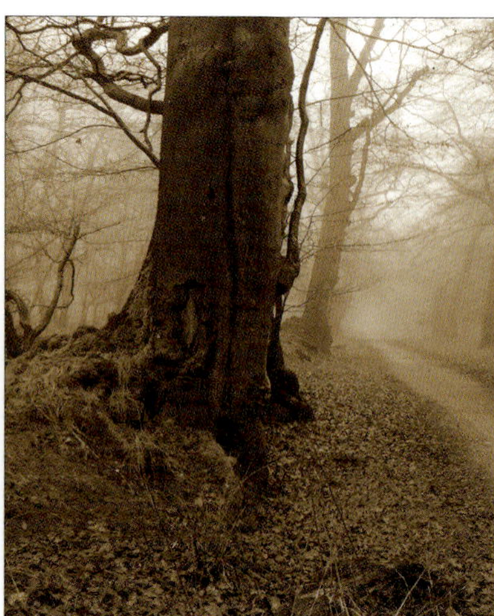

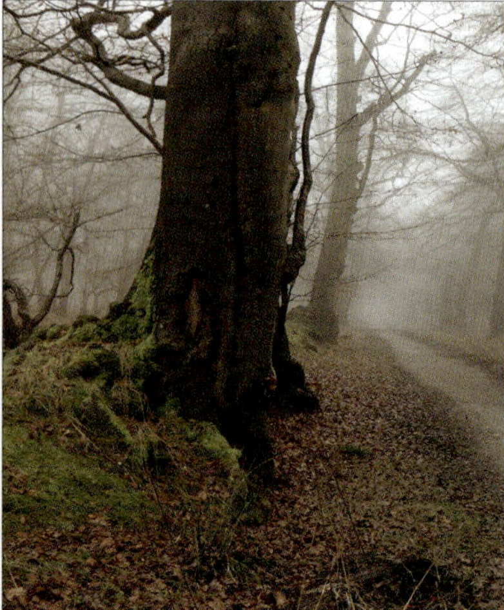

Fig 2.4 **A woodland scene with sepia toning and then blended with the original picture to produce a gentle autumnal effect.**

SPLIT TONING

Split toning is an editing technique that involves adding different colours to the shadows and highlights of an image. It creates very distinctive pictures and can add a cinematic or moody quality to a photo. As with the toning applications described so far, split toning can be utilised without removing all of the starting image colour. For example, a landscape scene could be adjusted so that the glow of a sunset sky could be warmed with an orange tone, while foreground rocks or water could be cooled using a blue tone. For this sort of application, the tools in Lightroom and Photoshop's Camera Raw filter (where it is called Color Grading) provide very versatile adjustments. Here, colour circles allow for selection of the hue to be applied to the image highlights, shadows and midtones. Sliders enable adjustment for the saturation of each colour, and a balance slider sets the division between highlights and shadows.

More dramatic split toning eliminates all of the original colour and, whilst usually retaining pure black and white at the ends of the colour gradient, adds new colours for all the intermediate tones. In Photoshop, the route to this split toning is in the Gradient Map Adjustment Layer (Layer > New Adjustment Layer > Gradient Map) introduced in Lesson 1 as a versatile tool for black and white conversion. When this is activated, a gradient from the foreground to the background colour (black to white by default) will be applied. Clicking on this opens the Gradient Editor. When the cursor is moved along the gradient it becomes a small hand and when clicked, a colour 'stop' is applied. A Color box also becomes active, and clicking on this opens the Color Picker so that the hue of that colour stop can be chosen. At this point a toned image is the result. However, for split toning, a further stop is added and a new colour applied. The stops can be moved along the gradient to adjust their impact on the resulting image.

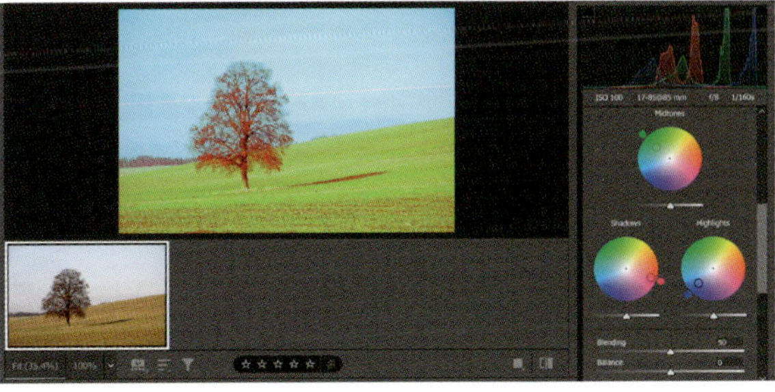

Fig 2.5 **A countryside picture opened in Photoshop's Camera Raw Editor (similar to the settings in Lightroom), with green toning selected for the midtones, blue for the highlights and red for the shadows. The starting picture is on the left.**

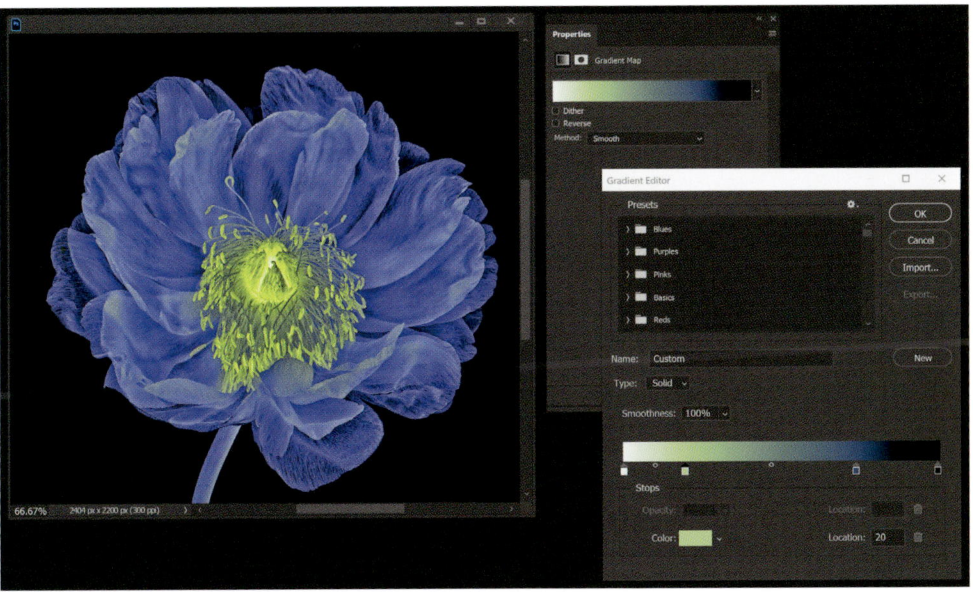

Fig 2.6 **A peony photograph split toned with Photoshop's Gradient Map Adjustment Layer using a blue colour stop for the shadows and a yellow stop for the highlights.**

In the Gradient Map adjustment, there is no requirement to limit the number of stops to two. As additional stops are applied along the gradient, the image can become quite surreal in appearance.

A quick start to the use of multiple stops is to try some of Photoshop's range of presets. These are set in colour groups and are designed to deliver harmonious colour combinations. They allow for further adjustment either by adjusting the position of the colour stops, or by adding additional stops. Once the new image is created, it is of course still available for adjustments of levels, saturation and contrast.

If even more wild application of multiple-stop split toning is desired, Photoshop has a setting that will deliver. This is to change the default mode in the Gradient Map from Solid to Noise. Noise toning applies a huge range of colour stops along the gradient and delivers curious, dramatic results. The range of colours is not set by the photographer, but randomly by Photoshop. If the result does not appeal, as is likely at first, there is a Randomize button that delivers a completely new set of colours. Repeated pressing of Randomize may eventually lead to a promising picture, and adjustment of colour sliders will enable fine tuning.

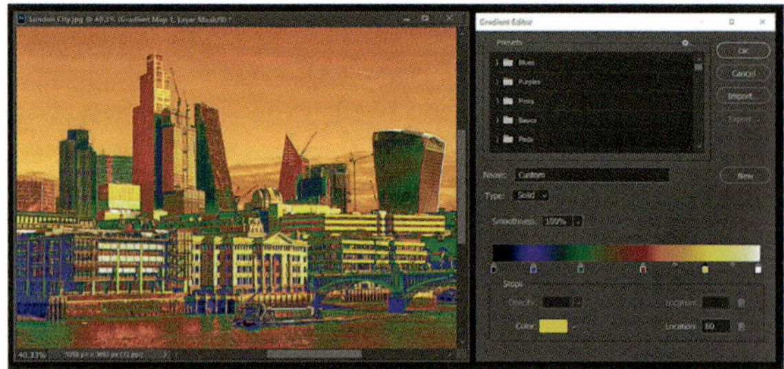

Fig 2.7 **A London city scene with a number of colour stops applied in Photoshop's Gradient Editor to produce a relatively abstract interpretation.**

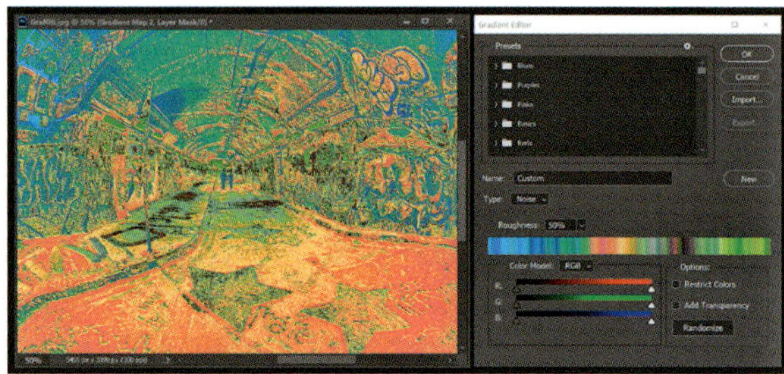

Fig 2.8 **With Photoshop's Gradient Editor settings changed from Solid to Noise, a huge range of colour stops is randomly applied. Here a picture of a tunnel adorned with graffiti takes on a surreal appearance.**

TONING – KEYS

A TONED image adds a colour along the tonal gradient of the picture. This was widely used in early film photography to apply a sepia tint to portraiture.

DIGITAL processing now enables any colour to be used in a toned picture. Orange and red tones produce a sense of warmth and blue tones contribute coldness.

MANY digital techniques can be used to tone photographs. When Photoshop Adjustment Layers are used, the result can be easily reversed.

COMBINING a toned image with the full-coloured original contributes a hint of the toned colour and can change the mood of the picture.

SPLIT toning adds two or more colours along the image gradient. The result is often dramatic and artistic.

A RADICAL split-toning method is to use Photoshop's Noise setting in Gradient Map. The results can be unpredictable but intriguing.

FACING PAGE
Fig 2.9 **A picture of the City of London with split tone treatment. The shadow colour is blue and the highlights yellow.**

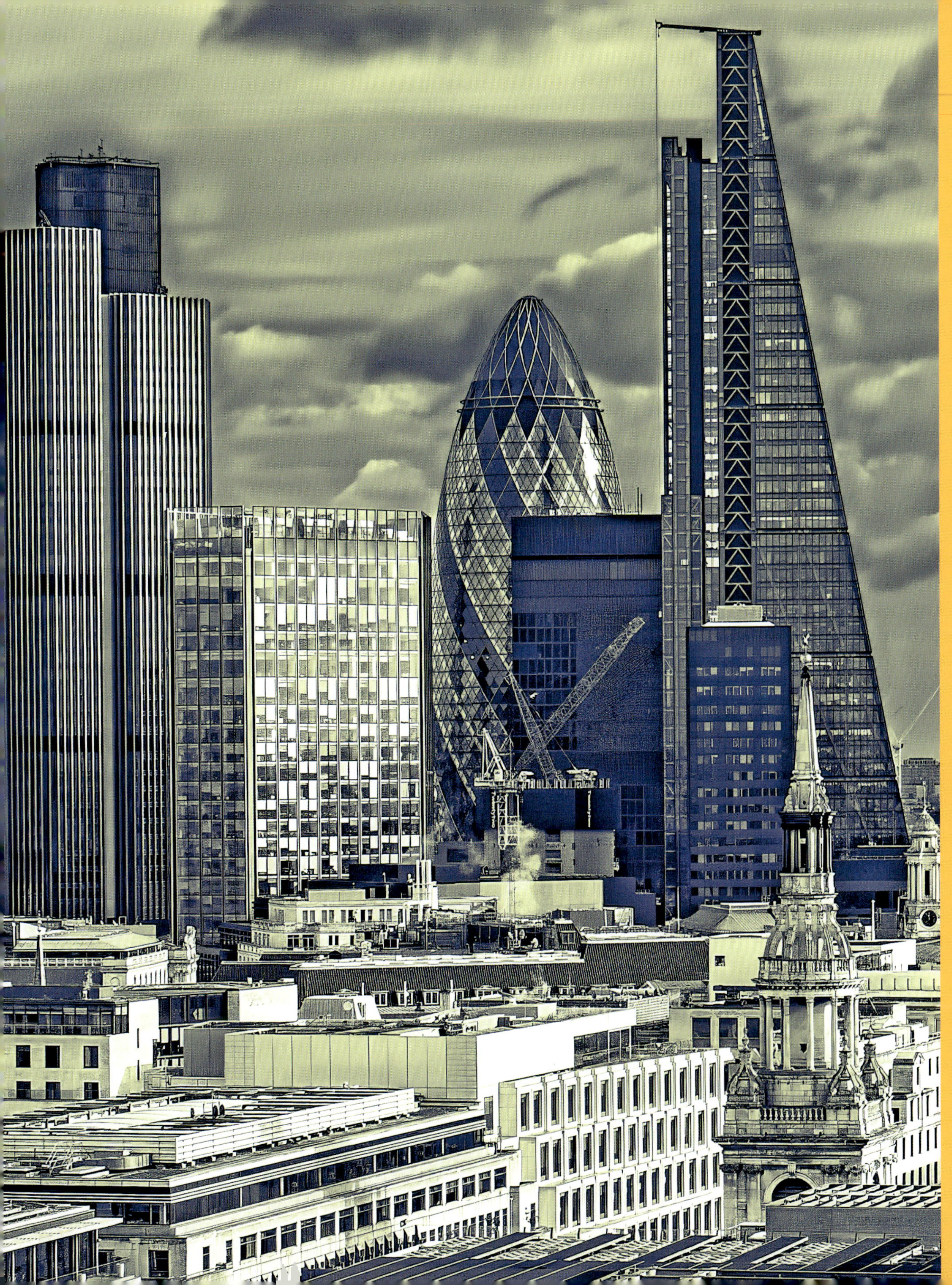

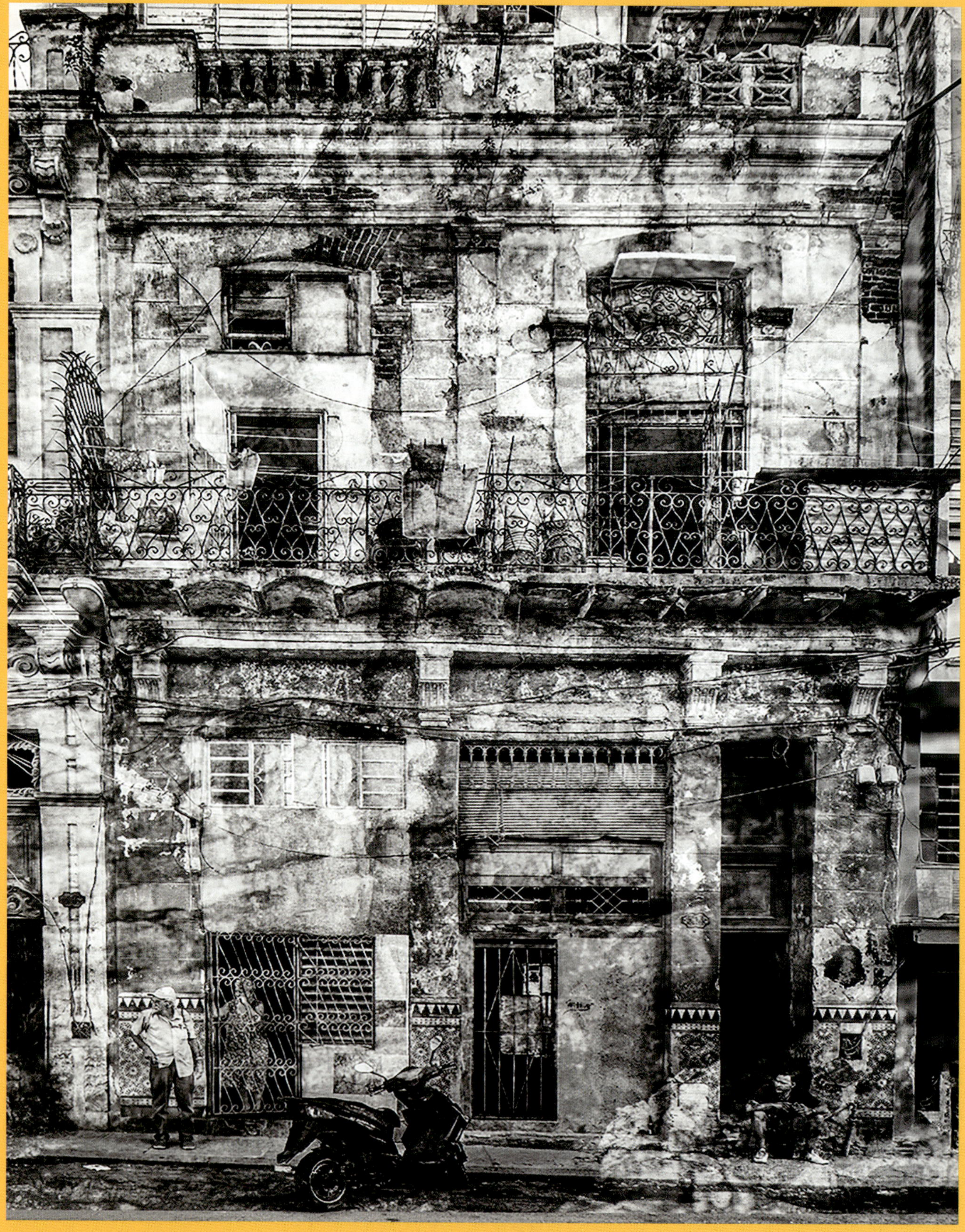

Fig. 3.1 **A building in Havana given a more graphic appearance by conversion to black and white (Lesson 1) and superimposed with a texture image of a rock surface.**

LESSON 3

TEXTURE

Texture is the surface quality of a substance. It is often described in tactile terms since real textures can be touched. Typical describing words are 'rough', 'smooth', 'furry', 'prickly', and so on. Although this Lesson is about transforming pictures to impart the appearance of texture, it is worth bearing in mind that many subjects are inherently textured and are worth photographing with directional lighting to emphasise their structure. Existing texture can often be enhanced using a tool, conveniently labelled Texture, in Photoshop Camera Raw and Lightroom. The slider in this setting can be dragged to the right to sharpen the edge contrast and emphasise the textural effect.

One way to add texture to a photograph is to print the picture on textured photographic paper. Many such papers are available, often replicating the canvas commonly used for painting. These are treated so that they will accept the ink from photographic printers. It is also possible to treat non-photographic paper with an ink-receptive coating, a layer that controls the spread of the printer ink droplets.

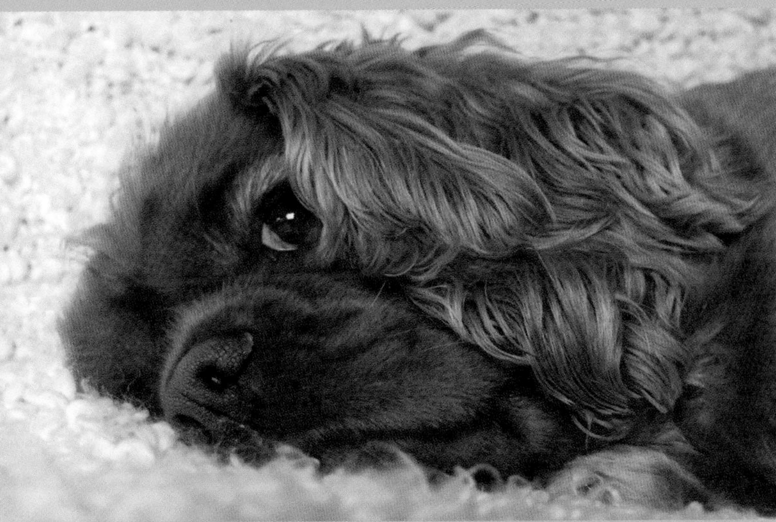

Fig. 3.2 **A photograph of Ted, whose naturally textured coat has been enhanced using the Texture setting in Photoshop Camera Raw.**

CREATING A TEXTURED EFFECT

As always, in the digital world it is possible to mimic the effect of texture in software. This texture cannot of course be felt by touching, but is an illusion usually created by adding the shadows and highlights of a separate texture image.

Adding texture can dramatically alter the appearance of a picture, and sometimes even rescue a picture that wasn't quite right at the start.

With texture in mind, it is worth looking out for textures and keeping their pictures in a separate folder. One day they will come in useful. If the pictures are to be used to 'texturise' a starting picture, it can help if they are converted to black and white. It will be then easier to envisage the effect they will have as a texture since it is the image tones and not the colours that will create the texture effect. Bear in mind that, for some Photoshop applications, texture files will need to be PSD files, so if they are JPEGs or some other format, open them and save a copy as a PSD (File > Save As; select Photoshop PSD in the drop-down menu).

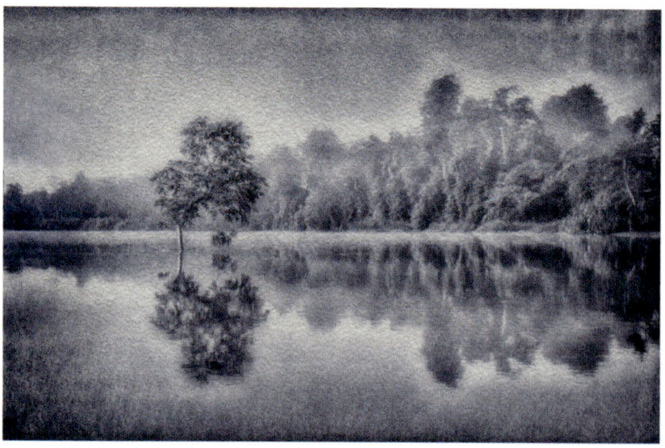

Fig. 3.3 **A scene of trees and water, toned as in Lesson 2 and with a canvas texture applied to replicate the effect of printing on textured paper.**

Fig. 3.4 **An iris flower with different texture treatments. The original is shown together with an applied texture of grasses, a canvas texture, and a rock texture as a background, toned to match the flower colour.**

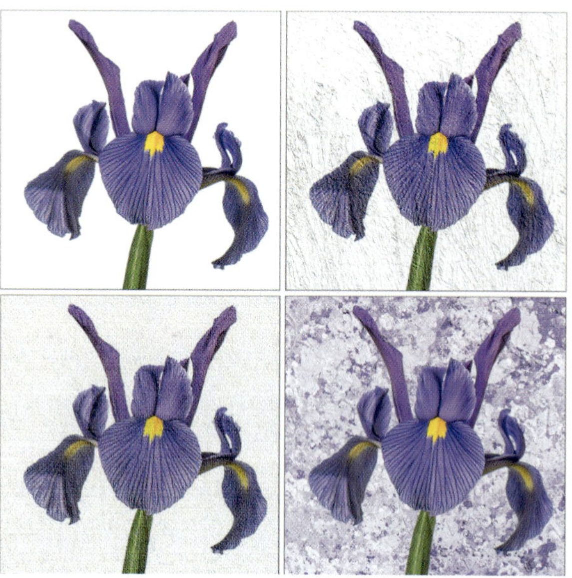

Fig. 3.5 **A range of useful texture images. It is easier to view their texturing effect when they are converted to black and white. For some Photoshop applications they should be saved as PSD files.**

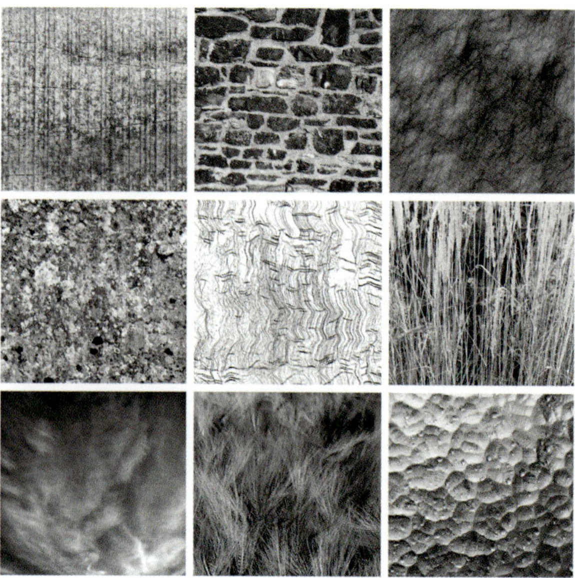

Texture can be a valuable pictorial asset as a background to an otherwise isolated subject. Textured backgrounds serve a similar purpose to out-of-focus backgrounds: they add interest and harmony without distracting from the main subject.

The methods for digitally adding a textured background are described later. However, a useful option is to separately print pictures of textures and to insert these as backgrounds at the taking stage. It helps if these are mounted on stiff card so they can easily be supported in place. They should be printed on matt paper to prevent giveaway reflections.

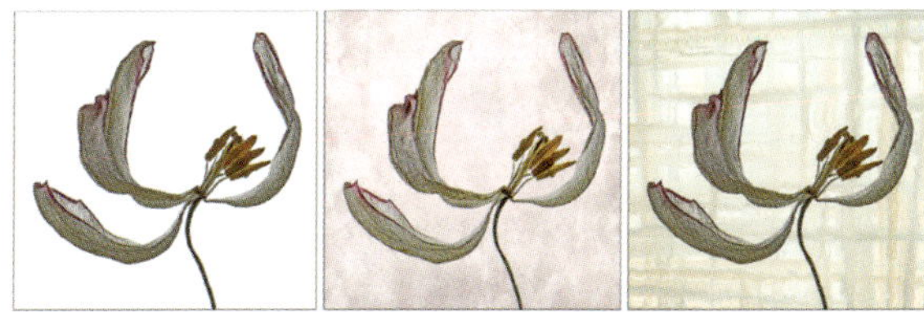

Fig. 3.6 **A dry tulip flower presented against two alternative texture backgrounds, both toned to match colours in the flower.**

Fig. 3.7 **Pre-printed textures enable small subjects such as flowers to be photographed in camera with textured backgrounds. These are about A3 size and printed on matt card.**

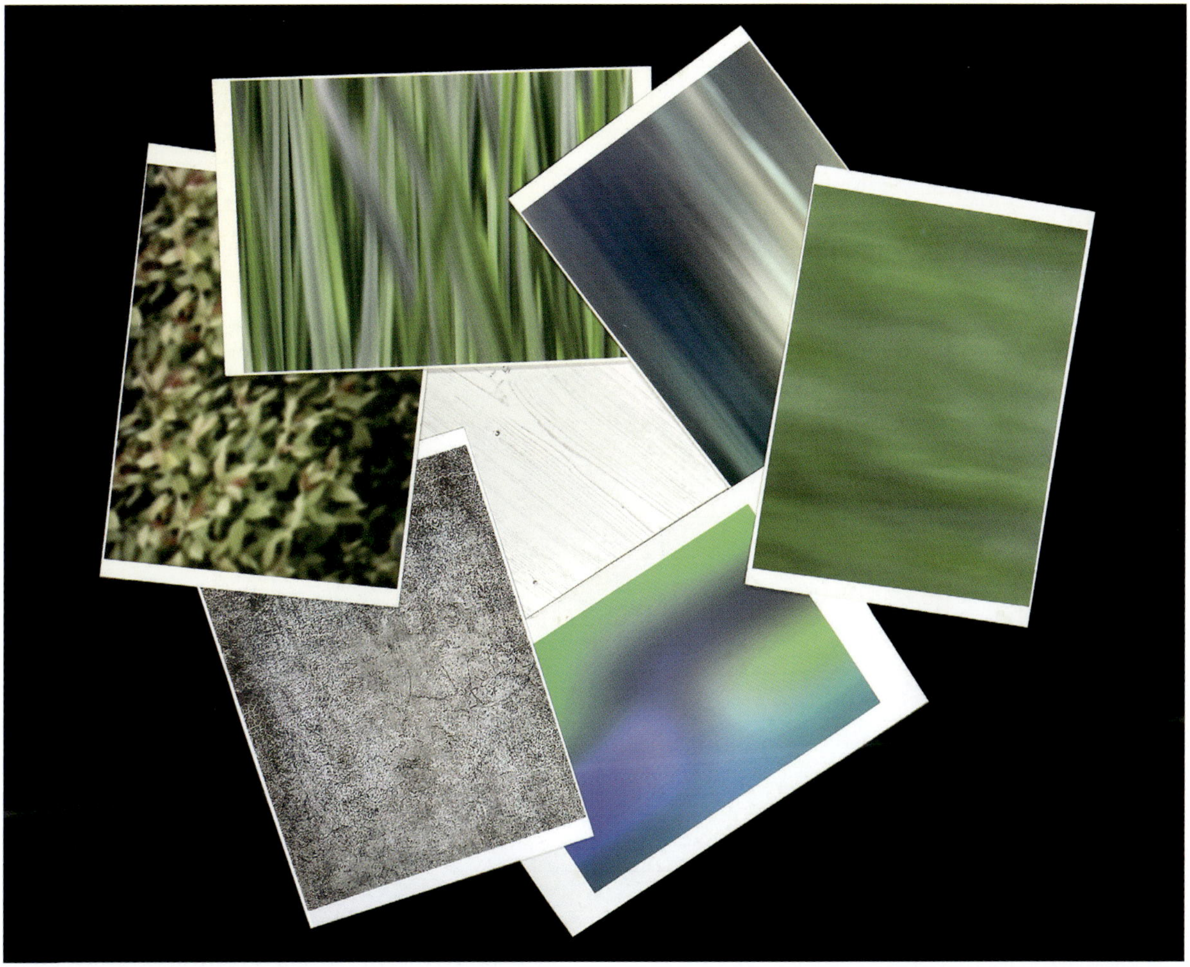

DIGITAL TEXTURE

There are many routes to adding texture using photo-editing software. A quick and straightforward method for creating texture images is to find a photograph that has a suitable mix of tones and colours and to apply one of the blur filters at high settings. It will often be necessary to lighten the result, for example by opening Levels in Photoshop and dragging the middle slider to the left. If the image is to be used to add texture to another picture, it should then be converted to black and white so that it contributes only its texture and not its colour.

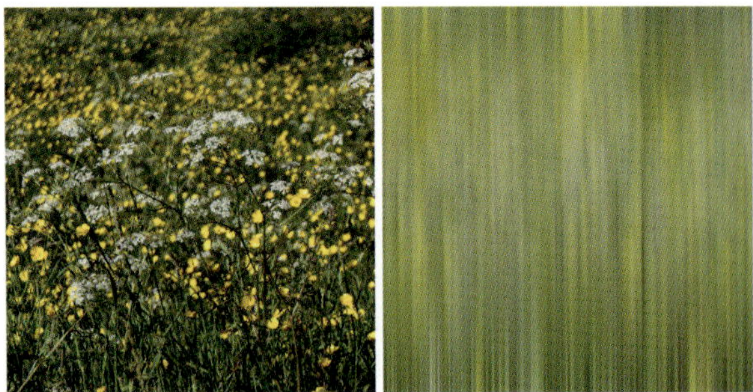

Fig. 3.8 **A flower meadow converted to a texture image with Photoshop's Motion Blur filter. The filtration angle is vertical (90°), and the Distance setting is 900 pixels, though this will vary depending on the resolution of the starting image.**

Adding a Texture Layer

Perhaps the simplest way to give a textured appearance to a photograph is to open a texture image, such as those in Figure 3.5 and place it on top of the starting picture (make the Move tool active and drag the texture onto the picture, then position and resize so it is a matching fit). It will now be a new top layer in Photoshop. Then select the Multiply blend mode for the texture layer. This will probably result in an excessive texture effect, so reduce the opacity of the top layer, perhaps to less than 50%, for a subtle impact. It is also worth trying other blend modes for this treatment, for example Overlay and Soft Light.

Fig. 3.9 **A beach scene textured by placing an image of a rock surface as a top layer in Photoshop and blending with the Multiply blend mode. The opacity of the texture layer has been reduced to modify the texture effect.**

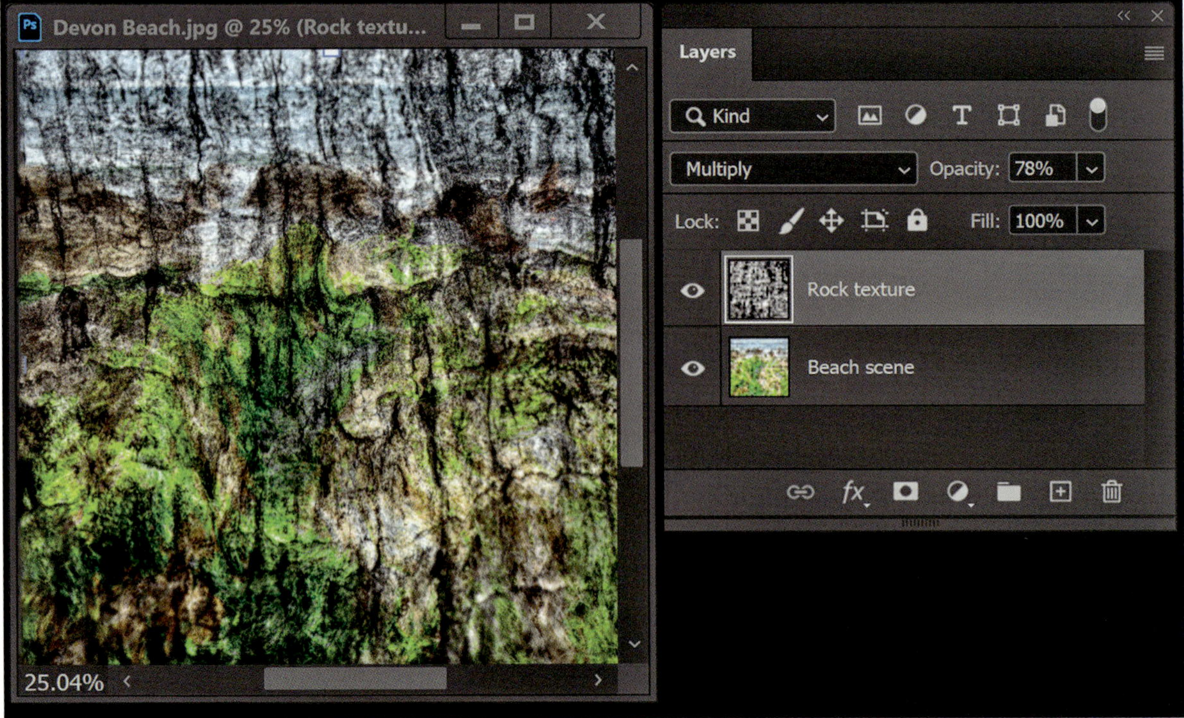

Using the Texturizer

Photoshop provides a dedicated tool for applying textures, the Texturizer. This is tucked away in the Filter Gallery (Filter > Filter Gallery > Texture > Texturizer). A menu box now opens that enables selection of the texture plus control over its application. The drop-down menu offers only a few preset textures (brick, burlap, canvas and sandstone). However, a box marked with horizontal lines is the Load Texture setting and, when clicked, allows any file saved in PSD format to be added as a texture. The sliders allow for Scaling, to control the size of the texture, and Relief, the amount of shine on the texture effect. If you find that the Texturizer, and indeed any of the other options in the Filter Gallery, is not working then it is possible that you are working with a 16-bit image. Convert this to 8 bits (Image > Mode > 8 Bits/Channel) and the Filter Gallery will come back to life.

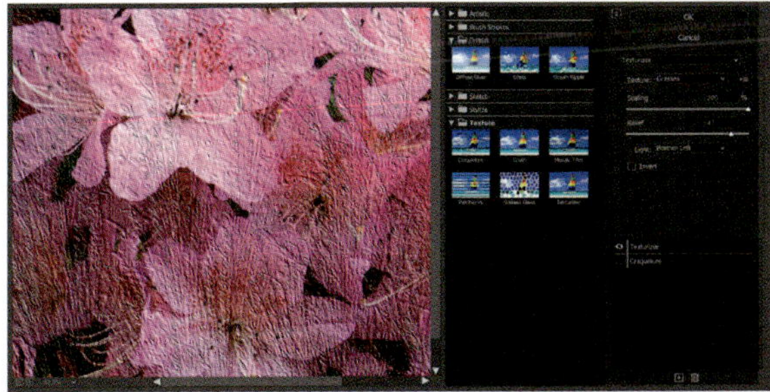

Fig. 3.10 **Photoshop's Texturizer, used to add texture to a picture of azalea flowers. The texturing image is a picture of grasses. This is not one of Photoshop's preset textures so must be loaded separately as a PSD file.**

Noise Texture

Noise is the digital equivalent of film grain and is generally regarded as undesirable. However, noise can be a useful artistic effect. It softens detail and can create a nostalgic feel to a picture. The simplest way to add noise is through Photoshop's Noise filter (Filter > Noise > Add Noise). Settings allow control of the amount of noise and a choice of two types, Uniform or Gaussian. Gaussian noise is more contrasty and gives sharper results. The Monochromatic box removes colour from the noise and is the best option for most texture treatments.

A non-destructive and controllable way to apply noise is to make a new layer on top of the original (Layer > New > Layer) and to fill that layer with 50% grey (Edit > Fill > 50% Grey). Then apply the noise to that grey layer and set the layer blend mode to Overlay. The noise will then be superimposed on the picture but can be modified by reducing the opacity of that layer.

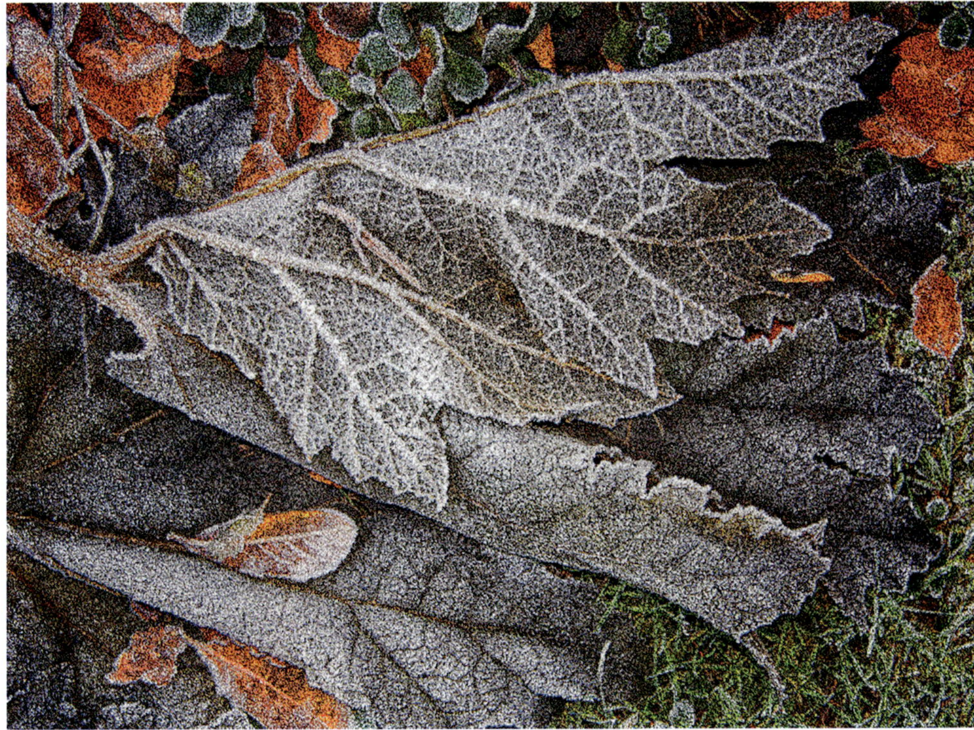

Fig. 3.11 **Frosty leaves textured by the addition of digital noise to enhance the impression of icy frost. The noise is monochromatic Gaussian with a setting of 35%.**

Selective Application of Texture

Sometimes uniform application of a texture is overkill, and a more elegant result is achieved by applying the texture to just a part of the picture. The most common combination is to apply texture to the image background and to leave the main subject untouched. This allows the subject to stand proud and can produce a three-dimensional feel. As noted above, this can be achieved at the taking stage by inserting a textured background behind the subject, but digital options are also available.

The usual digital tool for selective texture application is a layer mask. If the texture is a layer sitting above the subject picture then applying a layer mask (Layer > Layer Mask > Reveal All) and painting on the mask with a black brush will paint out selected areas of the texture. Reducing the opacity of the brush will result in a trace of the texture remaining and will enable controlled application of texture where it is wanted. A soft black brush should be used for this so that no hard edges can be seen. Brush hardness is set, together with brush size, at the top of the screen when the Brush tool is activated.

If the texture has been applied using the Texturizer as described above, then the texture is non-reversible. To modify the texture, save the textured image with a new file name and keep the original. Drag the textured image over the original to produce two layers, apply a layer mask to the top layer and paint with black, as explained above, where the texture is to be removed or reduced.

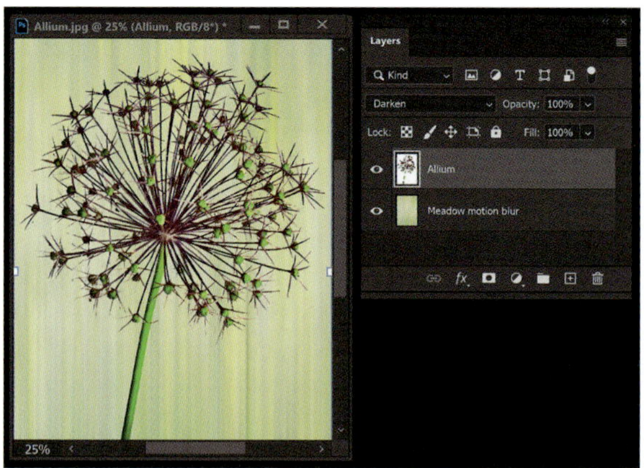

Fig. 3.12 **An allium seedhead superimposed on the flower-meadow texture background shown in Figure 3.8. Since all elements of the seedhead are darker than the background, the Darken blend mode ensures that both the allium and the background are visible.**

A useful alternative for applying a textured background is to use Photoshop's blending modes. If the subject is photographed against a light background and is on a layer above a light texture picture, then the Darken blend mode will result in the photographed background being replaced by the texture. If this is not quite right then the texture lightness can be increased in Levels until the subject is fully revealed.

TEXTURE - KEYS

TEXTURE is a tactile property and can be achieved in photography by printing on textured paper. However, the appearance of texture can be simulated by a number of photographic techniques.

TEXTURE images can be incorporated into photographs using digital overlay, or by applying texturizing tools designed for the purpose.

TEXTURED backgrounds add artistic style to a picture and can create a sense of depth.

NOISE, whilst often avoided in photography, can be an effective texture adding softness and a feeling of nostalgia.

DIGITAL techniques enable texture to be selectively added where needed.

FACING PAGE
Fig. 3.13 **A dry tulip flower set against a blurred texture background using a colour to harmonise with the flower petals. The flower has been textured by the addition of noise to give a crisper, more artistic appearance.**

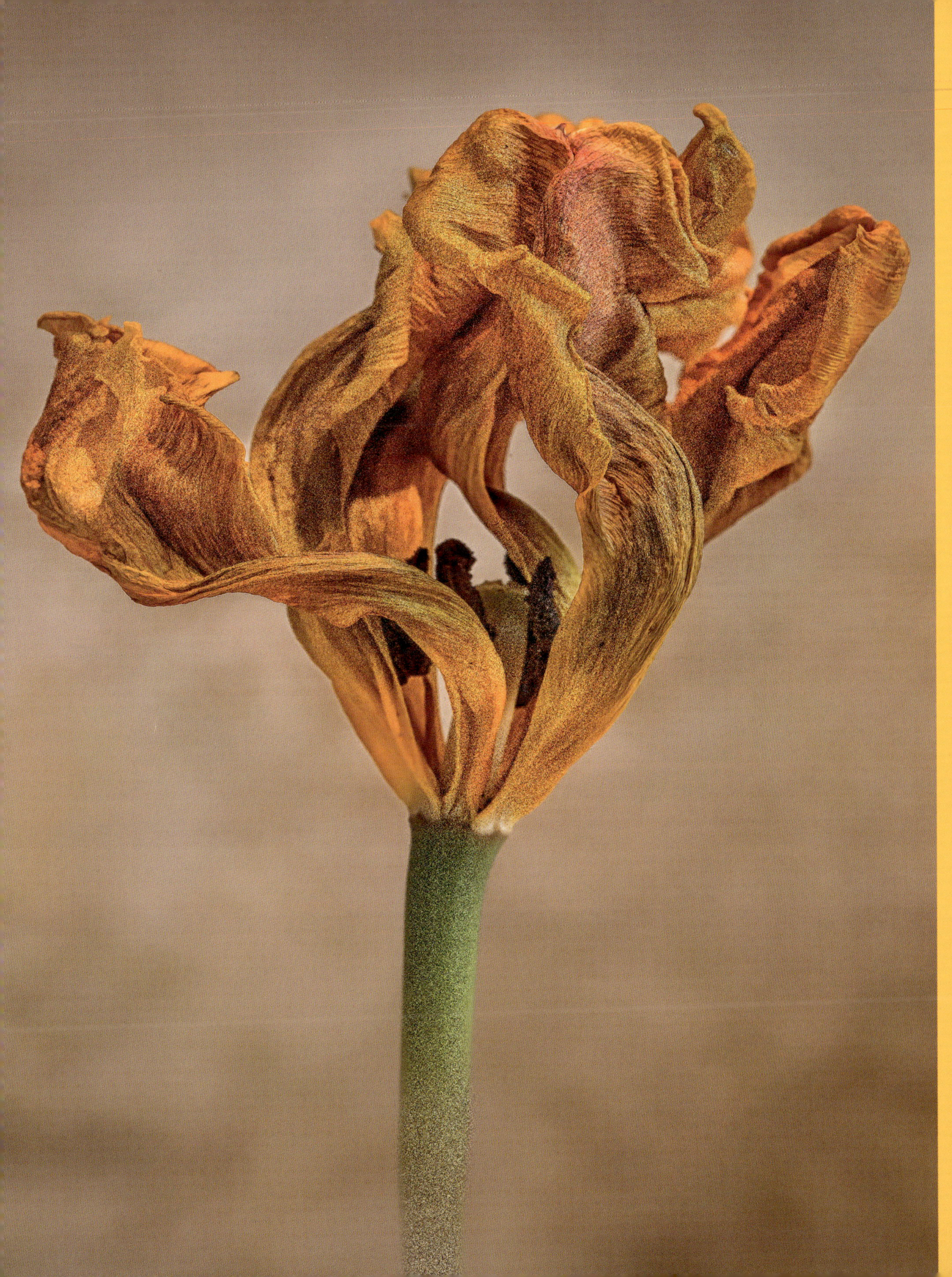

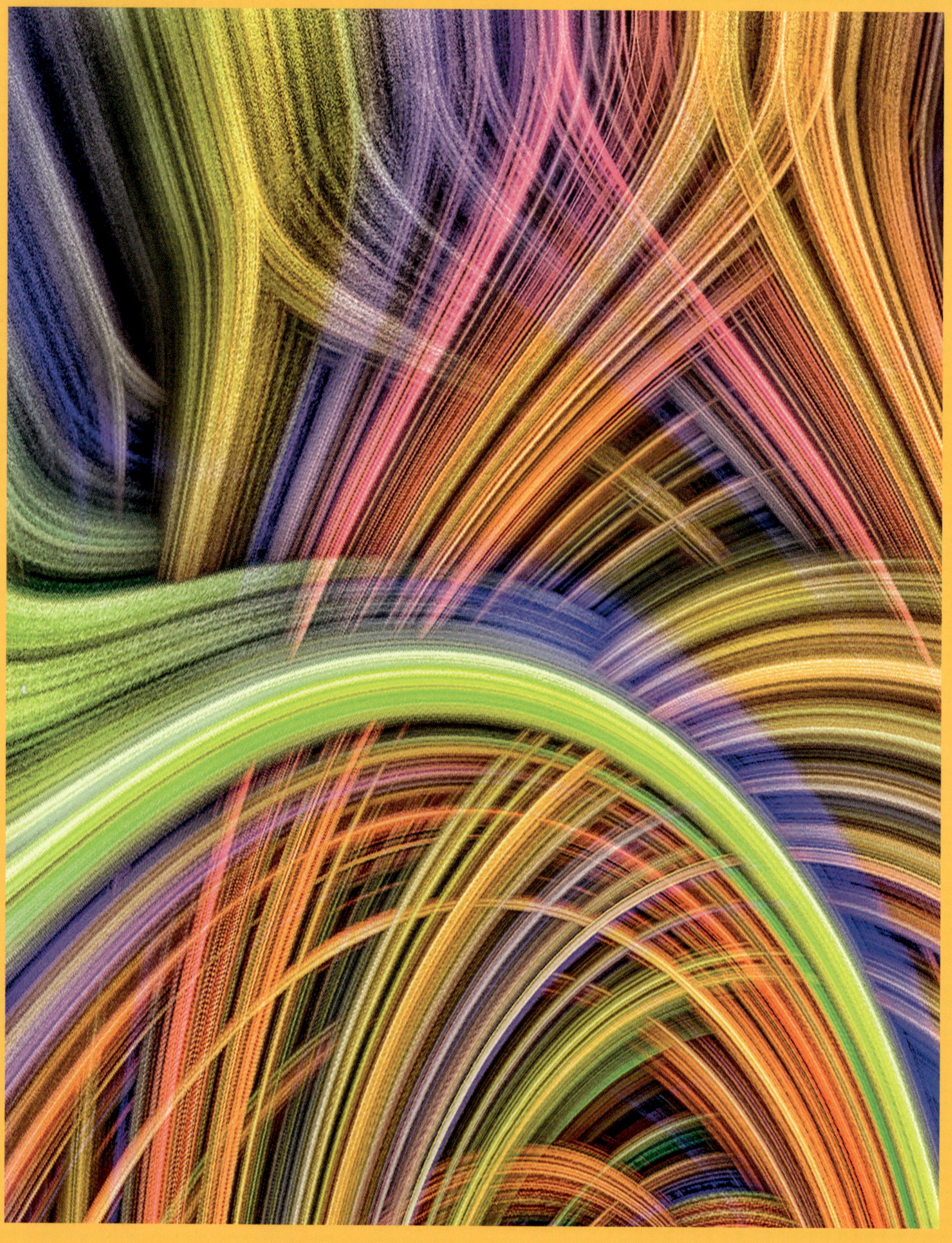

Fig. 4.1 **A picture of red-bricked buildings, with the twirl treatment described in this Lesson applied.**

LESSON 4

ABSTRACTION

Abstract photographs are pictures that do not have an immediate association with the world of objects. Instead, they rely on shapes and colours to achieve a pictorial result. This presents a challenge, often experienced when our abstract images are subject to external judging, namely to decide whether they have merit. The conventional rules of composition, and criteria such as image sharpness, may have to be set aside. Instead, the aim is to achieve an emotional impact and to appeal to our love of colours, shapes, lines and textures. We are not looking for an accurate depiction of reality.

There are countless routes to producing abstract images; for example simply extreme blurring of a starting image could convert it to an abstract. This, for more than any other photographic genre, means that it is open to endless experimentation. The creative right hemisphere of the brain is given free rein by being liberated from the need to portray reality. It also means that rules-based objections from the left hemisphere, often expressed as 'it's not photography' have to be resisted.

This Lesson sets out ways in which abstract images can be 'found' and methods by which conventionally taken photographs can be pushed towards abstraction. These are ideas and starting points for developing a personal style and heading off in new directions.

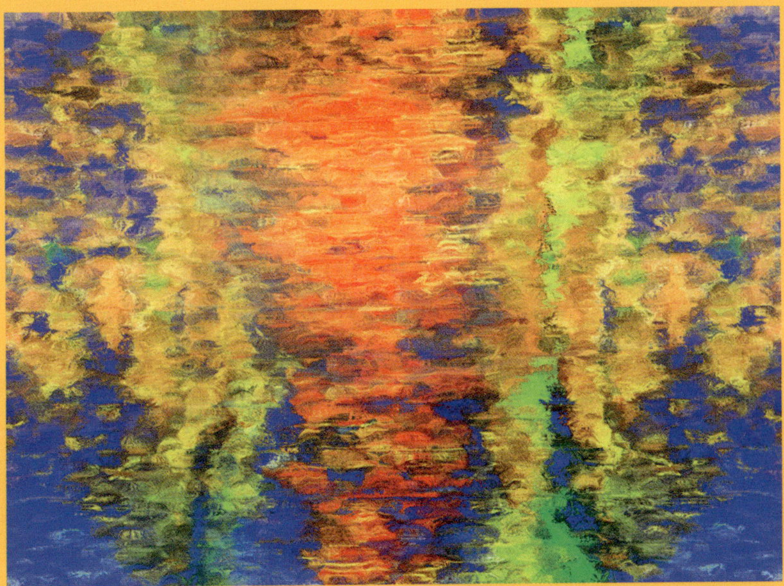

Fig. 4.2 **An abstract using a blend of images of a bridge reflection, relying on shapes and vivid colour for its impact.**

FOUND ABSTRACTS

It is surprising how many abstract pictures are all around us once we start looking for them. Examples include:

- Reflections in water
- Rusty metal surfaces
- Torn posters
- Ice and snow on windows and windscreens

As we get close to objects, their detail emerges and often presents abstract opportunities. Close-up photography invariably delivers abstract images, and it is helpful to have a camera and lens combination that allows for close-up or macro photography. These are considered in Lesson 13. This opens up a new world of detail and reveals abstract compositions in the surface of leaves, crumpled paper, tree bark and so on – in fact almost any surface on which we can focus at a close distance.

One especially rewarding source of abstract pictures is the surface of pressed flowers. Since these are completely flat, the image can be focused without any depth of field concerns. Pressing techniques are the subject of other books and websites, but it is worth noting that flower presses that can be placed in a microwave oven greatly speed up the pressing process.

DIGITAL ABSTRACTS

Imaging software such as Photoshop offers bewildering scope for turning an 'ordinary' photograph into an abstract picture. There is a temptation to keep on applying filters and adjustments and enjoy the dramatic abstract that emerges. However, it might then be difficult to backtrack and recall the steps that led to the masterpiece. To develop a personal style, record the steps along the way so that the process can be replicated with other pictures.

Fig. 4.3 **A range of 'found' abstract pictures: reflections of a boat in water, a rusty painted surface, a torn poster and a frost-covered windscreen.**

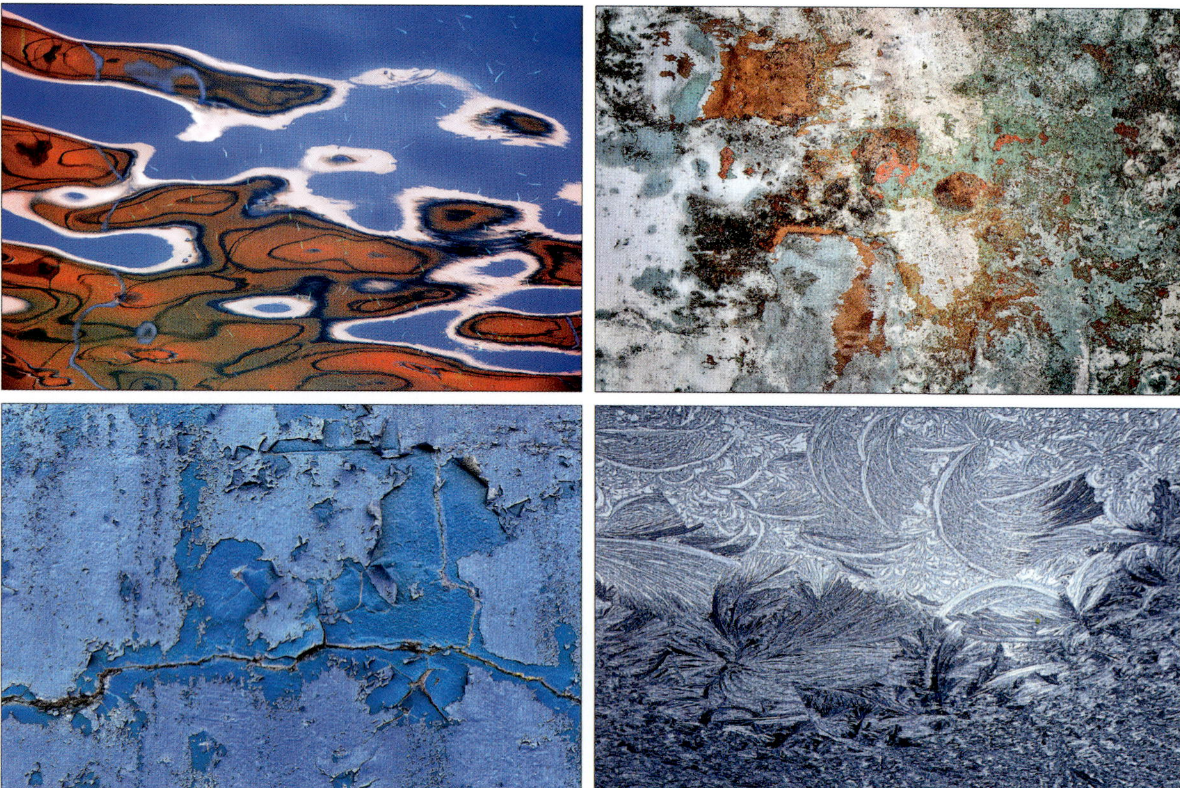

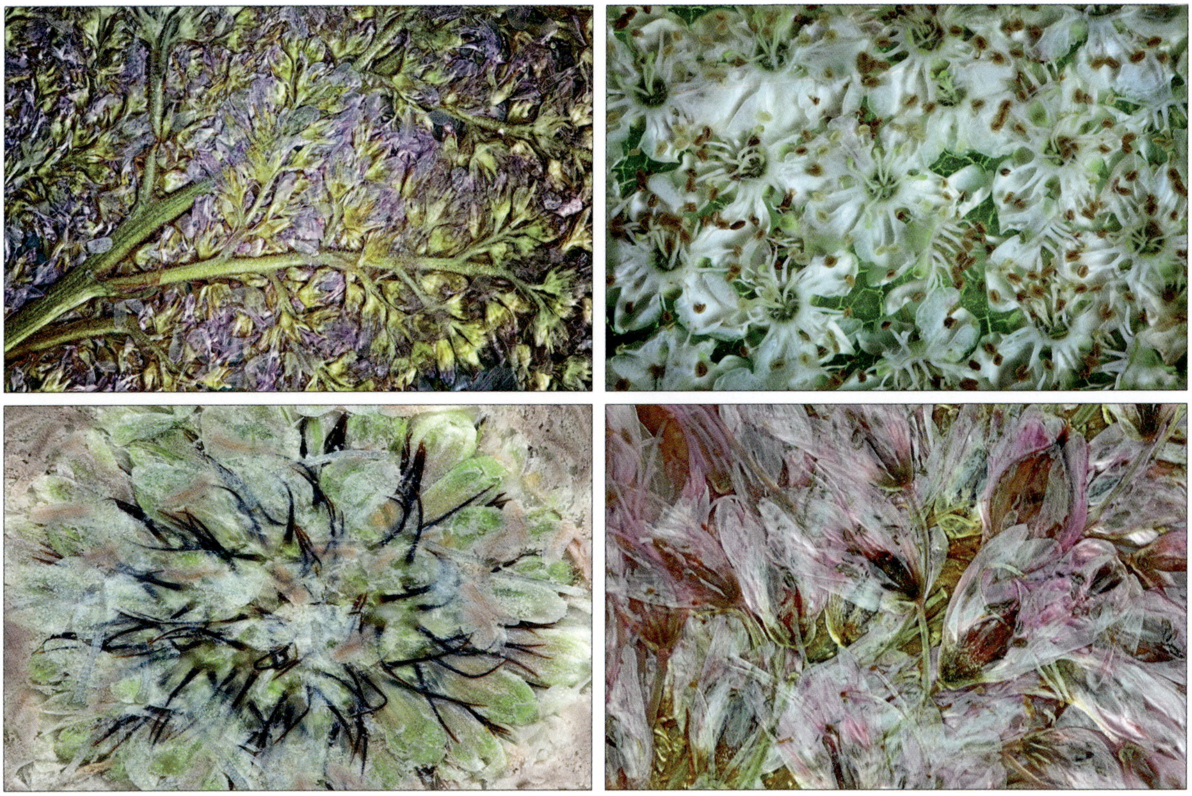

Fig. 4.4 **Abstract pictures from close-up detail of pressed flowers. An astilbe, firethorn, scabious and persicaria.**

As noted, pushing a filter such as one of the blur filters to extreme levels will move an image in abstract directions. If the result is disappointing it may be that the starting image has too many pixels. Today's digital images are often extremely high resolution, and the nudging of each pixel may be too small a proportion of the overall image size. So try again after significantly reducing the image size. If this delivers the desired result the image can then be resized upwards so that it is sufficiently large for its intended purpose.

Wave Filter

The Wave filter (Filter > Distort > Wave) is one of Photoshop's most complicated filters, with many levels of adjustment. However, this makes it one of the most versatile tools for abstracting photographs. It has three types of wave generator: sine, triangle and square. With each waveform there are settings for magnitude, wavelength and amplitude. Despite the many variables, the effect can be seen in a preview box as adjustments are made.

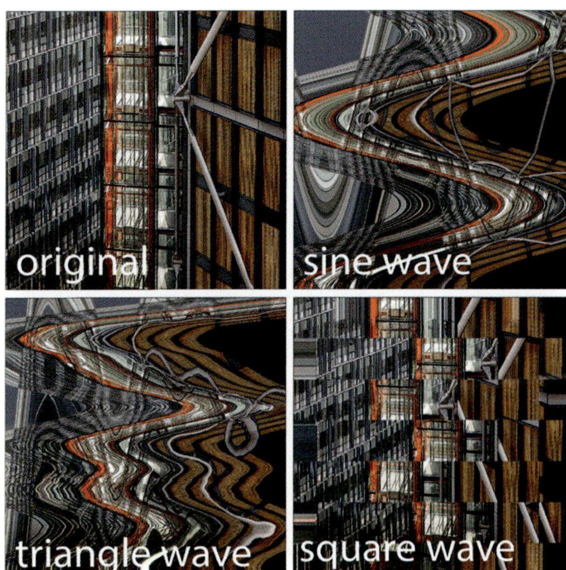

Fig. 4.5 **Abstract treatments of a picture of an office building using Photoshop's alternative settings in the Wave filter.**

Twirl Treatment

The twirl effect is an abstract treatment that produces lines of vibrant action. A starting picture should have bright, contrasty colours. Convert the image to simple horizontal lines using the Mezzotint filter (Filter > Pixelate > Mezzotint) with medium lines selected. Now apply radial zoom blur (Filter > Blur > Radial Blur) using the zoom method set at an amount of 100 with best quality. The zoom step can be repeated two or three more times to produce smooth zooming. Duplicate this layer (Layer > Duplicate Layer) so there are two identical copies of the zoomed version. With the background layer active, apply the Twirl filter (Filter > Distort > Twirl) with a positive number in the Angle box. An angle setting of 200 is a good starting point. Now make the top layer active and reapply the Twirl filter but with a negative setting of -200. This produces a twirl effect in the opposite direction. The two twirled layers can now be combined by applying a layer blending mode to the top layer. It is worth running through the blending modes to see which works best, but likely candidates are Darken, Multiply, Lighten, Exclusion and Difference.

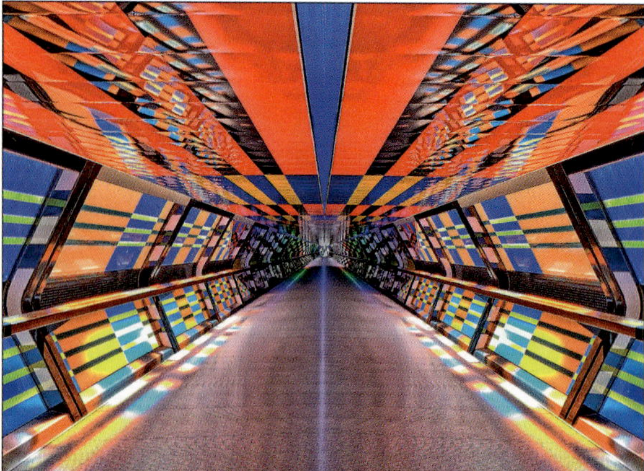

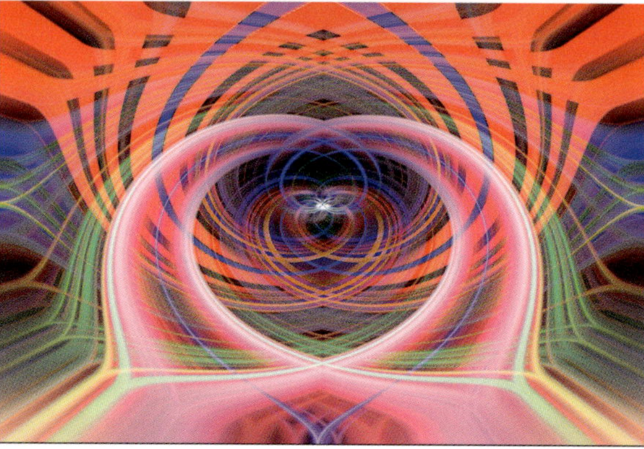

Fig. 4.6 **The twirl treatment applied to a picture of the illuminated tunnel in London's Canary Wharf.**

Orbs

An intriguing abstract can be created by two applications of Photoshop's Polar Coordinates filter. The resulting 'orb' resembles a circular glass paperweight. For a circular result, make the starting picture square. This can be achieved by cropping, or by resizing (Image > Image Size); unlink the connection between width and height and make both the same. Apply the Polar Coordinates filter (Filter > Distort > Polar Coordinates) with the Polar to Rectangular setting; this is not the usual starting setting for this filter so is not the default. Turn the image upside down (Image > Image Rotation > 180°) and repeat the Polar Coordinates transformation using the Rectangular to Polar setting. This will have applied a coloured background to the orb, and it is worth selecting the background and filling with black or white. A clean way to do this is to make a circular selection of the orb and invert the selection (Select > Inverse), then fill the background (Edit > Fill; choose black or white in the drop-down options).

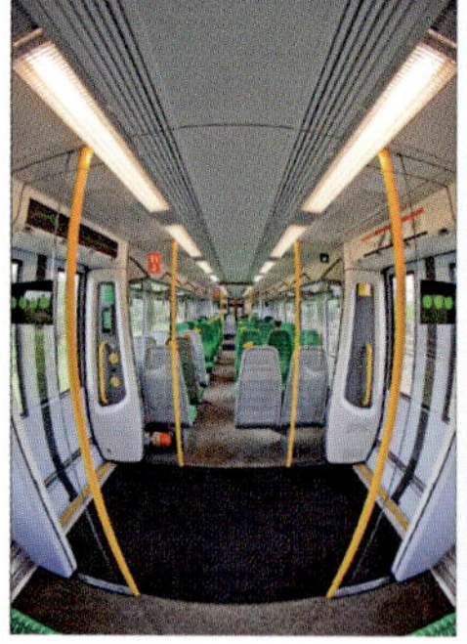

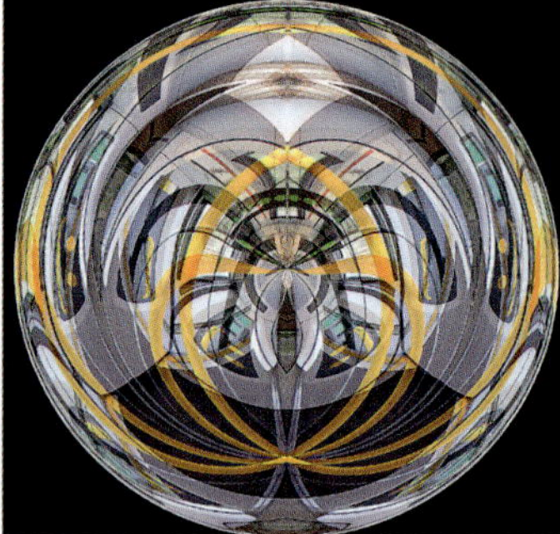

Fig. 4.7 **The orb conversion applied to a picture of a railway carriage. The original picture was taken with a fish-eye lens, and the yellow handrails add structural lines within the orb.**

Patterns

Photographic patterns are abstract images that have immediate appeal. A pattern is a design in which lines, shapes, forms or colours are repeated. Image-editing programs are the perfect tool for constructing pattern pictures. Once an image is on the clipboard (Edit > Copy), it can be repeatedly placed on the canvas (Edit > Paste) and arranged to create a pattern. Photoshop includes a pattern-making tool in which a selection of an image can be presented in a range of pattern formats. Make a selection from an image, copy the selection (Edit > Copy) and place the selected contents on a new layer (Edit > Paste). Give the selection a pattern name in the pattern dialogue box (Edit > Define Pattern). The selection will now be in Photoshop's pattern collection. Create a new blank canvas at a chosen size (File > New; enter the image dimensions and resolution). Fill the canvas with the selection using one of Photoshop's pattern options (Edit > Fill, with contents set to Pattern). The named pattern will be at the bottom of the Custom Pattern options. Choose the pattern type, such as Spiral Fill, from the list of options and click OK. A preview box will then appear; adjust the sliders to suit and click OK. This is likely to involve going backwards and forwards a few times to get the layout and scaling to match the chosen canvas size.

Additional software packages are available, either as stand-alone tools or as Photoshop plug-ins, that will deliver further pattern treatments. An intriguing option is PhotoSpiralysis (www.photospiralysis.com), which delivers the Droste effect. This is named after a brand of Dutch cocoa, which uses the effect in its product design. Droste treatment delivers a controllable spiral effect by repeatedly placing a shrunken version of the image on top of the original, rotating slightly each time. Detailed explanation of this technique can be found in Lesson 14.

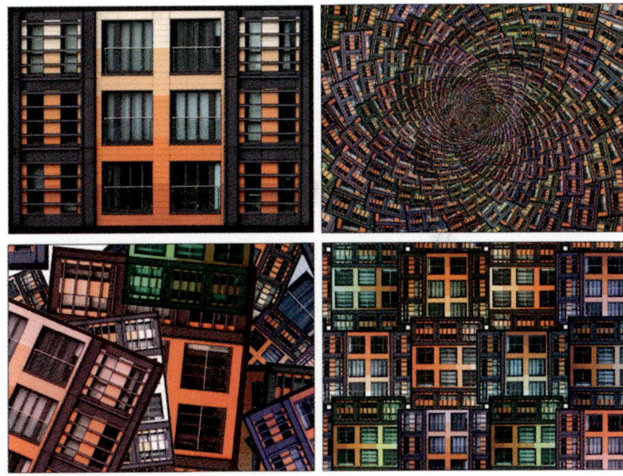

RIGHT
Fig. 4.8 **A colourful window with three different applications of Photoshop's pattern tool: the Spiral Fill, the Random Fill and the Cross Weave.**

Fig. 4.9 **The PhotoSpiralysis program, used to apply the Droste effect to a picture of a bird-of-paradise flower.**

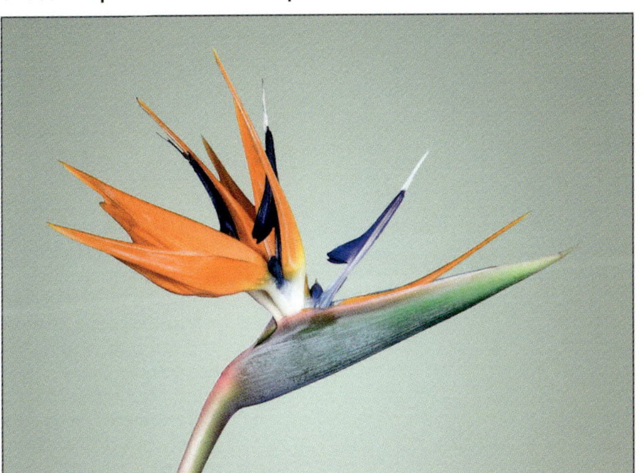

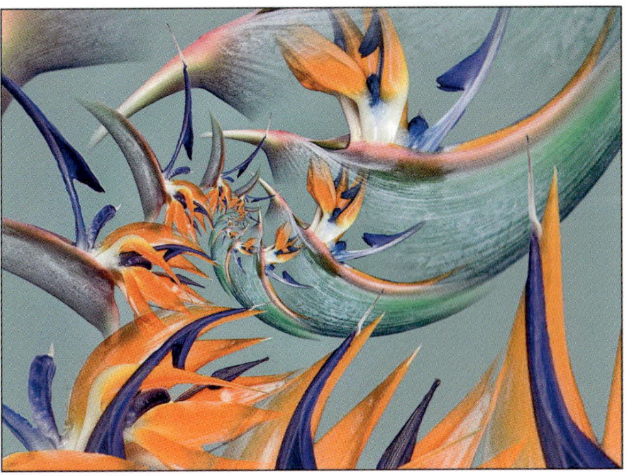

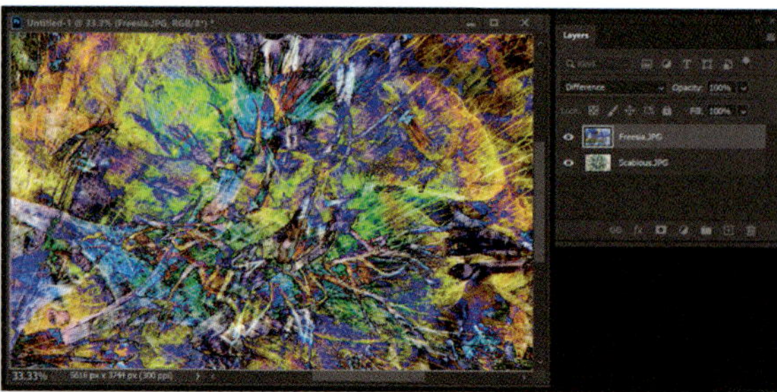

Fig. 4.10 **Photoshop's Difference blend mode used to combine two pressed-flower pictures to produce a dramatic abstract.**

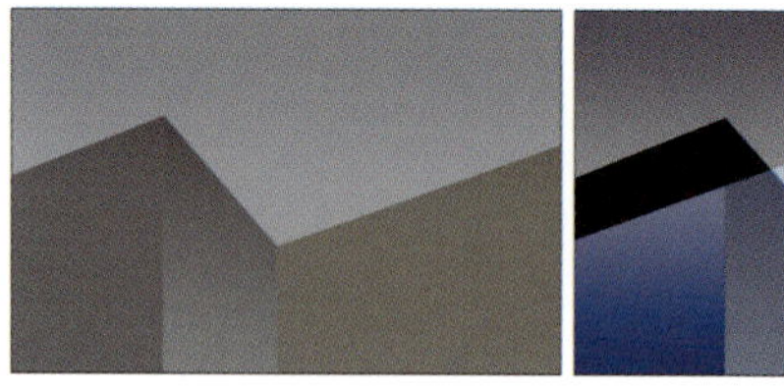
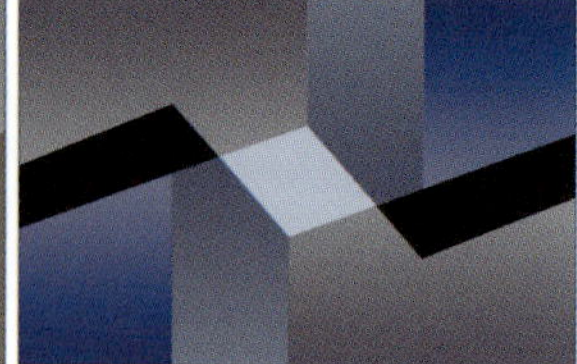

Fig. 4.11 **A geometric abstract based on a single image of the junction of a wall and ceiling. The picture was duplicated on a new Photoshop layer, rotated 180° and blended with the Multiply blend mode.**

Layer Blend Modes

Blending image layers together is a surefire route to abstract images. Almost any two images when loaded as separate Photoshop layers will become abstract when blended together. The only real requirement is that the two images are not the same. It can be difficult to anticipate exactly what result each blend mode will produce so it is worth running through them. This can be done by clicking on one of the drop-down blend modes and then using the keyboard arrow keys to scroll through the options. Often the Multiply or Difference modes will produce the most dramatic transformations, with new colours being created in the process.

An option, illustrated in Figure 4.11, is to use the same picture on each layer but to rotate one layer so that it does not align with the layer below.

There are many other routes to image abstraction than those described here. Other Lessons, particularly those on double exposure and displacing, describe techniques that can be used to produce abstract pictures.

ABSTRACTION - KEYS

ABSTRACT photographs do not attempt to portray reality; they rely on shape, colour and form for their impact.

ABSTRACT pictures do not lend themselves to assessment using conventional compositional guidelines. Instead, they will be judged for their emotional impact.

MANY abstract images can be found in the natural environment, especially when photographed with close-up and macro equipment.

THERE are countless routes to producing abstract pictures using digital techniques, and this is a rewarding area for creative experimentation.

PATTERNS are a particularly pleasing form of abstract image and can be created with several digital techniques.

FACING PAGE
Fig. 4.12 **An abstract assembled from images of rotated sections of a graffiti-painted wall combined in Photoshop layers and merged with the Darken blend mode. Adjustments were then made in Levels to brighten the result.**

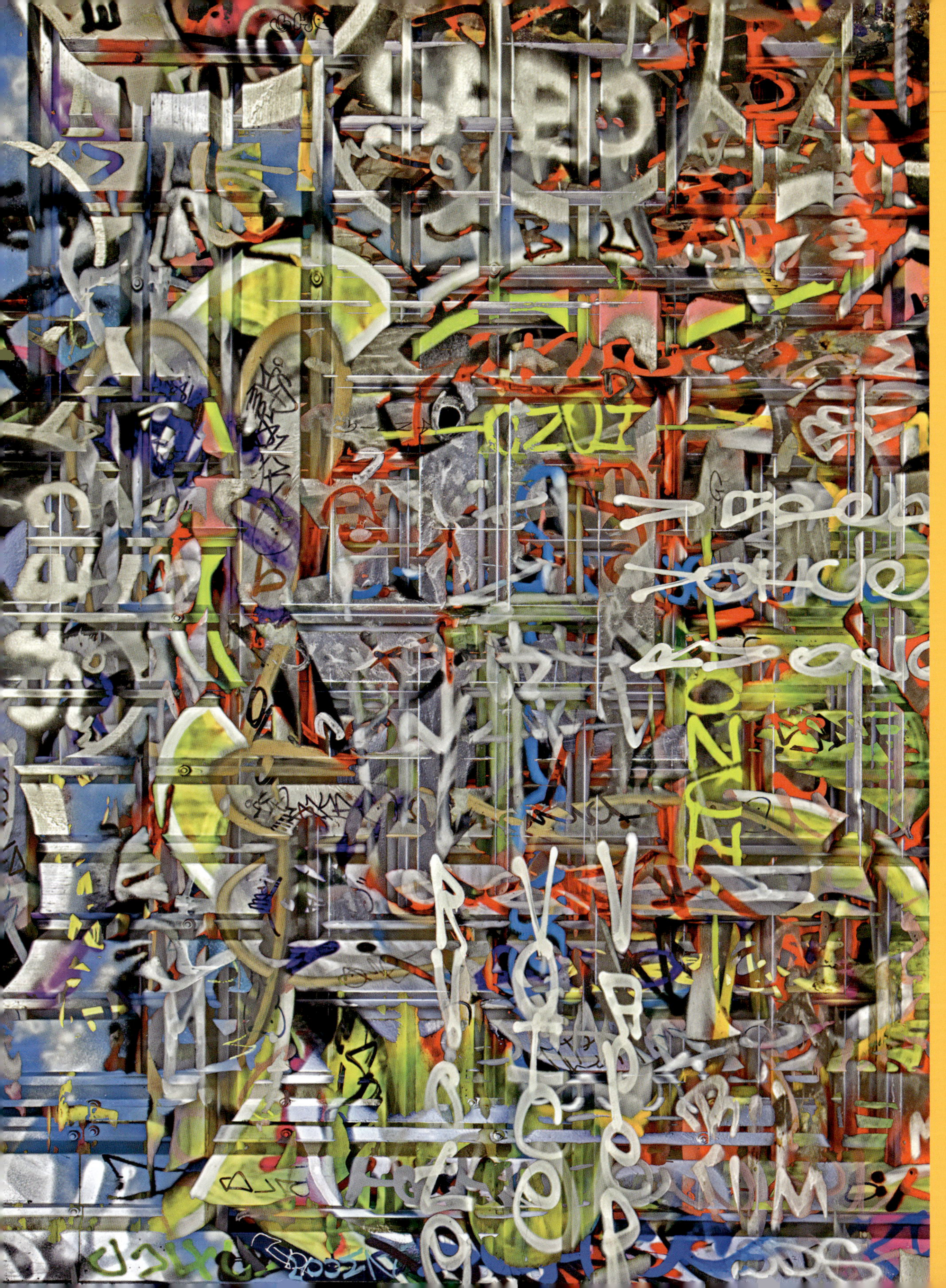

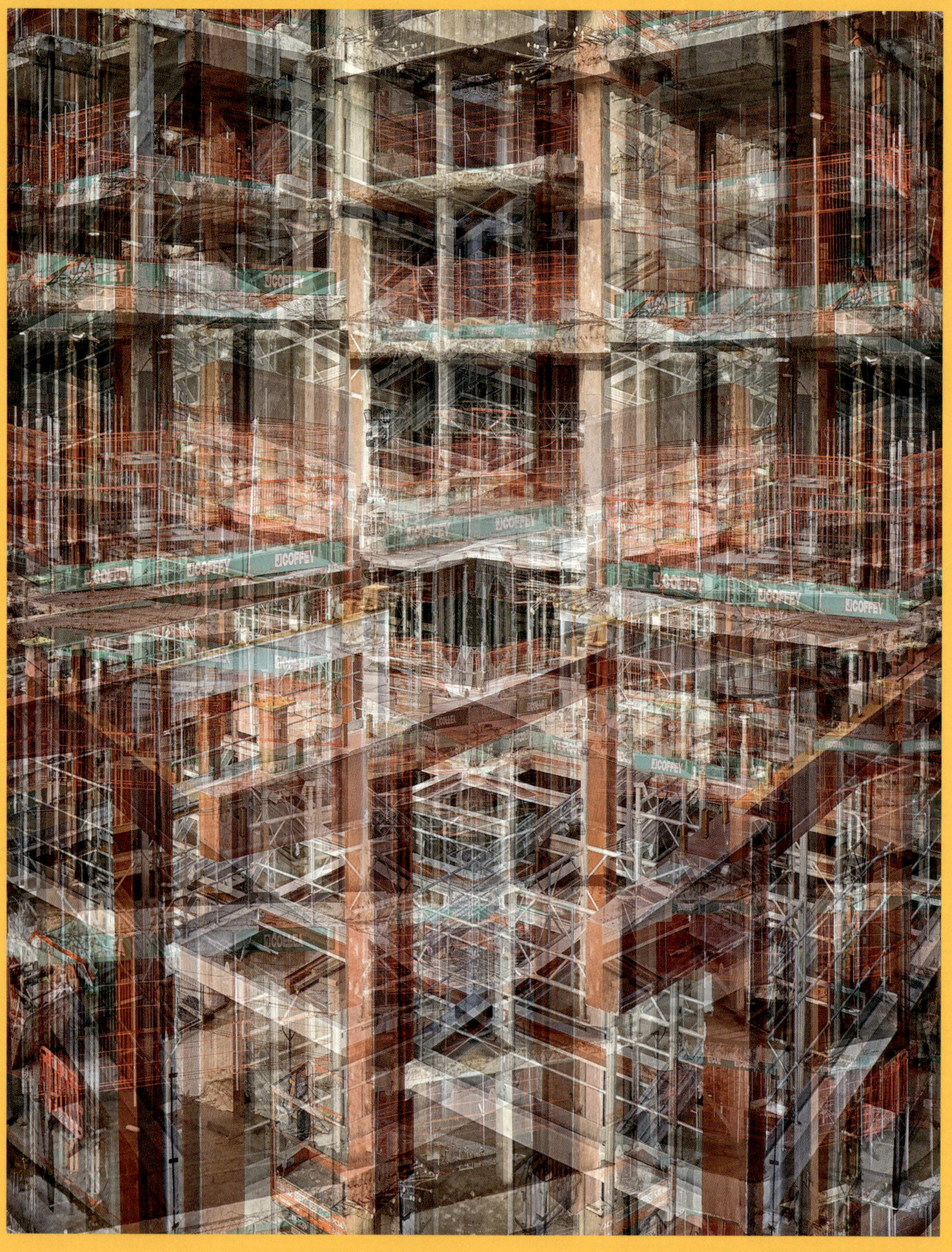

Fig. 5.1 **A double exposure of a section of a building site, also used in Figure 5.10, giving a sense of detail and depth.**

LESSON 5

DOUBLE EXPOSURE

Double and multiple exposures were some of the earliest special-effect treatments in photography. They were achieved by exposing one picture in camera and then taking another without winding the film on. This could also be delivered in the darkroom by printing two or more negatives that were sandwiched together. These options are still open for film-camera users. However, with the use of digital techniques much greater flexibility is offered, and very artistic results can be achieved.

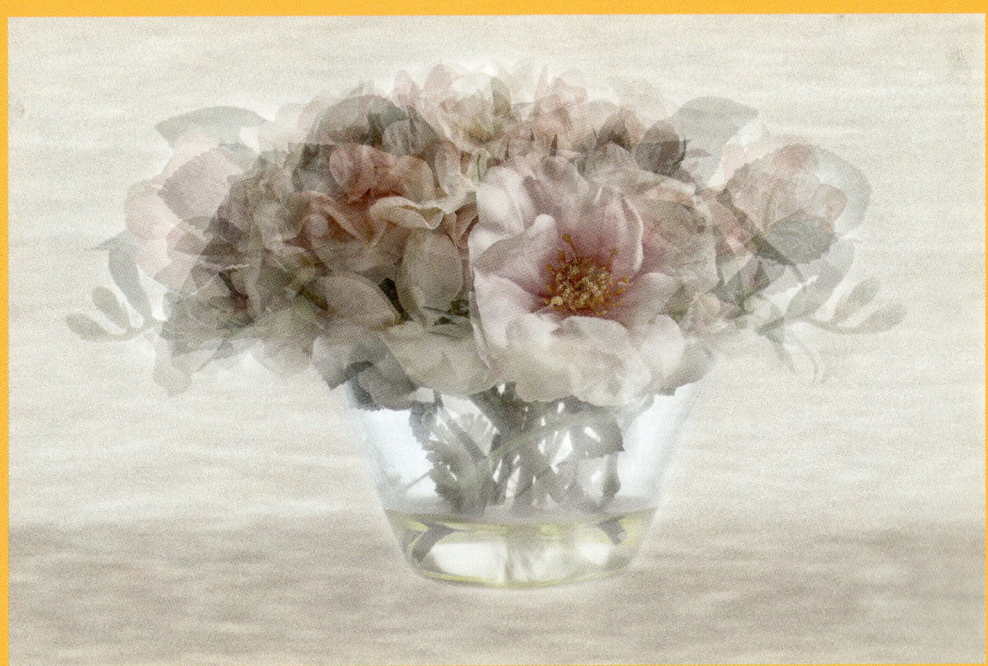

Fig. 5.2 **A floral composition consisting of three merged images with the visibility of the central rose increased to give a focal point. Texture has been selectively added as presented in Lesson 3.**

IN-CAMERA TECHNIQUES

Although the film route is still an option for double-exposure images, digital cameras offer considerable advantages. Most modern digital cameras include a setting by which images can be combined in camera. Digital menu settings can present something of a labyrinth to negotiate but buried away there is likely to be a setting called Multiple Exposure. Once it is activated there are other decisions to be made. The first is to set the number of exposures that will be combined. Although it is tempting to go for the maximum, perhaps up to nine, it is safer to settle for two or three. High numbers of exposures can result in over-complicated pictures. The other main setting controls the way in which the exposures will be combined. This will vary from camera to camera but replicates the layer blending modes in Photoshop. A typical default setting is called Additive, in which each shot is given full exposure. A safer starting point is a setting usually called Average, by which each image is automatically underexposed so that the final image is then correctly exposed. Finally, it is possible to ensure that each image is separately saved as well as the composite. This is ideal if some of the individual pictures have merit and gives the option to reprocess the merged picture in software for additional adjustments.

Image blending can also be achieved in the camera that is always with us, the smartphone. There is a range of phone apps that can be used for double and multiple exposure, some free and some paid for. They include PhotoSplit, Snapseed, Image Blender, Double Exposure and Photo Blend. This is not a comprehensive list, and new apps are often added. As with the in-camera options, the result can be seen building up on the viewing screen. There is a further advantage that the number of images to be combined does not have to be pre-set and exposures can be added until the result looks right.

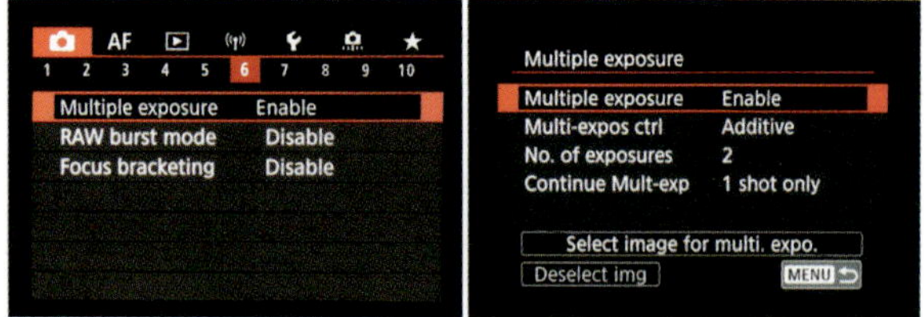

Fig. 5.3 **Typical settings within a digital camera menu to enable multiple-exposure photography. When Multiple exposure is selected, the blend mode and the number of images to be combined can be set. In this illustration, the blend mode is Additive, and two images will be combined.**

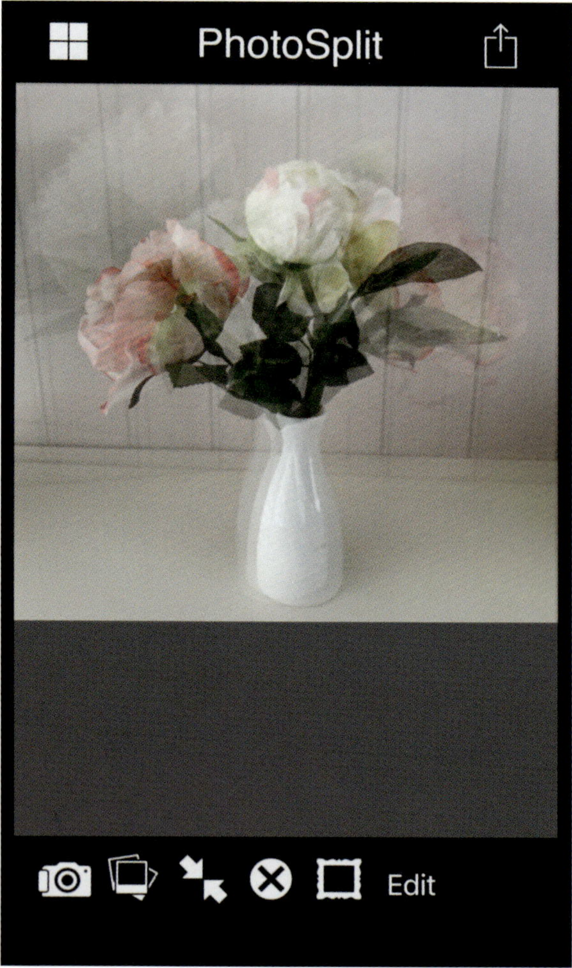

Fig. 5.4 **The smartphone app PhotoSplit is one of many for multiple-exposure photographs. Here it is used for a vase of flowers and shows the challenge of aligning the edges of a vase.**

DIGITAL METHODS

As ever, there is no shortage of digital techniques for this treatment. They generally rely on layers-based software such as Photoshop, in which each of the pictures to be blended is loaded into a layer and then combined using one of the digital options. Photo software enables control over the process, both in terms of the precise positioning of each image and the relative visibility of the separate images.

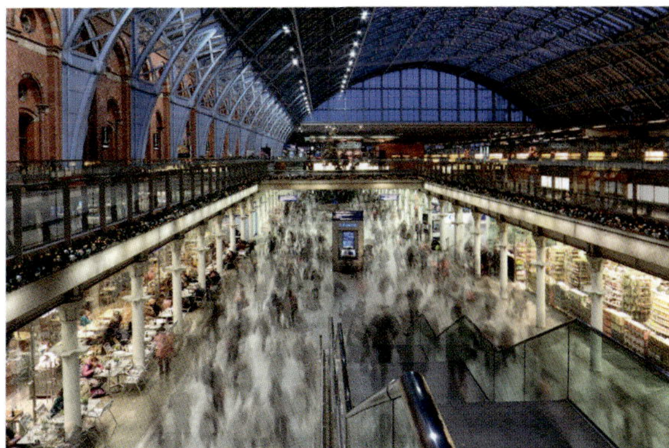

Fig. 5.5 **A multiple-exposure picture of London's St Pancras Station, designed to give the impression of busy movement. Each image was loaded in a Photoshop layer and adjusted for opacity. Since tripods cannot be used in these public spaces, the pictures were handheld and had to be aligned in software (Edit > Auto-Align Layers > Auto).**

Opacity Adjustment

The first step is to place all the images to be combined on separate layers. The impact of each layer is then adjusted by changing the opacity of the upper layer or layers. Images can be combined as layers in a single image file by clicking and dragging them onto each other. If the Shift key is pressed at the same time, the images will be centred. So, if they are the same size, they will be precisely aligned. An option that is useful if several images are to be used is to access a tool that automatically opens and centres images in layers. In Adobe Bridge, the widely used software for image filing, the tool is at the top of the screen (Tools > Photoshop > Load Files into Photoshop Layers). To adjust opacity, a starting point is to give each layer equal impact. If there are just two layers, simply set the top-layer opacity to 50%. For more layers, the opacity is a progressively increasing fraction of the number of layers. So, if there were five layers, the top layer would be set at 1/5 opacity, the next layer down at 1/4 opacity, the next at 1/3, the penultimate layer at 1/2 and the bottom at full opacity. To make life a little more complicated, the fractions must be entered as percentages. The opacities can then be tweaked to produce the desired contribution of the various layers. More fine tuning can be undertaken by placing a layer mask on a layer and painting on the mask with a soft low-opacity black brush to reduce the impact of selected areas.

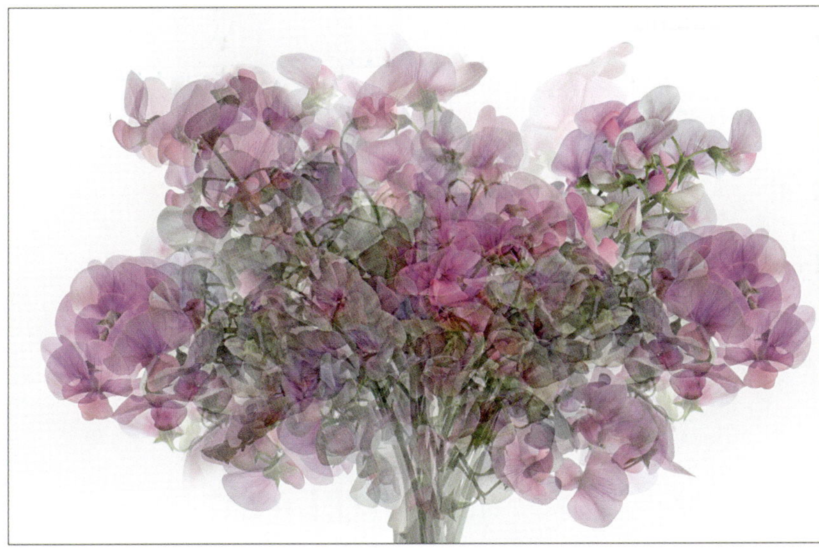

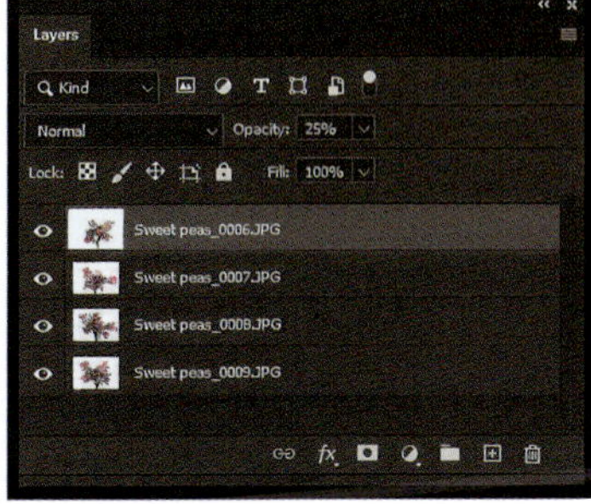

Fig. 5.6 **Four pictures of a vase of sweet peas showing the layer settings for blending by adjusting layer opacity. The top-layer opacity is shown at 25%; the next layers down will be 50%, 75% and 100%.**

Blending Modes

As with several of the techniques covered in this book, great flexibility and creative opportunity is offered by the blending mode features available in any imaging software that allows for layers-based processing. When the blend for the top image in a layer stack is set to Normal, there is no blending into the images underneath and only that top layer is visible. When the blend mode is set to Darken, only tones that are darker than the next layer down will be visible. The naming of other blend modes is often less obvious. For example, the very useful Soft Light mode darkens or lightens the colours, depending on the blend colour. The result can be an attractive soft, diffused effect.

Other blend modes often produce very different results. For double-exposure effects, as with producing abstract images in Lesson 4, it is often worth running through the different modes to produce a result that appeals.

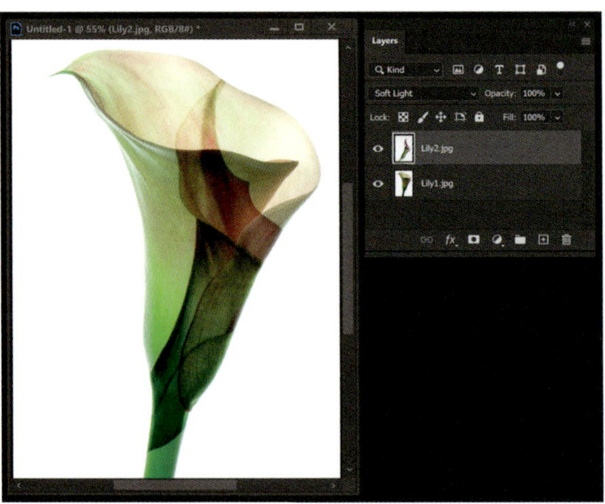

Fig. 5.7 **Two pictures of a lily combined using the Soft Light blend mode.**

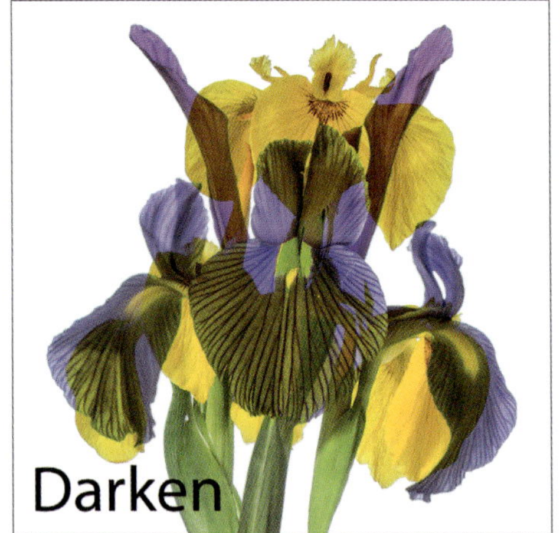

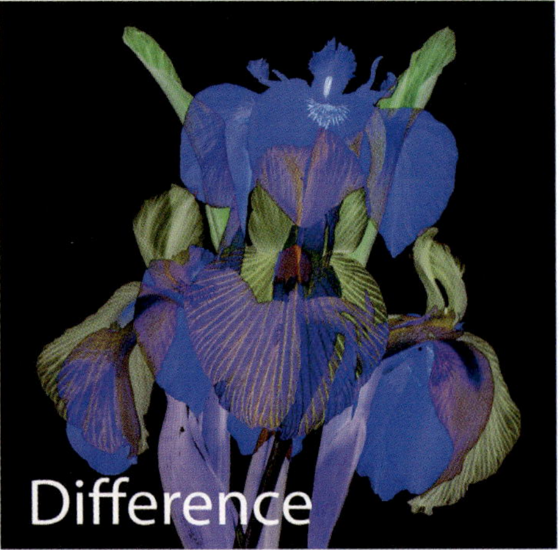

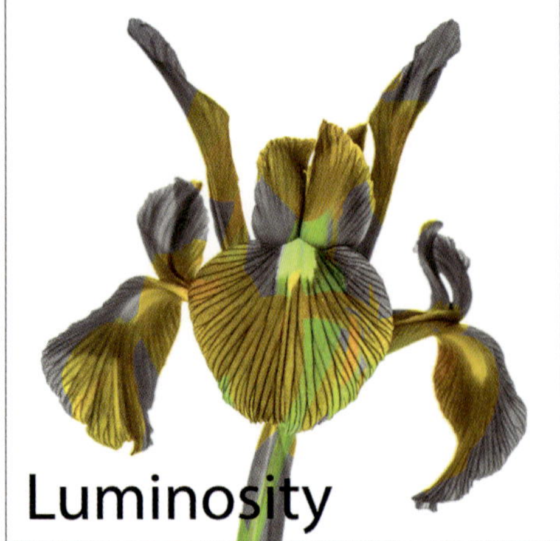

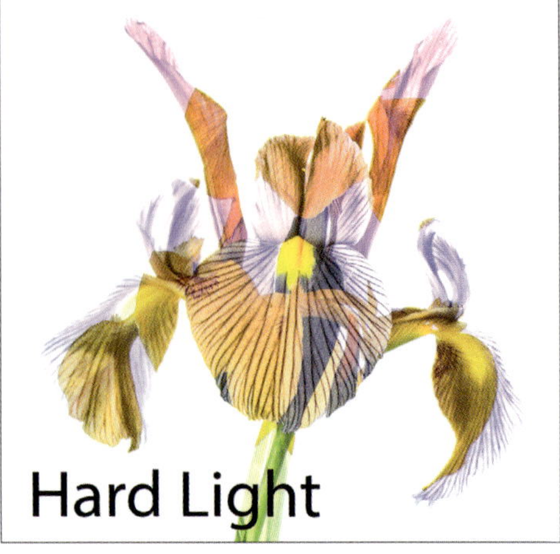

Fig. 5.8 **A purple iris as a top layer above a yellow iris, showing the effect of different blend modes.**

SUBJECTS FOR DOUBLE EXPOSURE

Double and multiple exposures enable us to view subjects in new ways, to add interest and depth. Double exposure can often be used to emphasise the innate characteristics of a subject.

Flowers

Flowers take on a more gentle, floaty appearance when double exposed. Vases of flowers are particularly successful when treated in this way. However, it can be a challenge to ensure that the diffused appearance of the flowers is not carried over to the vase, so the rim and edges of the vase should be aligned in each picture. Digitally this can be achieved by nudging the layers in software so that they coincide. When taking the pictures, it is sometimes helpful to place the vase in the centre of a turntable so that it is always centred as it is rotated for each picture.

Buildings

Double-exposed buildings can become dramatic and three-dimensional. It is also possible to create a sense of place, for example by combining a record shot with a signpost showing the location. One option, illustrated in Figure 5.1, is to take a section of a building and superimpose it on another section. In Figure 5.10, the original image was flipped horizontally, as explained in Lesson 11, placed on a new Photoshop layer and combined by reducing the opacity of the flipped image.

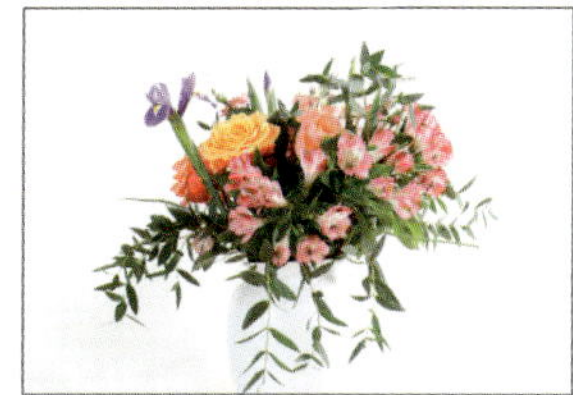

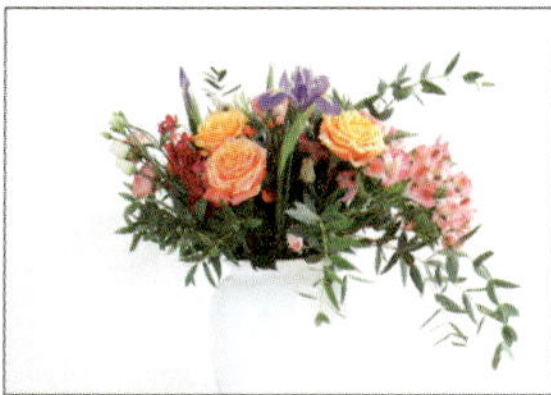

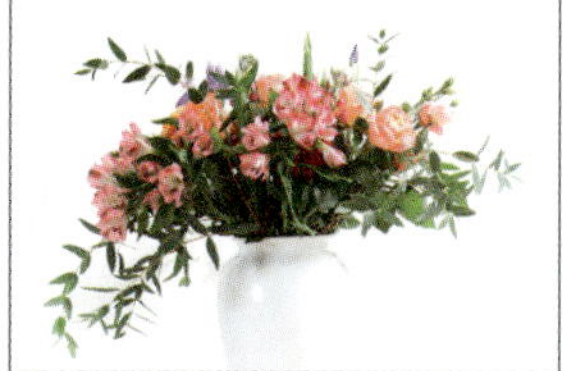

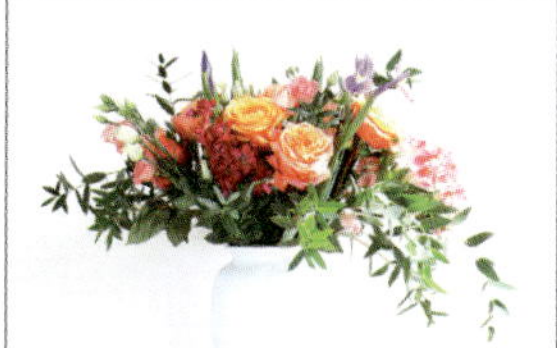

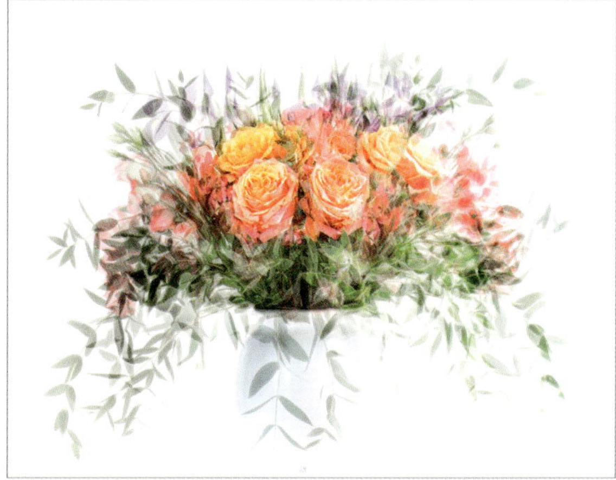

Fig. 5.9 **Four pictures of a vase of flowers taken from different angles and combined using layer-opacity adjustment. The challenge is to ensure that the position of the vase is consistent throughout the sequence.**

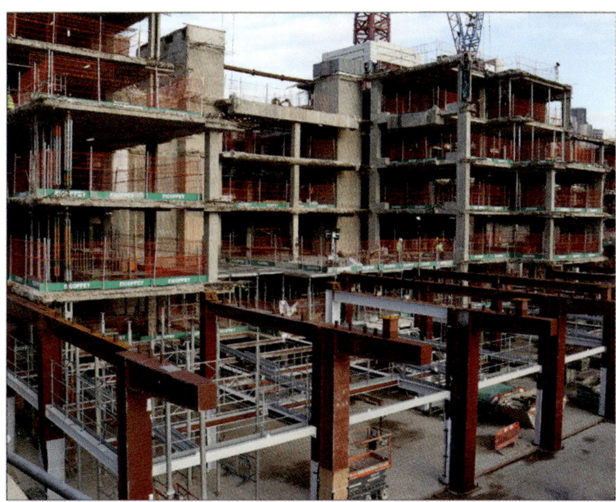

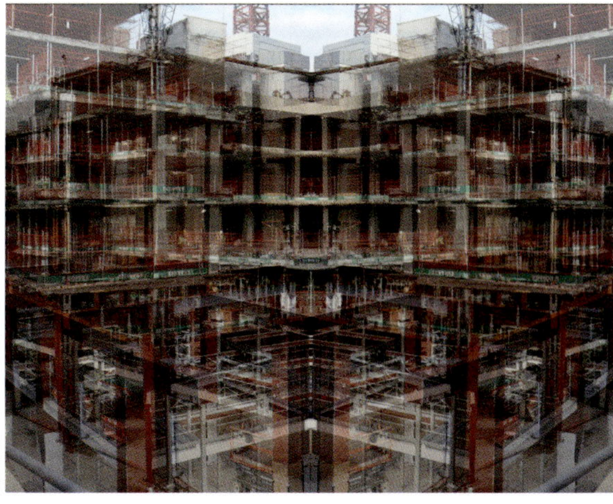

Fig. 5.10 **A building site combined with a horizontally flipped version of itself and blended using reduction of the top-layer opacity. A cropped and adjusted version of this picture is shown in Figure 5.1.**

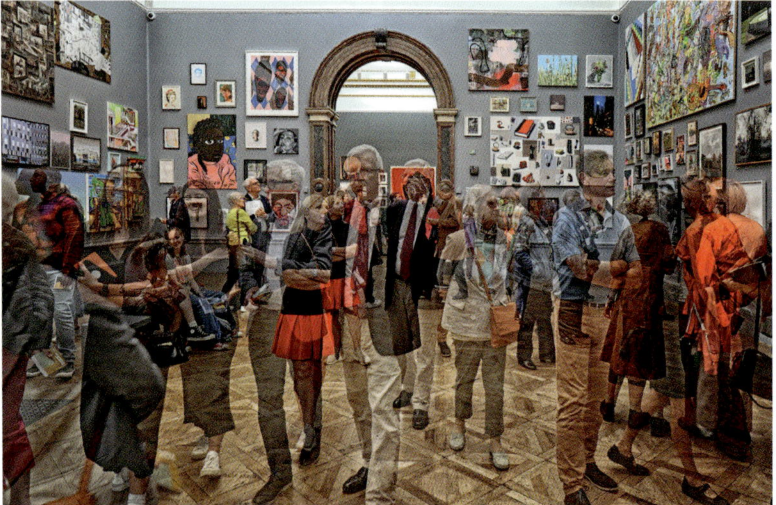

Fig. 5.11 **A double exposure of the Summer Exhibition at London's Royal Academy.**

People

People in double-exposed pictures will become translucent. We see through them to their background or to some other image. This can give them a ghostly appearance. The intensity of the effect can be controlled by adjusting the opacity of the layer on which they appear. If there are a number of pictures of an environment through which people are passing, such as the railway station in Figure 5.5 or the art gallery in Figure 5.11, there will be a sense of the urgent movement of people through crowded spaces.

These subject suggestions are far from comprehensive. This approach is wide open for creative experimenting. Double exposure can create dreamy landscapes, mysterious close-ups and evocative street pictures.

DOUBLE EXPOSURE - KEYS

DOUBLE and multiple exposure is achieved in film cameras by exposing a number of pictures without winding on the film.

DIGITAL techniques allow greater flexibility over the control and final appearance of double-exposed pictures.

IN layers-based software, images can be combined either by adjusting the opacity of the layers or selecting appropriate blending modes.

MULTIPLE exposure can be used to enhance the inherent qualities of subjects such as flowers, buildings and people.

MULTIPLE exposure is particularly suited to creative experimentation.

FACING PAGE
Fig. 5.12 **A bunch of sweet peas photographed from three different positions, placed on Photoshop layers and combined by adjusting the opacity of the top and middle layers.**

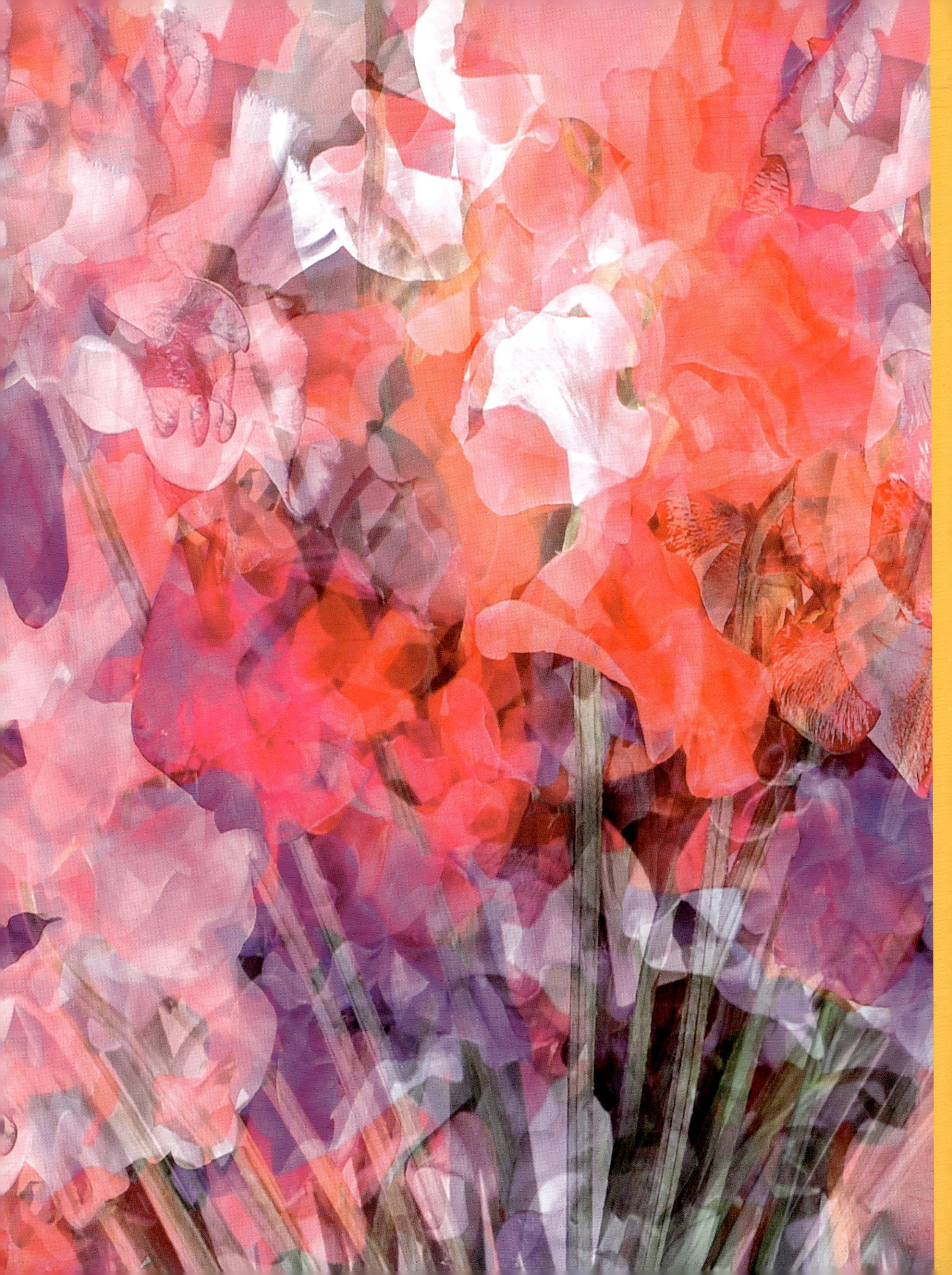

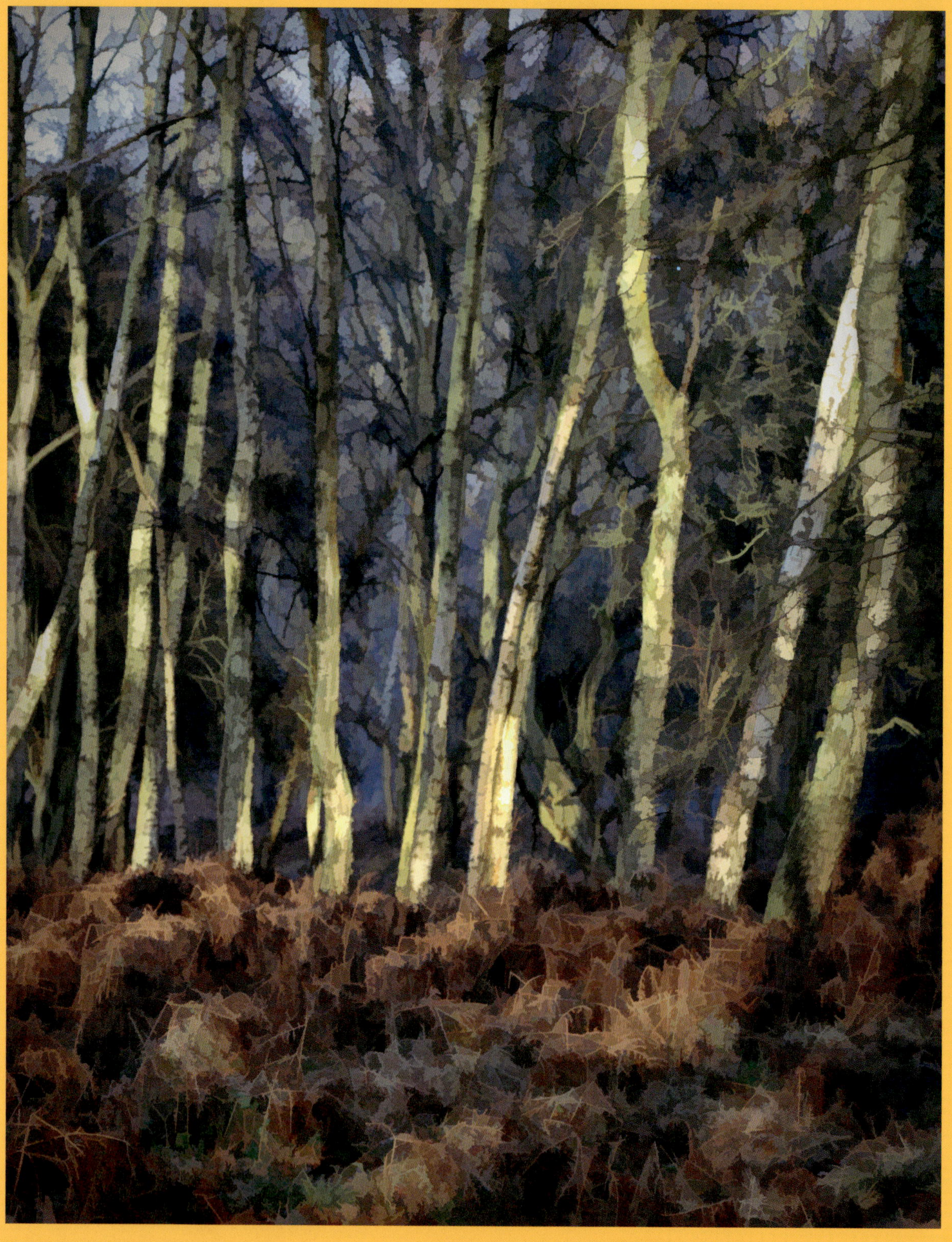

Fig. 6.1 **Brightly lit beech trees with detail removed using the Photoshop Cutout filter.**

LESSON 6

SIMPLIFYING

Simplifying in photography means removing elements in the picture space that distract from the main message. It's often tempting to try to include everything we see in the picture. However, although the detail may have added to our experience at the time, in a picture it may be distracting clutter. It is also easy to be lured by the capability of modern cameras that can deliver very high-resolution images with acute sharpness. Desirable though this can be, it is not always the route to artistic images. This Lesson considers ways in which detail can be removed from photographs so that the composition can be appreciated for its balance of colours, shapes and forms.

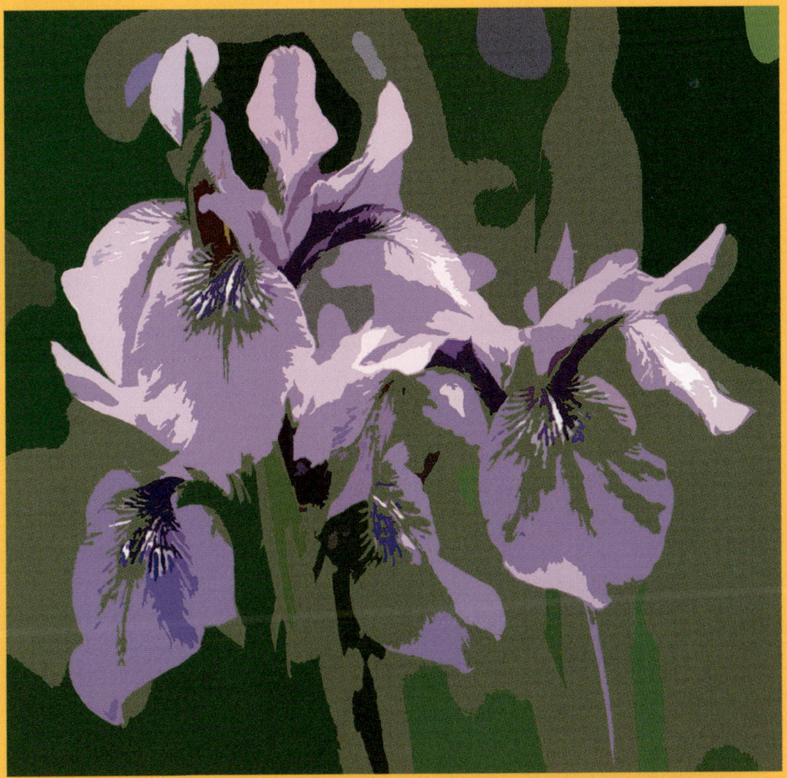

Fig. 6.2 **An iris flower simplified by removing detail to give a more striking and graphic presentation.**

RESOLUTION

Resolution is the level of detail in an image. For digital images, this is measured in pixels per inch, ppi. For prints the measure is dots per inch, dpi. These two measures are often confused! The higher the resolution, the more detail and definition in the image. An image is generally considered high resolution at 300ppi or more. This would mean that an A3 picture (42 × 29.7cm or 16.5 × 11.7in) would need an image size of around 5,000 × 3,500 pixels, an area of 17.5 million pixels (or megapixels). This is within the resolution delivered by most modern cameras.

Reducing Resolution

It may seem outrageous to invest in high-resolution photographic equipment and then to deliberately reduce that resolution. Of course this is not something to do routinely. However, as resolution decreases, different and sometimes intriguing pictures emerge. As the identity of the subject fades, the shape and colour distribution of the picture become evident.

To reduce resolution, it is necessary to change the image size (Image > Image Size). A box will display the image dimensions with options of displaying in a range of units including pixels, centimetres and inches. The image resolution is also displayed. Enter a reduced dimension size; for example change the width in Figure 6.4 from its original 3,648 pixels to 1,500 pixels and see if this delivers the desired result. The image height will be reduced proportionally, provided the width and height link is left at its default position.

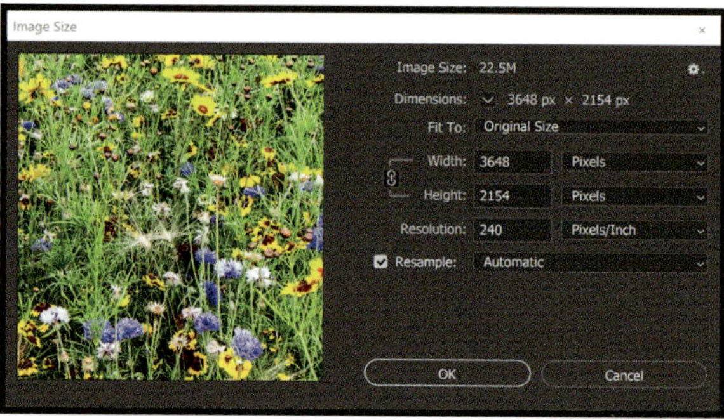

Fig. 6.4 **The image-size setting in Photoshop. Displaying the resolution in pixels as shown here gives the true image size and can be used to reduce resolution if needed for some of the techniques in this Lesson.**

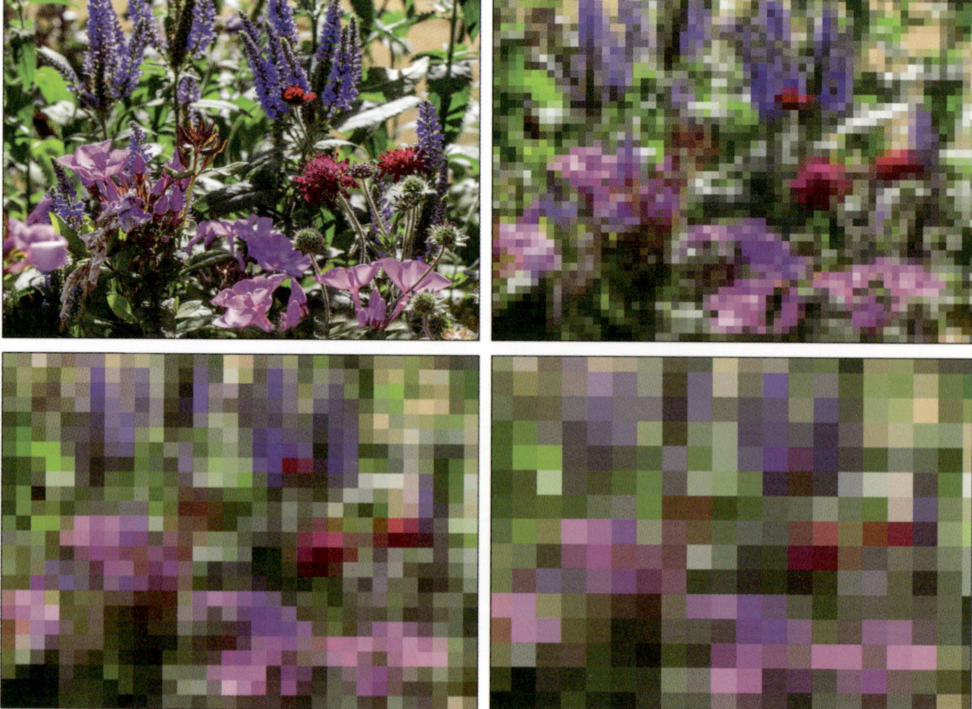

Fig. 6.3 **A garden-flower picture with progressively reduced resolution, firstly to simplify the shapes and eventually to show only the distribution of colour.**

It is worth noting here that reduced-resolution images can be extremely helpful when applying some of the digital filter treatments described later and in other parts of the book. Photoshop filters can deliver disappointing results when applied to high-resolution pictures because there are simply too many pixels for the effect to be apparent.

Once the resolution has been reduced to give the desired visual result, the image may now be too small for its intended purpose, perhaps to print. So it is now necessary to interpolate the picture back up to a suitable size. To do this, revisit the image size setting, tick the Resample box and enter the appropriate larger dimensions. However, to preserve the image appearance, do not use the default resample setting of Automatic since this will lose the intended blocky appearance. Instead use the drop-down options and select Nearest Neighbor (hard edges). This will deliver the increased image size without changing the appearance.

The Digital Short Cut

A Photoshop filter can deliver the reduced-resolution appearance without actually changing image resolution. This is the Mosaic filter (Filter > Pixelate > Mosaic). A slider marked Cell Size can now be adjusted to give the desired effect. Note that this does not actually change the image resolution so would not be the step to take if you are reducing resolution in order to get greater impact from other filters.

Combining Low- and High-Resolution Images

An interesting effect can be produced by combining a low-resolution image with its high-resolution original using one of the blending methods described in Lesson 5. This results in a distinctive image effect in which the 'blocks' from the low-resolution version affect the tones of the underlying original, giving an intriguing checkerboard appearance.

DIGITAL FILTERS

Most digital filters, including the blur filters reviewed in Lesson 10, effectively simplify the image. In the process they often add directional lines for creative effect. In addition, some filters are specifically designed for simplification by removing detail.

Median Filter

The Median filter (Filter > Noise > Median) is a long-established Photoshop tool and is one route to reducing image noise. The process used is complex: it discards pixels that differ too much from adjacent pixels and replaces a centre pixel with the median brightness value of the adjacent pixels. The Radius slider can be adjusted for the strength of the filtration and once pushed above a few pixels, goes well beyond noise removal and produces distinctive simplified pictures.

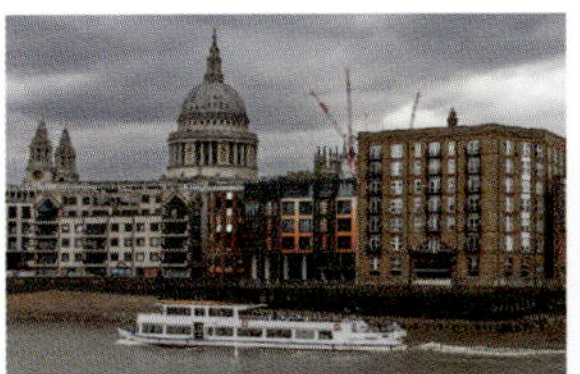

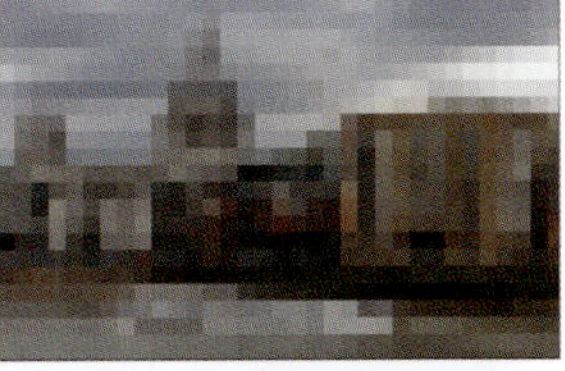

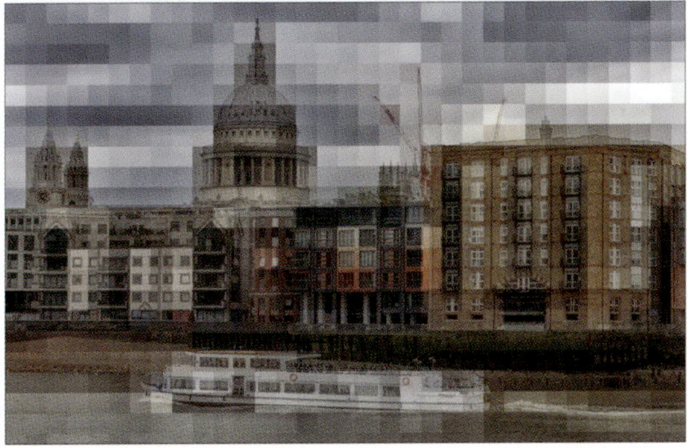

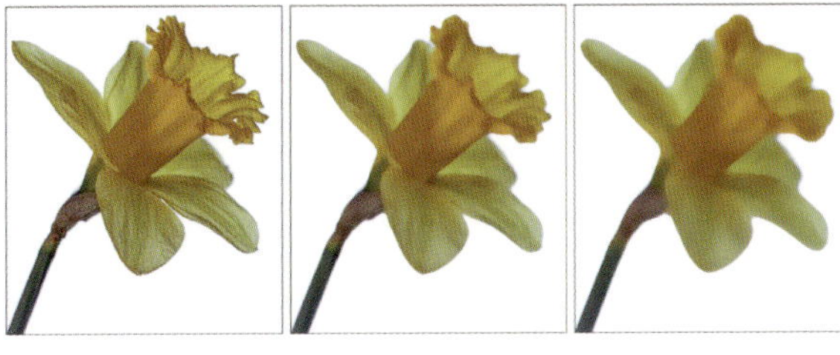

TOP
Fig. 6.5 **A picture of St Paul's Cathedral in London alongside a low-resolution version of the same picture. The final image is a blend of the two pictures achieved by combining them in Photoshop layers and reducing the opacity of the top layer.**

BOTTOM
Fig. 6.6 **The smoothing effect of the Median filter applied to a daffodil at increasing strengths.**

Cutout Filter

The Cutout filter is accessed via Photoshop's filter gallery (Filter > Filter Gallery > Artistic > Cutout). It portrays an image as though it were made from layers of roughly cut coloured paper. The level of simplification can be set with sliders for the number of levels (of simulated paper), the fidelity and the simplicity of the 'torn' edges. The results can be striking and artistic.

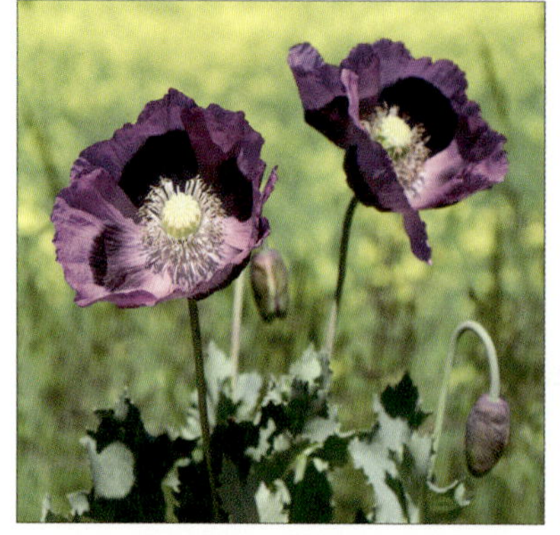
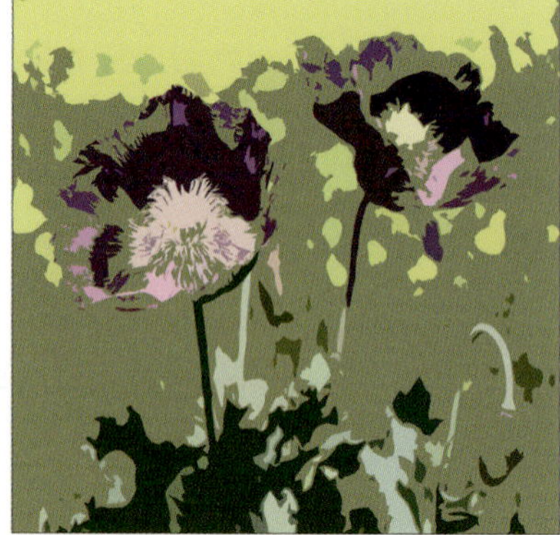
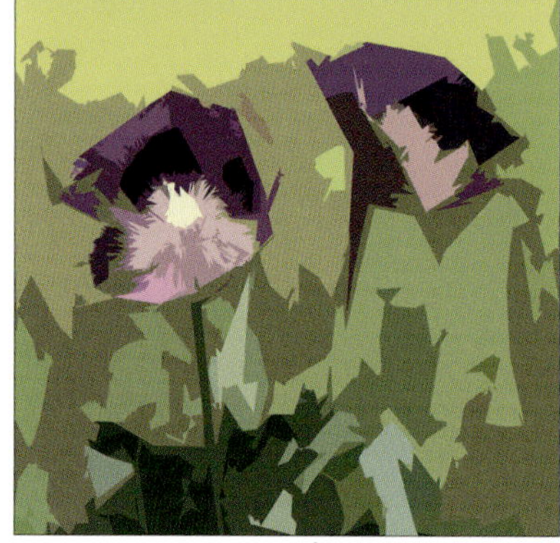
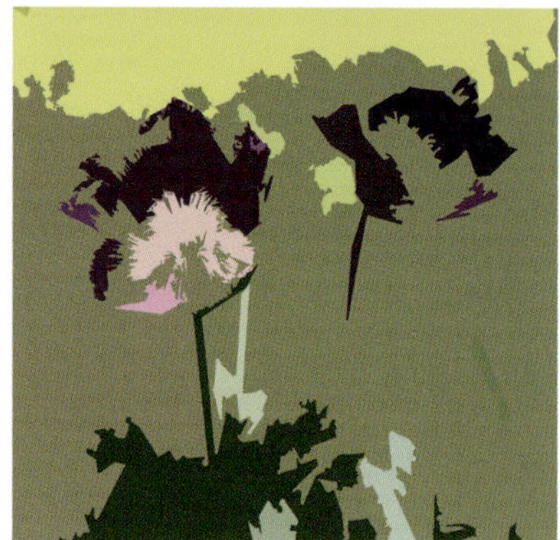

Fig. 6.7 **Photoshop's Cutout filter applied to a picture of poppies at increasing levels of simplification.**

Oil Paint Filter

The Oil Paint filter (Filter > Stylize > Oil Paint) simplifies in a distinctive way and is designed to create the appearance of a classic oil painting. Whether it achieves this is questionable, but the resulting images can be unusual and attractive. Directional lines in the starting picture are smoothed and stretched. Settings sliders control the extent of the stylisation and the addition of 'shine', which adds the appearance of directional lighting on the simulated oil paint. This filter is particularly responsive to changes in the starting resolution of the image and as previously noted, it can be worth reducing resolution to achieve the maximum effect.

Fig. 6.8 **The Oil Paint filter applied to a picture of a bluebell wood. The simplified image is stretched along directional lines.**

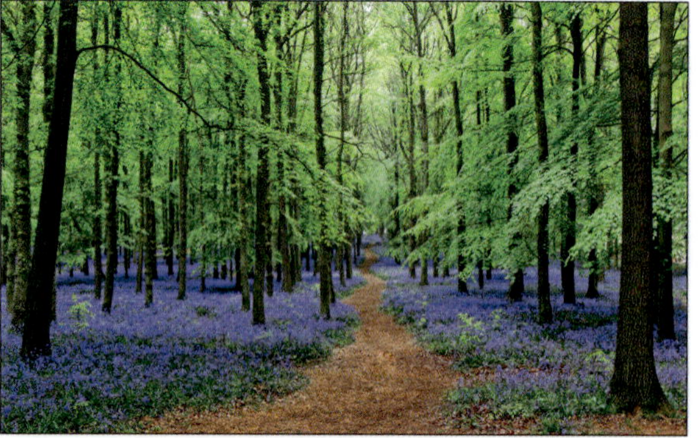
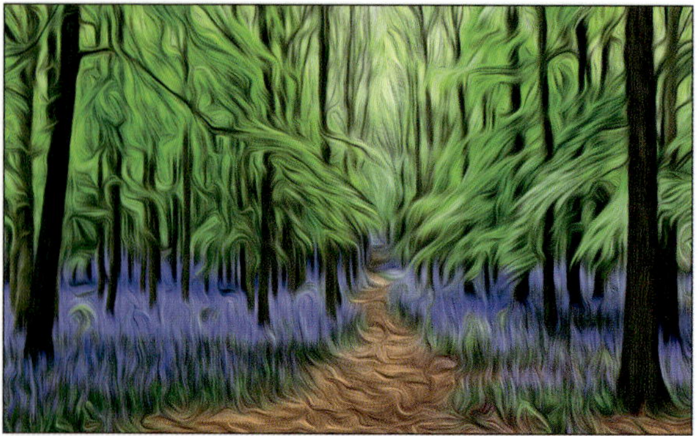

COMPOSITION

Simplified pictures remove distracting details and draw attention to the structure and composition of the image. This presents challenges but also opportunities.

Removing Imperfections

All photographers have the experience of producing a picture that is 'almost right'. However, it is marred by some blemish or imperfection. Simplification techniques may come to the rescue. Removing detail will focus attention on the composition and result in a more artistic presentation of the subject. In some cases this can be achieved by cloning over unwanted areas or by using tools such as Photoshop's Spot Healing Brush.

A particularly useful application of simplification is in the photography of artificial flowers. These can be excellent subjects with ideal colours and shapes and can be flexibly positioned for photography. However, they often look undeniably artificial, often with frayed edges on fabric petals. Digital filters will conceal the artificial structure and add an artistic appearance.

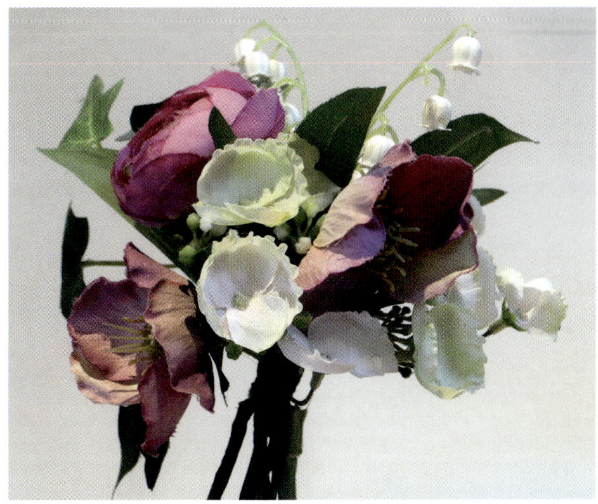

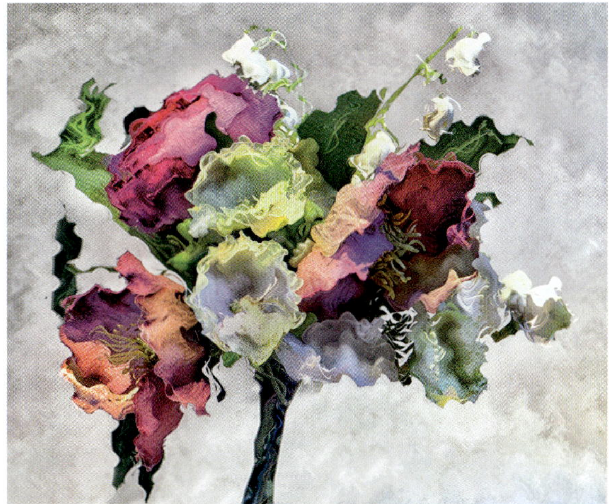

Fig. 6.10 **The fabric construction of these artificial flowers means that the original photograph does not stand up to close scrutiny. Application of the Wave filter distorts the frayed edges and results in a more artistic interpretation.**

Fig. 6.9 **A photograph of a South African street before and after removal of blemishes and unwanted distractions using cloning tools and the Spot Healing Brush. Image saturation has then been increased to enhance the overall impact.**

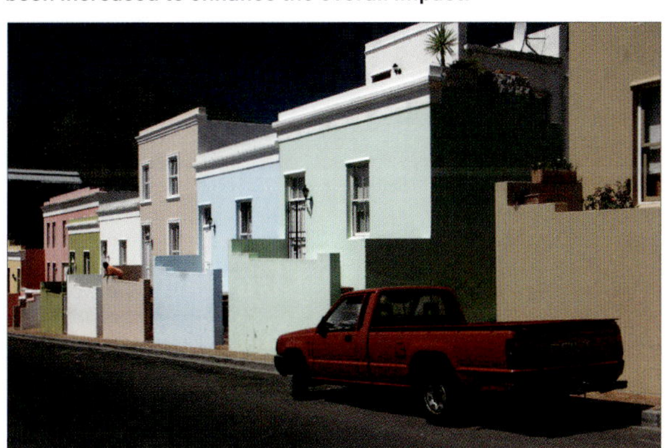

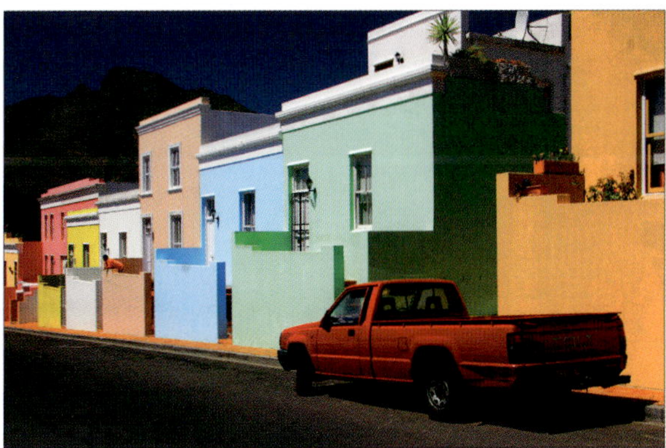

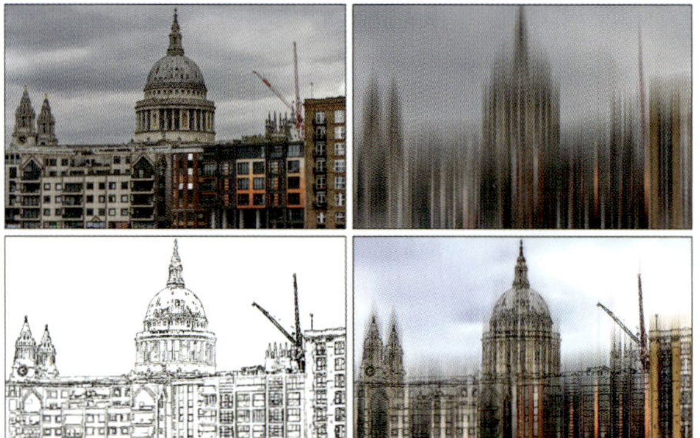

Fig. 6.11 **St Paul's Cathedral with a high level of vertical motion blurring. The line edges of the original picture are combined with the blurred image to restore some structure. This is particularly valuable to ensure that well-known landmarks can still be identified.**

Restoring Structure

There is a risk of simplification pushing a picture too far towards abstraction. If this is not the desired intention, it can be useful to bring some structure back into the image. This is particularly the case when photographing well-known landmarks. Here the aim is to ensure that the identity of the subject is still retained despite the simplification. One possibility, explored earlier, is to blend the original and the simplified pictures together. Another technique is to record the line edges of the original picture and to superimpose them back on the simplified version. The tool to produce crisp line edges is tucked well away in Photoshop. It is a setting in the Smart Blur set (Filter > Blur > Smart Blur; set Quality to High, and Mode to Edge Only). Sliders allow adjustment of the precision of the edges and the number of edges to be found. This will produce white edges on a black background and, since we want black edges, this should be inverted (Image > Adjustments > Invert). Make the edge image a layer on top of the simplified picture and combine them by using the Darken blend mode on the edge layer. The edges will now be superimposed on the image and structure restored. Reduce the opacity of the edge layer to reduce its impact if needed.

SIMPLIFYING - KEYS

SIMPLIFICATION removes distractions and blemishes from images and enables appreciation of the distribution of colours and shapes.

MODERN cameras can produce very high-resolution photographs, which can be a barrier to image simplification.

REDUCING image resolution can be necessary to achieve maximum impact from digital filters.

MOST software filters simplify images, usually adding artistic treatment such as directional lines in the process.

IT may be desirable to restore some structure to highly simplified pictures, for example by superimposing the line edges from the starting image.

FACING PAGE
Fig. 6.12 **A picture of sweet peas with a combination of simplification techniques including Oil Paint, Cutout and application of line edges. Overall saturation has been reduced to give a softer impression.**

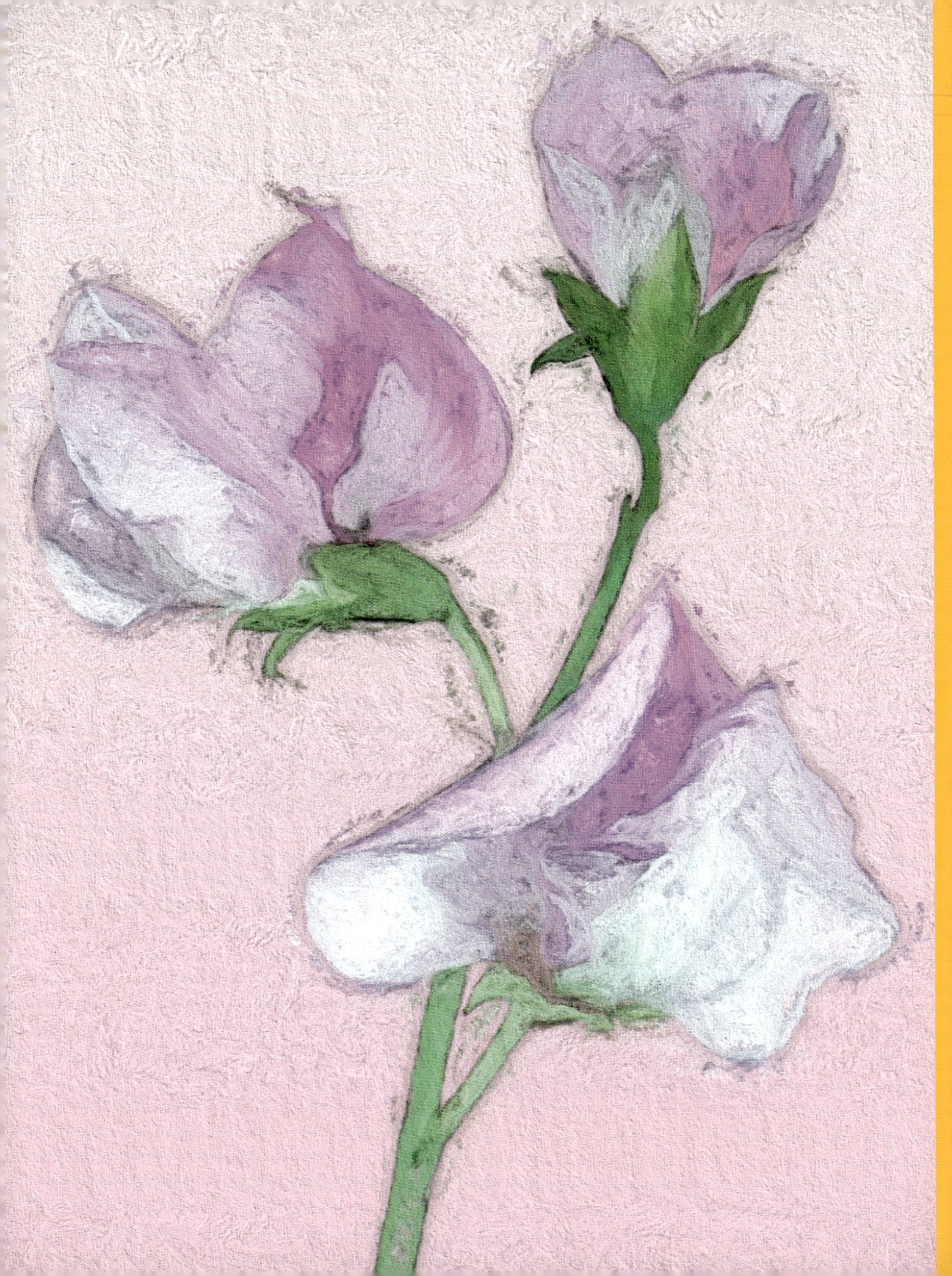

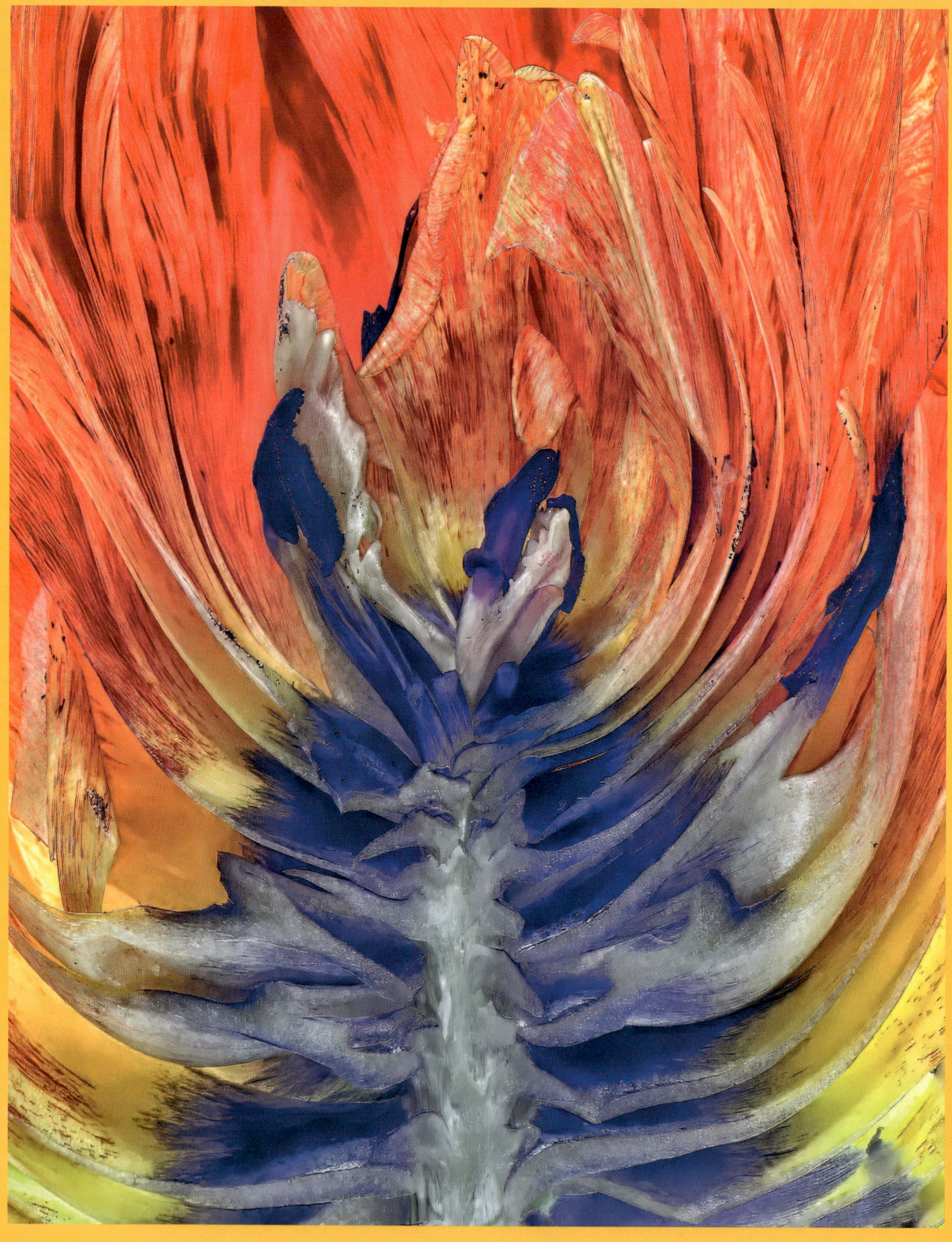

Fig. 7.1 **A cut section of a tulip. The impact of the composition is enhanced by the three primary colours of red, blue and yellow.**

LESSON 7

COLOUR

Colour is often behind our emotional reaction to a picture. Colour combinations can create drama and excitement, or harmony and calm. Colour theory can be extremely complex but is usually based on Isaac Newton's colour wheel. This presents the primary colours of red, yellow and blue around a circle. Between them are the secondary and tertiary colours made by mixing the primaries. The continuous range of hues can be coded in various ways. In Photoshop they are assigned a number based on their number of degrees around the circle. So red is 0, yellow 120 and blue 240. Figure 7.2 shows the colour wheel with named colour blocks, although in reality it is a smooth continuum.

Adjustment of colour in Photoshop, for example in the toning techniques in Lesson 2, usually opens the Color Picker. A vertical column shows the range of hues and clicking on this opens a full box of that hue. Moving the cursor horizontally in the box changes the saturation of the colour and governs its shade. Moving left reduces the saturation, while moving right increases the saturation, making the colour more vivid. Moving vertically changes the brightness of the colour. Moving up makes the colour brighter, while moving down makes it darker. In Figure 7.3 the box displays a hue (H) of 287°, a shade (S) of 56% and a brightness (B) of 60%. Other tables show different ways of defining a colour, for example the proportions of red, green and blue.

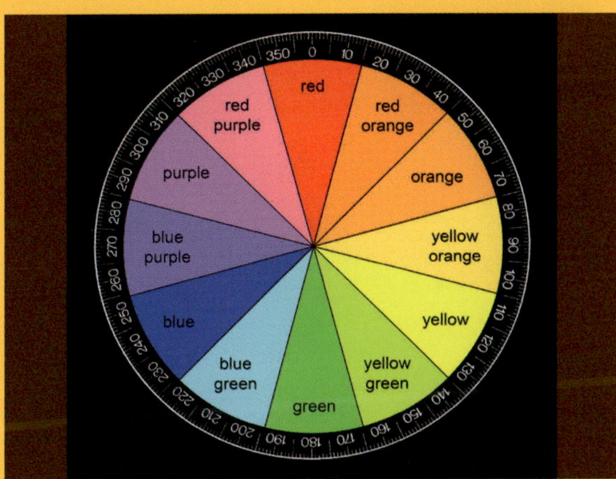

Fig. 7.2 **The colour wheel, devised by Isaac Newton in 1706, is the basis for much colour theory. The primary colours of red, yellow and blue are equally spaced and the secondary colours in between result from combinations of the primaries. Opposite colours on the wheel are complementary and give the greatest contrast. Colours adjacent to each other give harmonious combinations.**

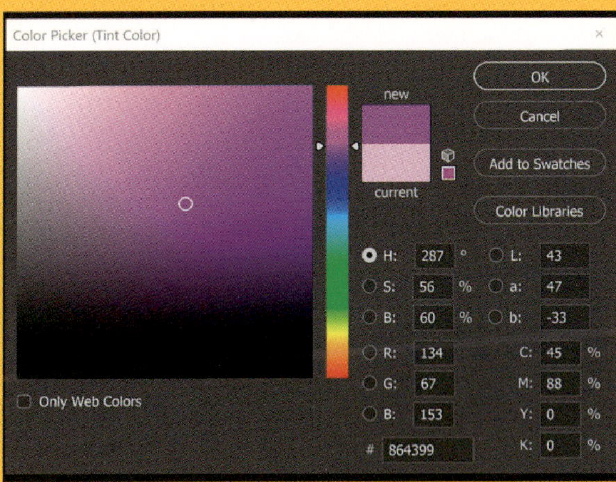

Fig. 7.3 **Photoshop's Color Picker showing a purple hue. The hue can be changed in the vertical bar on the right. The saturation and brightness of the selected hue can be adjusted by moving the cursor within the large square box.**

COLOUR COMBINATIONS

Broadly speaking, the warm colours red, orange and yellow will tend to be prominent in an image. The cool blues and greens will be more recessionary and more suited as background colours. Since these are the colours of sky and foliage, this may happen naturally but may also benefit from digital tweaking. The greatest visual contrast and drama is produced by combining complementary colours in a picture; these are colours that are opposite each other on the colour wheel. Examples are the contrasting colours in the tulip section in Figure 7.1 and the tomato in Figure 7.4.

Harmony in pictures is achieved when the colours are next to each other in the wheel; these are analogous or adjacent colours. This is achieved in Figure 7.5 with a mix of green, orange and yellow colours.

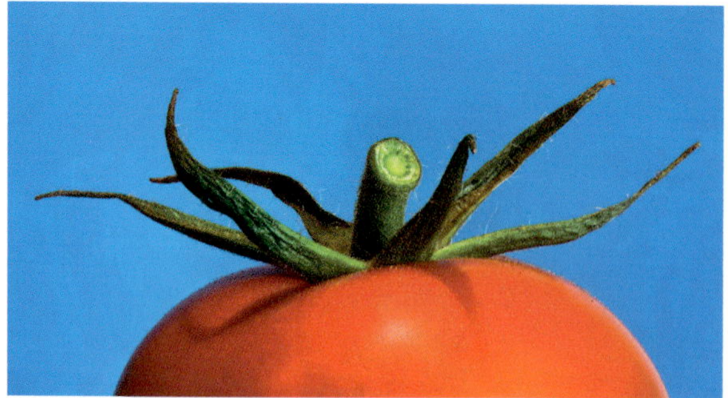

Fig. 7.4 **The simple picture of a tomato gains its impact by using primary colours at high levels of saturation.**

Fig. 7.5 **The woodland scene is a harmonious mix of colours close to each other on the colour wheel.**

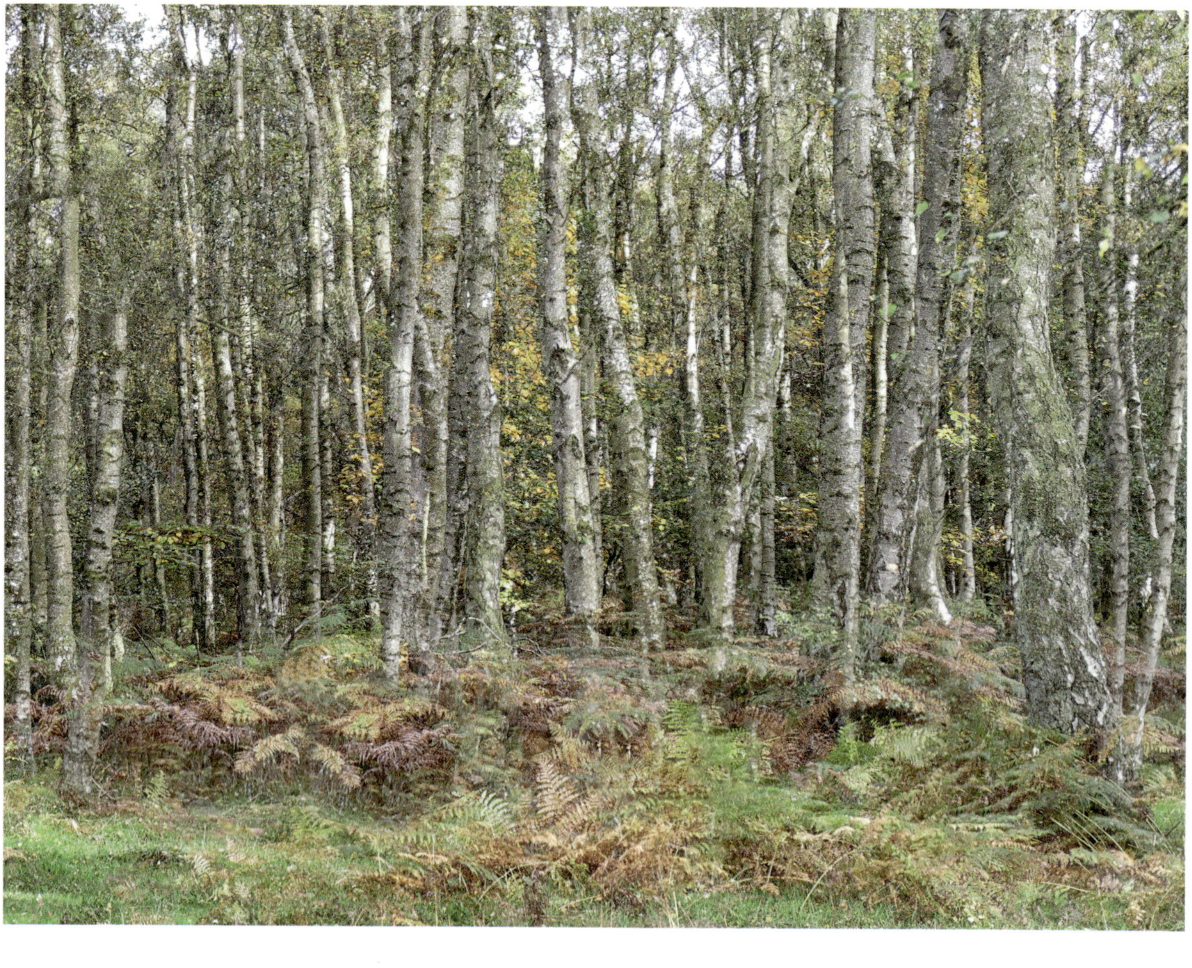

COLOUR IN SOFTWARE

Photo-editing programs such as Photoshop offer considerable scope for revisiting 'as seen' photographs and making colour adjustments. These might be simple tweaks to correct the colours to the way they were intended, or dramatic colour shifts to completely change the impact of the image.

Changing Hues

A versatile tool for making colour changes is in the Photoshop settings for hue and saturation (Image > Adjustments > Hue/Saturation). This opens a control box for the picture's hue, saturation and lightness. The settings also provide another option for the image toning presented in Lesson 2, by clicking the Colorize box. In Figure 7.6 the adjustments have been set to apply only to the cyan colours in the image as described later.

The Hue slider makes dramatic changes and, if moved to the extreme right or left, will convert all colours to their complementary colours. The image changes can be viewed as the sliders are moved and the picture will move from realism to the psychedelic. This is a particularly useful adjustment for abstract pictures, where realism is unlikely to be important.

Saturating and Desaturating

As well as changing hues, the Hue/Saturation settings can deliver drama or calm to an image by adjusting saturation and lightness. As with hue adjustments, the slider controls allow the effect to be viewed during the adjustments. Saturation is the intensity of the hue from grey, no saturation, to the pure vivid colour, high saturation. If the saturation slider is fully to the left the picture has no colour and is one route to conversion to black and white. Lightness is a measure of the relative lightness or darkness of each colour. The slider fully to the left gives a pure black image, and to the right pure white. Adding lightness this way can result in an attractive soft pastel effect. It is easy to overdo these adjustments. Increasing saturation can look exciting, but for natural subjects might move too far from realism. This is especially the case with grass and foliage, where a vivid green will be unconvincing.

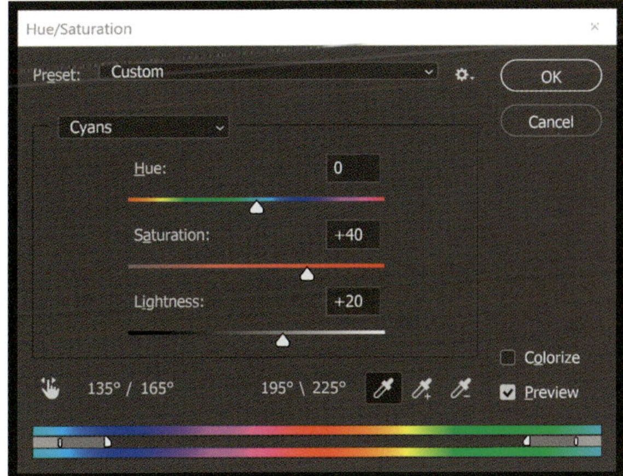

Fig. 7.6 **The Hue/Saturation settings in Photoshop allow independent control of hue, saturation and lightness using variable sliders. Here they are set to increase the saturation and lightness of the cyan colours only.**

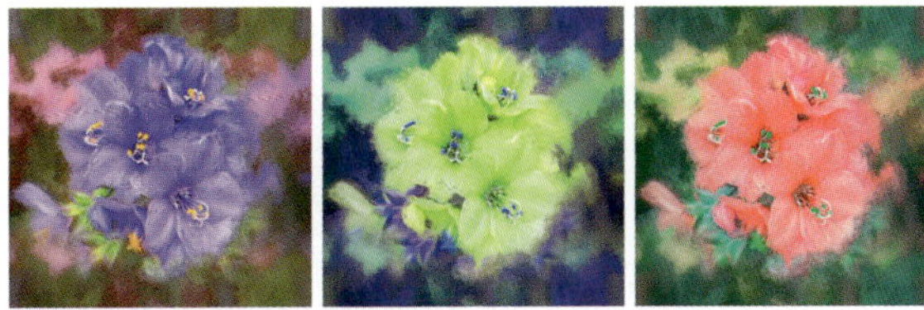

Fig. 7.7 **The polemonium flower picture on the left is dramatically changed by moving the hue slider in Photoshop's Hue/Saturation settings.**

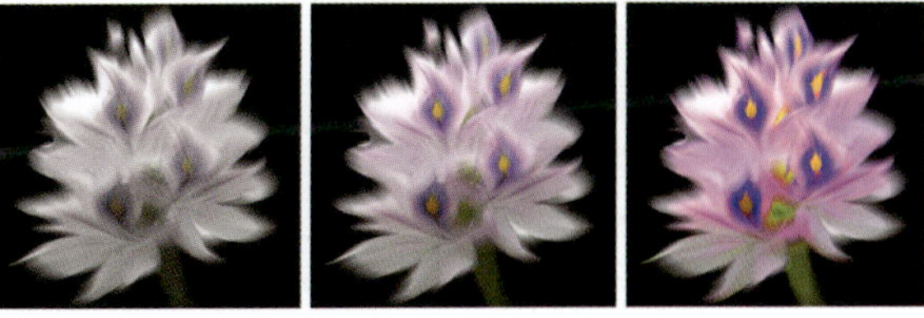

Fig. 7.8 **A picture of a water hyacinth (centre) adjusted with the saturation slider in Photoshop's Hue/Saturation settings. Sliding to the left gives the subtle low-saturation image. To the right gives a dramatic oversaturated result.**

Selective Colour Adjustment

It is often the case that the complete overhaul of colours using the Hue slider in its default position is not what is wanted. Instead, only one colour or one part of the picture is to be adjusted. For example, the colour of a flower might benefit from adjustment but not the background. In this case, the drop-down options next to the arrow key by the word Master allow specific colours to be selected for adjustment. If, for example, the Cyans option is selected as in Figure 7.6, only cyan hues in the original will be changed. If you are not sure of the name of the colour to be changed, pick any of the colour names and click on the desired colour in the image. The name will change to that colour and will become the only colour affected by the slider.

Fig. 7.9 **If the pink colour of the original dahlia picture is selected in Hue/Saturation, by selecting a colour in the drop-down menu and then clicking on the pink, it can be changed to any other colour, without affecting the background, by adjusting the hue slider.**

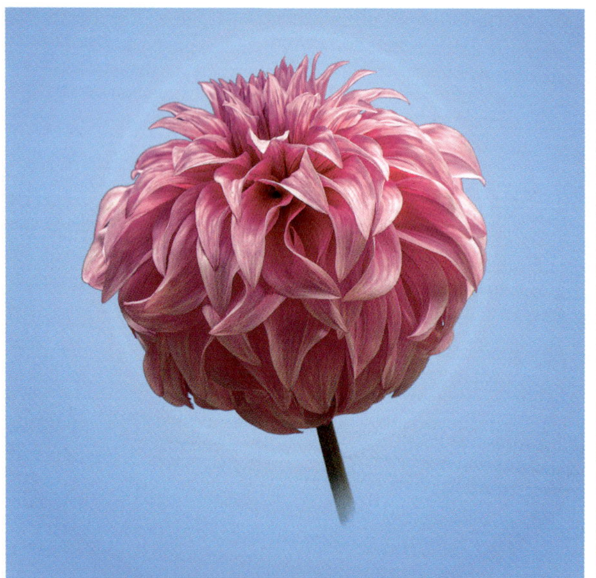

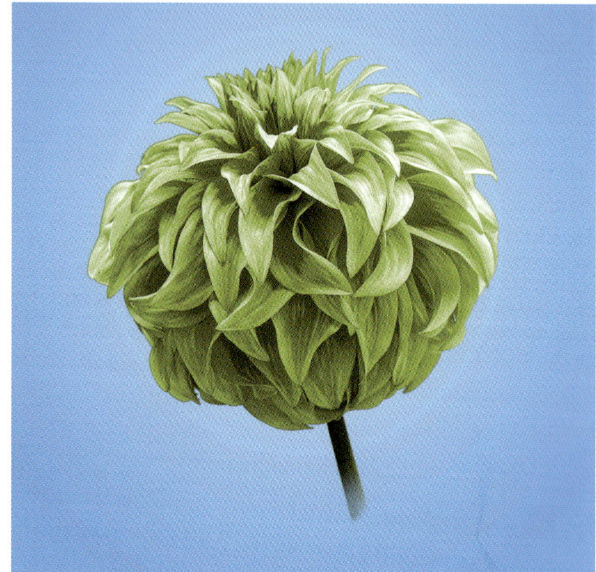

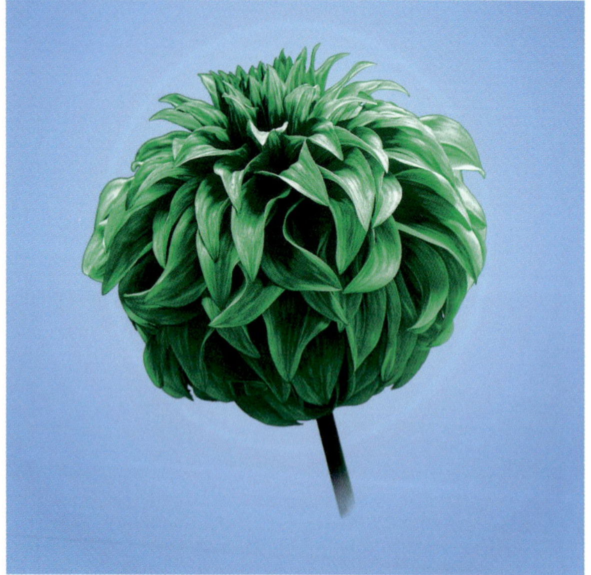

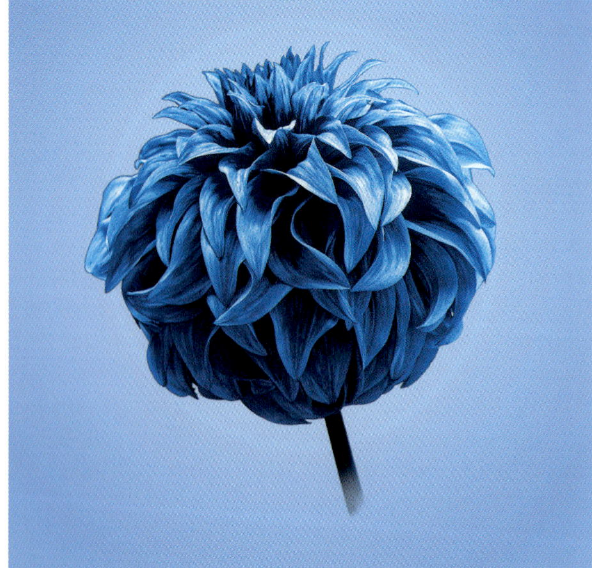

Spot Colour

An effective artistic treatment for some subjects is to convert an image to black and white (Lesson 1) and then restore colour to selected areas. The coloured item then becomes the strong focal point in the picture. Subjects might be a red telephone box in a black and white street scene, a single green leaf on a black and white tree, or bright-blue eyes on a monochrome face. It can then be worth experimenting with the introduction of just a hint of colour in other parts of the picture. This can add a sense of depth and translucency. The process here is to make two copies of the starting picture as layers in Photoshop. Make the top layer black and white using one of the methods in Lesson 1 (for example Image > Adjustments > Black & White). Then apply a layer mask to the black and white layer (Layer > Layer Mask > Reveal All). With a black brush set at 100% opacity, brush on the mask to reveal the underlying colour in the selected areas. To now add the areas to which the hint of colour is to be added, set the opacity of the brush to a lower level, say 25%, and brush where needed. It is very easy to overdo this, since repeated brushing will risk a return to full colour. To avoid this, set the brush colour (the top colour of the boxes at the bottom of the Tools panel) to grey rather than black, this will limit the intensity of the colour that can be applied. This treatment is illustrated in Figure 7.10.

Fig. 7.10 **Some physalis fruits in their papery husks. The original conversion is to black and white and is made a new layer in Photoshop. Painting at full opacity on a layer mask restores the colour of the fruit. Painting at low opacity provides a gentle hint of colour and adds a feeling of depth and translucency.**

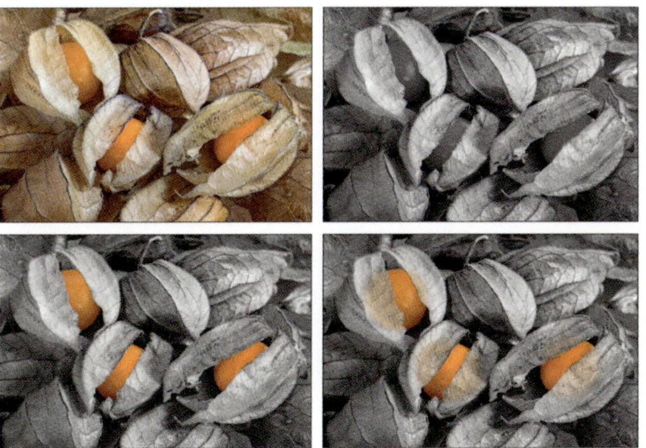

COLOUR NEGATIVES

New and unexpected pictures can emerge when we revisit old images and view their negatives. In Photoshop this is called 'inverting' (Image > Adjustments > Invert). In film days the negative was generally the starting point of the picture, and the film negatives had to be converted to positives during the printing process. Inverting a colour image makes two changes: dark tones become light tones and vice versa, and colours become their complementary colours. So black becomes white and red becomes green. The result is surprising and often mysterious and attractive.

Fig. 7.11 **A picture of a cup alongside its colour negative (Invert in Photoshop). Colours become their complementary colours. Light tones become dark and dark tones become light.**

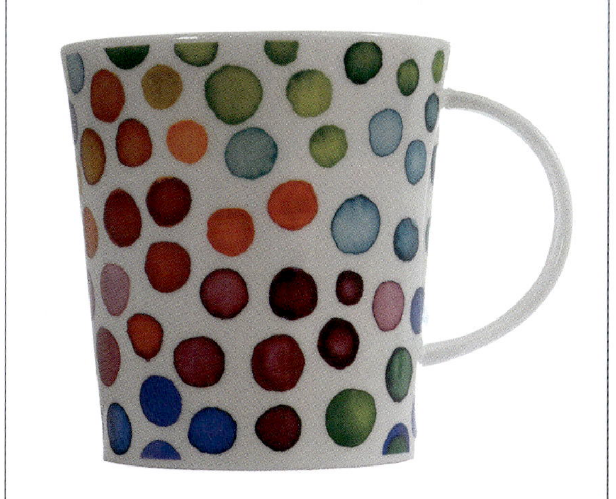

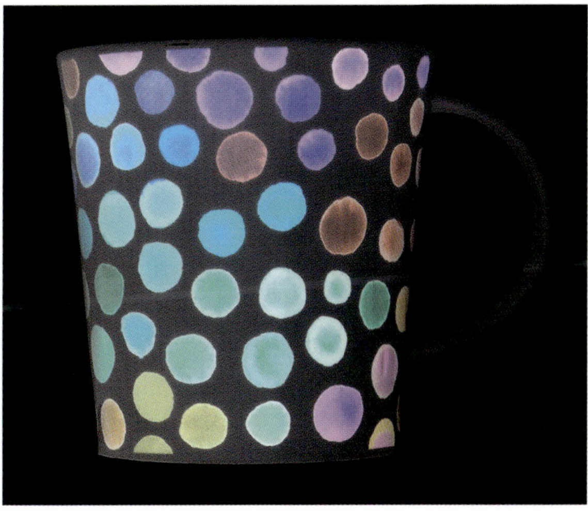

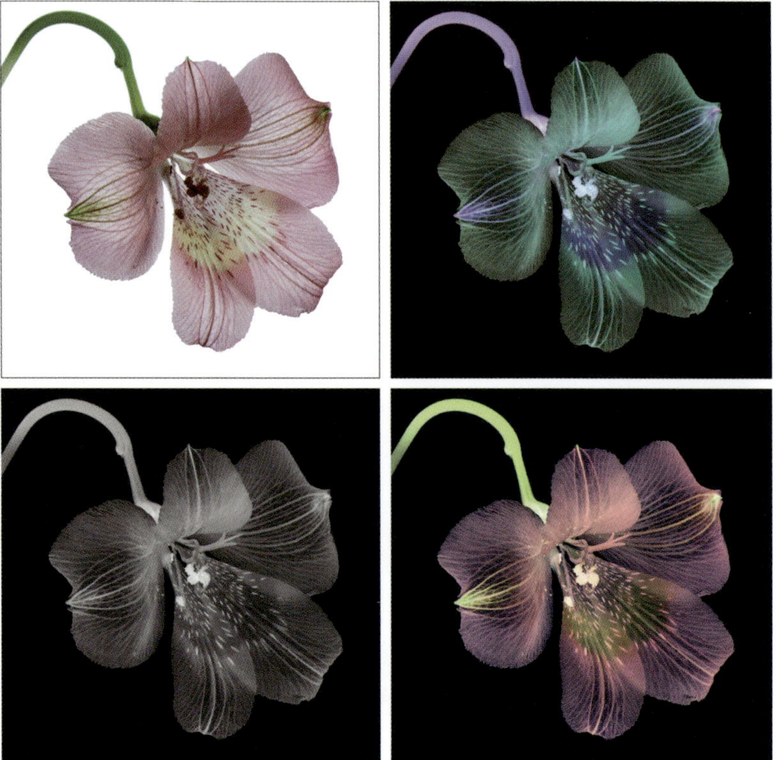

Fig. 7.12 **An alstroemeria flower beside its colour negative. Since the new colours are unnatural, they are concealed by conversion to black and white in the bottom left version. This is an effective way to convert a white background to black, or vice versa, without making complex selections. The bottom right version has the original colours restored by moving the Hue slider to its extreme position, but the tones are still inverted so dark areas become light and light areas dark.**

It is not uncommon for the inversion of tones to be effective, for example a dark background becoming light, but the colour change doesn't work. In this case it can be worth converting the inverted image to black and white so that the tonal changes are delivered but the colour conflict is removed. An alternative is to restore the original colours as described above by moving the Hue slider in Hue/Saturation to the extreme left or right. This restores the colours but not the tones so, for example, a light-blue sky in a starting picture will become a dark-orange sky when inverted, then a dark-blue sky when the Hue slider is moved to its extreme. The result of inverting the tones but not the colours will be unusual and offers considerable scope for experimenting.

COLOUR - KEYS

COLOUR in photography helps create mood and trigger emotion, ranging from harmony to drama.

COLOUR theory is based on the colour wheel, which shows the primary colours and the intermediate colours resulting from mixing the primaries.

COLOURS opposite each other on the colour wheel are complementary colours and provide the greatest visual contrast. Colours close to each other are analogous colours and deliver calm and harmony.

AN effective artistic treatment is to convert an image to black and white and to reintroduce colour to selected areas. Adding additional subtle colour can contribute a sense of depth and translucency.

CONVERTING a colour picture to its negative through digital inversion produces results that can be attractive and surprising.

FACING PAGE
Fig. 7.13 **A sweet pea converted to black and white, with radial blur added to each flower. To provide a gentle colour effect, a layer mask is placed on the black and white layer and a low-opacity brush used to restore a little of the original colour.**

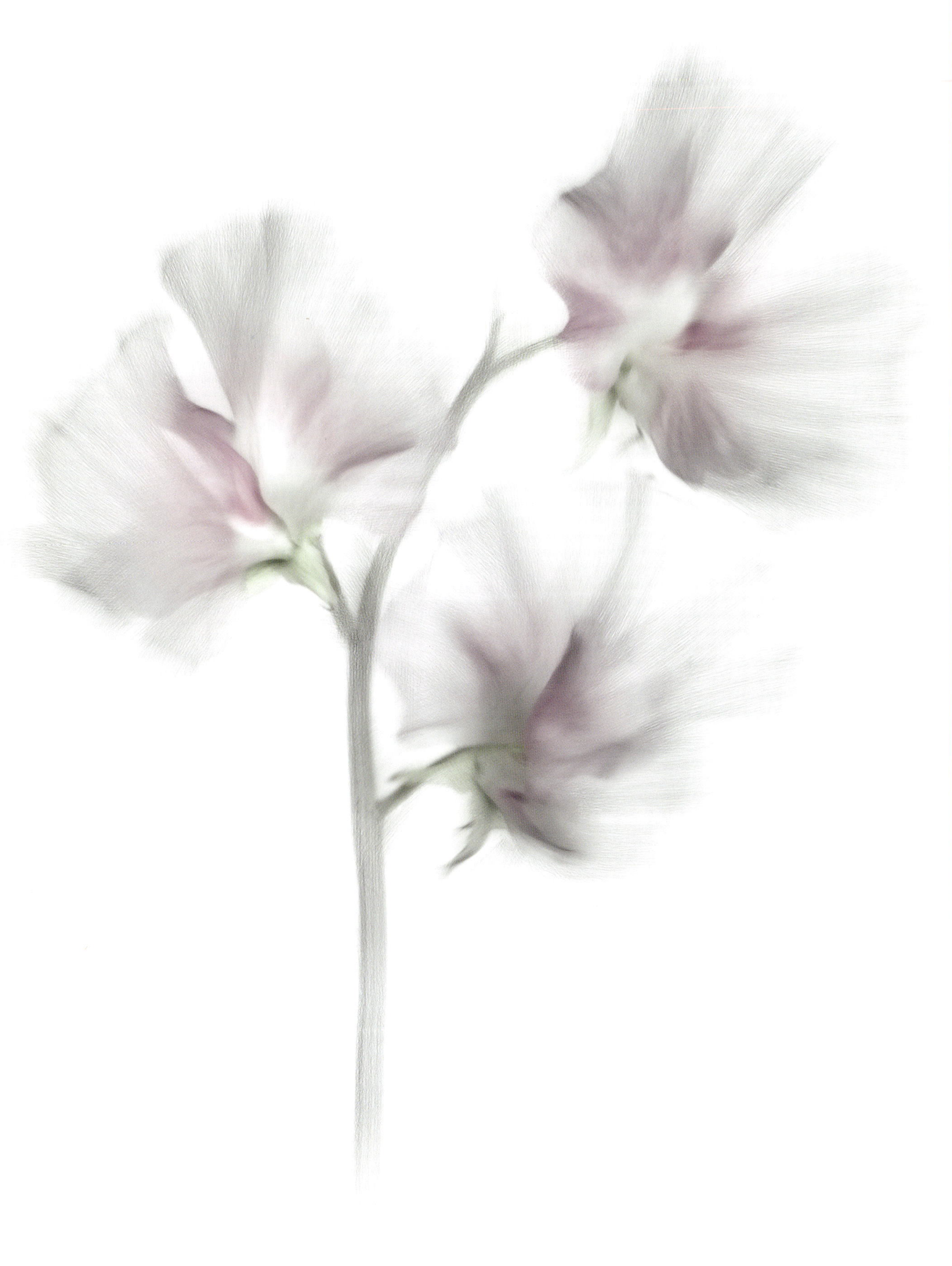

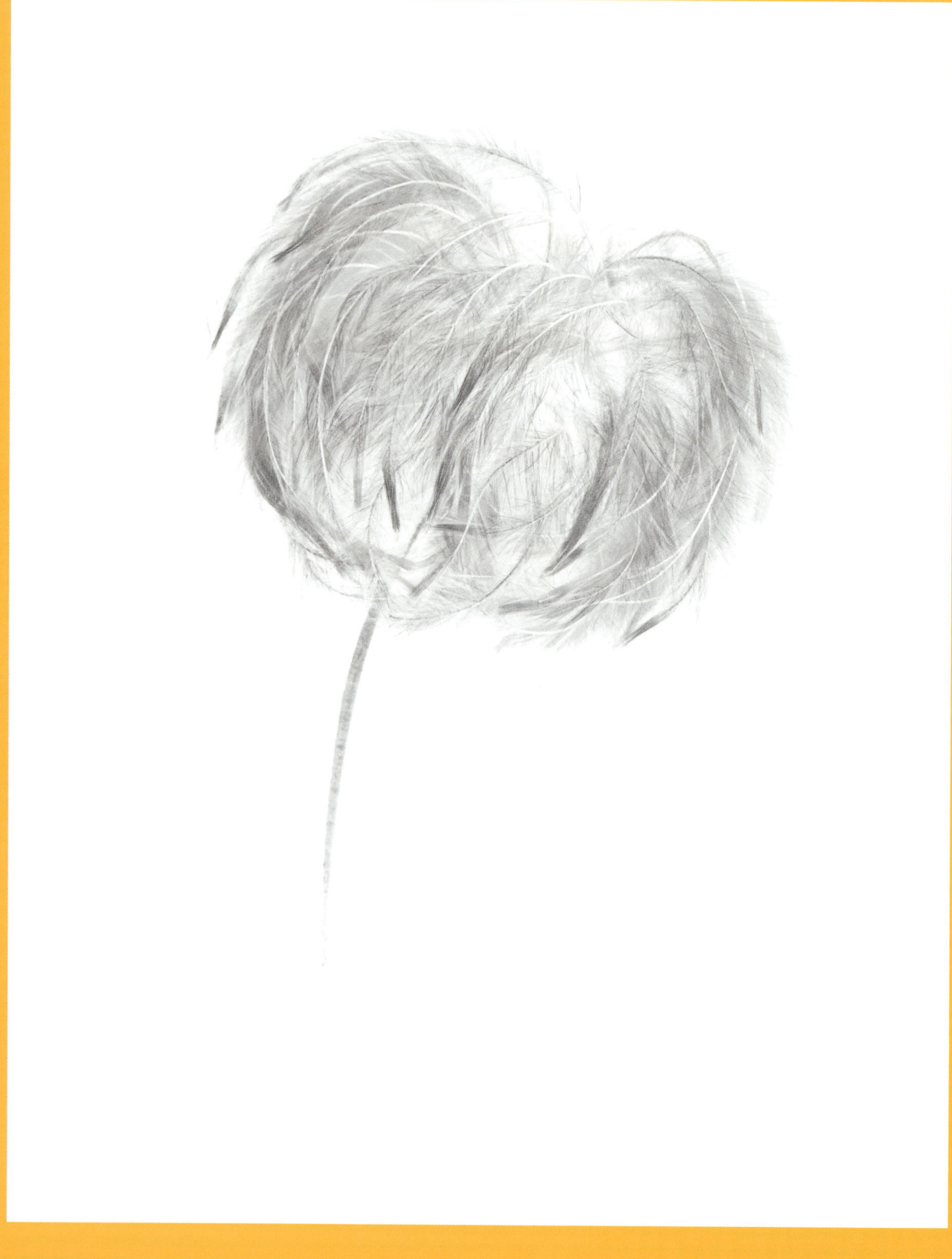

Fig. 8.1 **A clematis seedhead isolated on a white background, converted to black and white and lightened through adjustment in Photoshop Levels.**

LESSON 8
MINIMALISM

Minimalist photography aims to strip a subject down to its most elegant and basic form. It emphasises the essentials and relies on simple lines, shapes, colours and negative space to create clean, uncluttered images. When successful it can convey a sense of calm, peace and order.

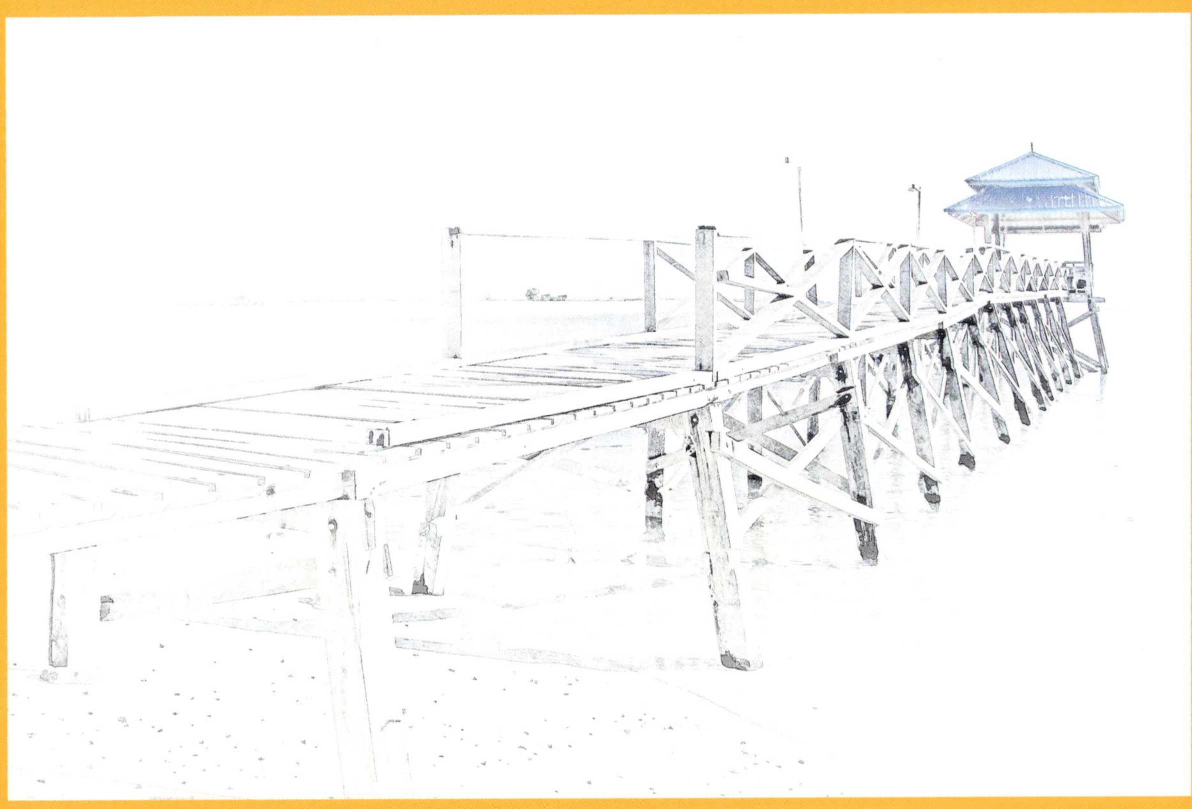

Fig. 8.2 **A wooden pier in Borneo, simplified using Photoshop's Cutout filter, lightened using Levels adjustment, and with blue toning introduced in selected areas.**

THE POWER OF NEGATIVE SPACE

Negative space is a common characteristic of minimalist photography. It emphasises not just the subject but also the space around it. Attention is drawn to the main figure, but there is awareness of the surrounding emptiness. The use of negative space can also aid composition. A widely used composition guideline is the 'rule of thirds', in which subjects should be positioned horizontally or vertically on imaginary lines that divide the frame into three. Imagine a noughts and crosses grid imposed on the scene. This is so generally accepted as a way to bring harmony to a picture that it is common for software and camera screens to display this grid to aid composition at the taking or processing stage. In practice many subjects present themselves centrally and the emptiness resulting from moving them to one side can feel unnatural. Once accepted though, the newly created breathing space will become a feature of the composition.

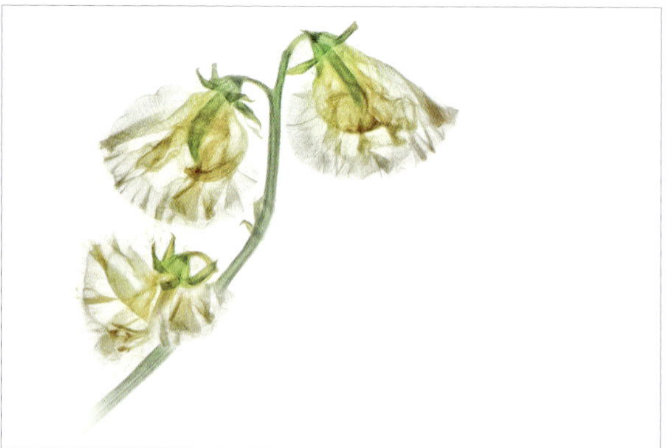

Fig. 8.3 **A pressed sweet-pea flower photographed on a lightbox and positioned on a blank white canvas to allow an area of negative space.**

MINIMALIST COLOUR

Colour in photographs can become very compelling when used sparingly. Colour can be faded so that it gives just a hint of the original. An example is in Figure 8.4. A simple adjustment for this is in Photoshop's saturation adjustment (Image > Adjustments > Hue/Saturation; drag the middle slider to the left).

Another approach is to desaturate the picture but to restore colour to a limited area as in Figure 7.10. The desaturated area is the equivalent of negative space, drawing attention to the main subject. Scenes that are predominantly muted but have a single coloured element, as in Figure 8.5, can be effective minimalist photographs.

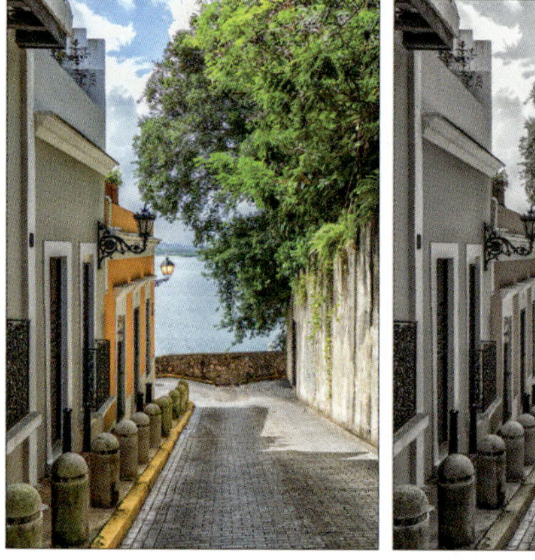

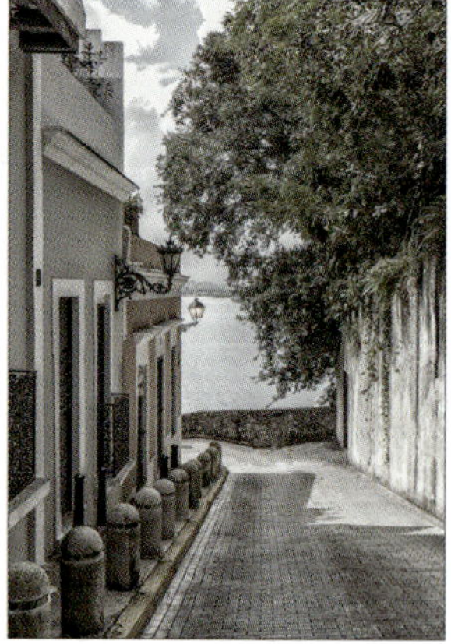

Fig. 8.4 **A colourful street scene in San Juan alongside a very desaturated version giving a more minimalist interpretation.**

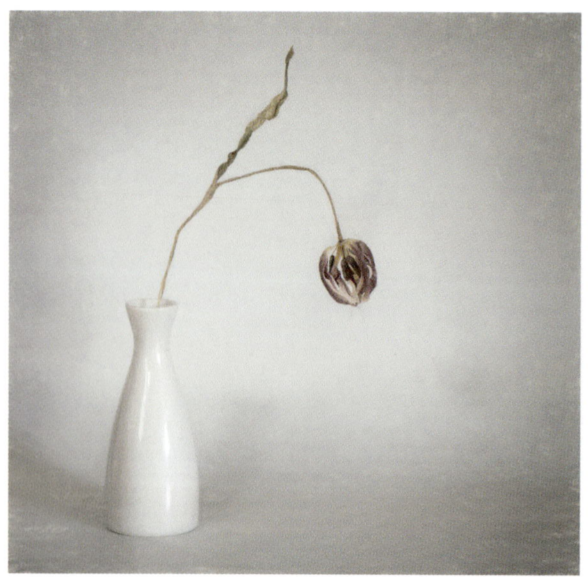

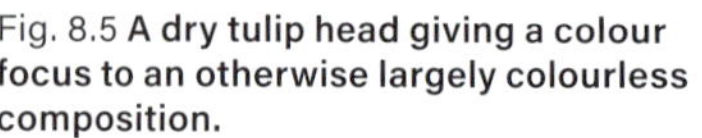

Fig. 8.5 **A dry tulip head giving a colour focus to an otherwise largely colourless composition.**

MINIMALIST ABSTRACTION

Minimalism and abstraction can work well together. In the art world this can be contentious, with largely empty canvases attracting comments like 'this isn't art'. A minimalist photograph certainly runs the same risk, and this is a genre that divides opinion. However, as photographic images become simplified using the techniques in Lesson 6 and Lesson 10, they will often move towards abstraction and the results can be artistic and striking. The aim is to identify a combination of shapes, shades and textures that deliver a harmonious or contrasting composite.

Fig. 8.6 **A stretched and blurred seascape removing any detail from the subject and relying only on colour and simple minimalist composition.**

MINIMALIST CLOSE-UP

As we get close to any object, concentrating on its detail, the subject becomes less important, and the lines and shapes take over. The result is likely to offer scope for minimalist compositions. Close-up and macro photography can be a specialist subject requiring dedicated equipment. However, many standard camera and lens combinations will enable sufficiently close focusing to deliver minimalist results. This includes modern smartphone cameras. Further information about equipment options is presented in Lesson 13. In addition, there is great scope for cropping in to a small section of a photograph, looking for simple shapes. This will of course result in some sacrifice of image resolution, but for a minimalist picture that might be acceptable. After cropping, increase the image size to whatever is needed for display or printing (Image > Image Size; enter the new dimensions) and see whether the result delivers the desired quality. If it doesn't then specialist AI software discussed in Lesson 13 may come to the rescue.

Fig. 8.7 **Close-up detail of the edge of an old book using directional lines for image structure. The image is sepia toned to reflect the age of the subject.**

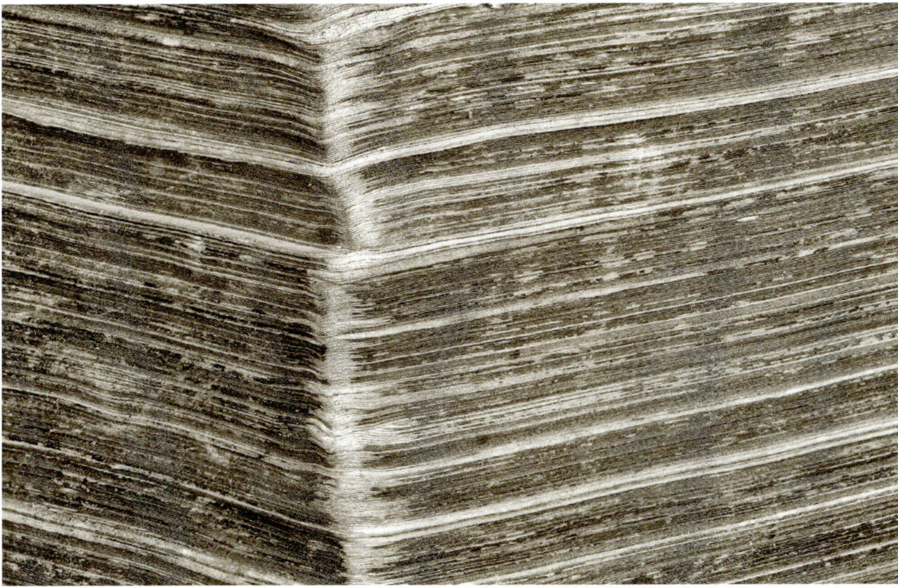

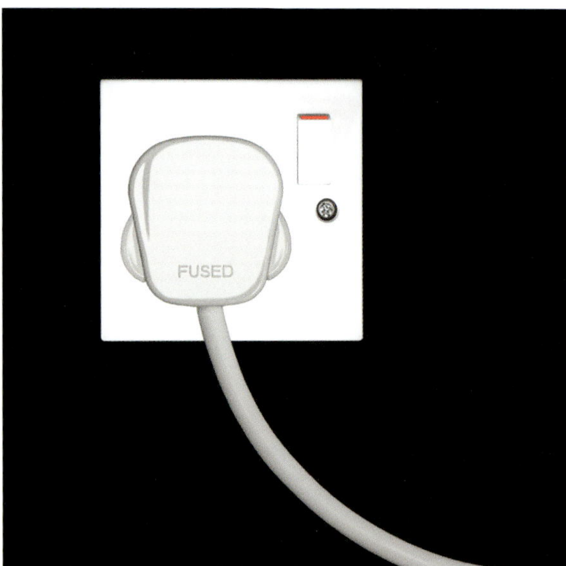

Fig. 8.8 **A simple picture of an everyday plug and socket, relying on the lead-in line of the cable for composition, and a single area of red as an image focal point.**

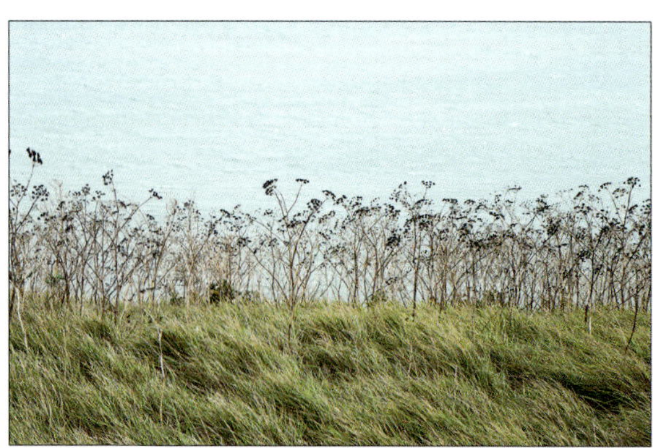

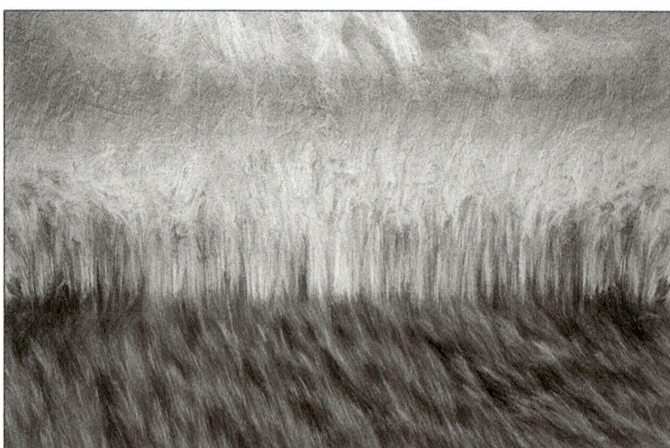

Fig. 8.9 **A picture of coastal grassland given minimalist treatment through conversion to black and white, and directional blurring using Photoshop's Oil Paint filter.**

SUBJECTS FOR MINIMALISM

As with all creative photography, there are no real restrictions in the search for minimalist images and they often emerge in unlikely places. This might involve a change in outlook since photographers can be drawn to colour, clutter and complexity. However, once minimalism is the goal, its pictures are everywhere. The following suggestions offer starting points but are by no means comprehensive.

Everyday Objects

The things we take for granted often take on a pictorial quality when inspected through a photographer's eye. Carefully positioned and lit, they may be perfect for a minimalist canvas. Almost anything can fit the bill, though it might take time for the picture to emerge, and adjustments to focus, saturation, lightness and so on could be needed to fit the minimalist brief. The kitchen is a good place to start, with forks, spoons and graters offering gentle lines and textures. Utilitarian subjects such as the plug and socket in Figure 8.8 might not have been designed with art in mind but turn out to have an elegant beauty of their own.

Landscape

Landscape photography is at its most effective when stripped of unnecessary detail. This enables the overall structure to be seen and appreciated and allows focus on key elements in the scene such as foreground rocks, buildings or plants. The background can then become the negative space, adding context without being distracting. This is also the photographer's opportunity to make the most of bad weather. Rain, mist and cloud will diffuse the light and eliminate harsh shadows, as well as adding a blurring filter effect. If nature doesn't provide this, digital treatment might come to the rescue, as in Figure 8.9.

Flowers

In a minimalist flower photograph, the flower is singled out for attention. This can be achieved in studio photography by isolating the flower against a plain or diffuse background such as those in Figure 3.6. An alternative is to take the picture in a natural environment but to ensure the composition and the camera settings do not distract from the subject. It is helpful to use a large lens aperture if possible (the small f numbers, usually from f2.8 to f5.6), so that the depth of field is limited, and the surroundings of the flower are out of focus. A useful approach for field-flower photography is to use lenses with a long focal length (100mm and beyond). These isolate the flower and minimise background distractions. Smartphone photography can be a challenge here since smartphones deliver high depths of field and tend to keep everything in focus. Use the portrait setting on the phone if available; this creates an artificial shallow depth of field, and the flower will become prominent.

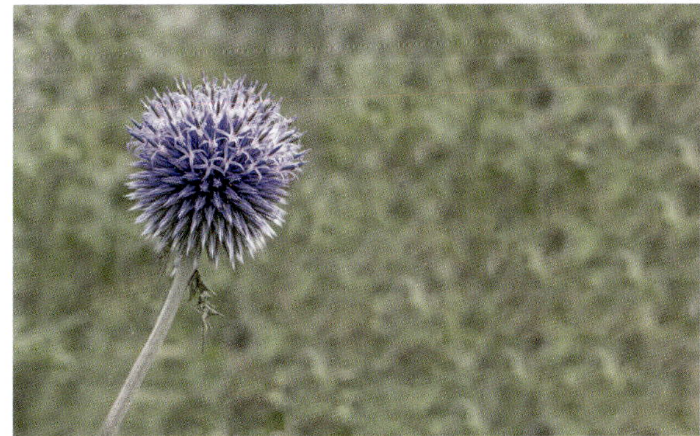

Fig. 8.10 **A globe-thistle flower photographed in the field and isolated against an out-of-focus background. The flower is positioned off centre to provide an area of empty space.**

MINIMALISM TECHNIQUES

Digital software offers a range of options for taking a starting photograph and converting it to minimal elements. Many of the techniques and filters described in this book tend to reduce detail and move the image in a minimalist direction.

Line Edges

A Photoshop tool to isolate the edges of an image is described in Lesson 6 and illustrated in Figure 6.10. (Filter > Blur > Smart Blur; set Quality to High, and Mode to Edge Only, then invert the result: Image > Adjustments > Invert). In that Lesson the edge tool is used to restore structure to a simplified picture by combining the edges with the modified original. However, the edges on their own can be effective minimalist pictures.

Shadows

When a subject is isolated in space with little other content, it becomes the sole focus for attention. It is then important to ensure that its lighting and positioning are just right. As already noted, guidelines such as the rule of thirds will help with positioning, but fine tuning of lighting effects may be needed to make the most of the subject. Adjusting shadows can be critical here. Shadows can help to focus attention on the subject and will create a sense of depth. A useful tool here is in Photoshop's layer styles (Layer > Layer Style; select Drop Shadow). To apply layer styles, the subject must be on a new layer, above the background layer. The drop-shadow settings allow the depth, intensity and diffusion of the shadow to be adjusted. The shadow can be manoeuvred into position by dragging it on screen.

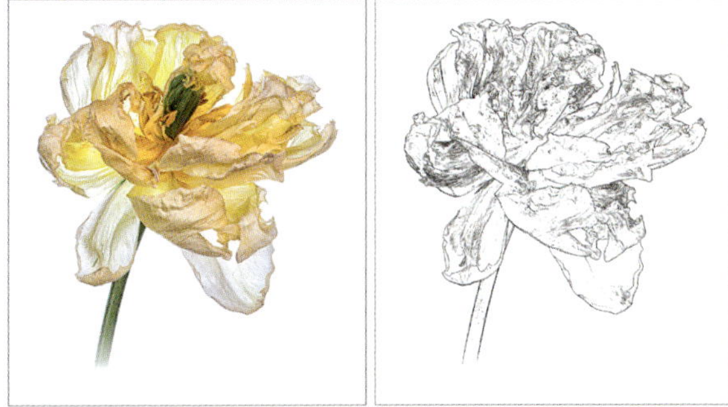

Fig. 8.11 **A tulip flower alongside a minimalist treatment consisting only of the line edges from the starting picture.**

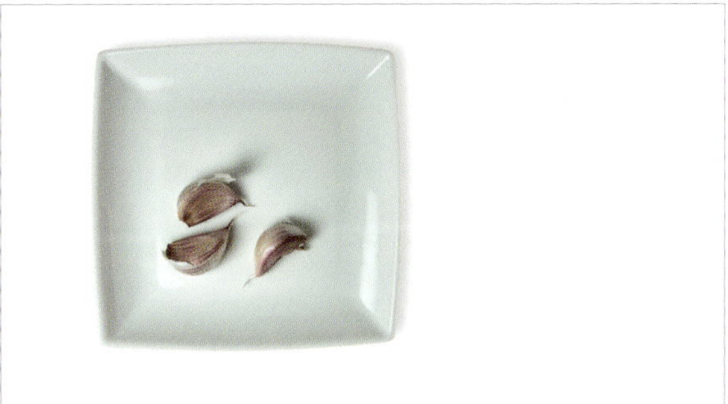

Fig. 8.12 **A white saucer with three garlic cloves. The positioning allows compositional space, and a shadow has been added to the saucer using Photoshop's Layer Styles to match the garlic shadows and to add a feeling of depth.**

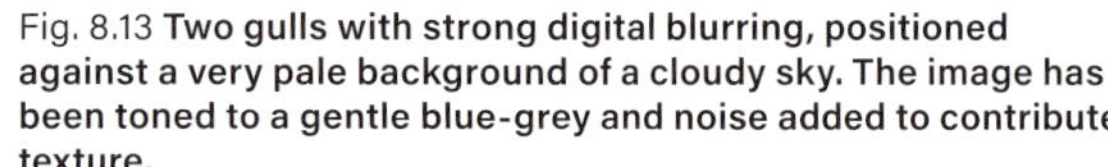

Fig. 8.13 **Two gulls with strong digital blurring, positioned against a very pale background of a cloudy sky. The image has been toned to a gentle blue-grey and noise added to contribute texture.**

Click and Drag

A starting point for a minimalist composition might be a simple empty frame. This can be created at any desired size and resolution (File > New; set the required width and height, or choose one of the presets such as A4). If some texture or colour is wanted, select the canvas (Select > All) and fill with a soft colour (Edit > Fill, with Contents set to Color). Texture can be added to the colour in the Filter Gallery (Filter > Filter Gallery > Texture > Texturizer). To make the texture more diffuse, add Gaussian blur (Filter > Blur > Gaussian Blur). Now the canvas is set to receive the subject. Open the subject picture and drag it onto the new canvas (set the Photoshop tool to Move, usually the top option on the toolbar). It will now be a new layer with adjustable-size edges and can be sized and positioned to suit. If the background of the subject picture is unwanted it can possibly be removed using a layer blend mode (the drop-down options at the top of the Layers panel). For example, if the background of the subject image is white, then a blend mode of Darken will ensure that only the subject is visible in the final picture.

MINIMALISM - KEYS

MINIMALIST photographs aim to reveal the essence of a subject. They rely on simple shapes, lines and negative space for their impact.

THE use of negative space places particular emphasis on composition. Often the rule of thirds will provide a useful compositional guideline.

ABSTRACT images can be well suited to minimalist treatment. The absence of a recognisable subject offers flexibility over composition.

SUBJECTS for minimalist photographs include everyday objects such as kitchen utensils, and isolated flowers.

LANDSCAPE photography takes on a minimalist form in poor weather when mist and rain obscure details.

PARTICULARLY useful digital techniques for minimalist images include the use of line edges, shadow creation using layer styles, and click-and-drag composition on a blank digital canvas.

FACING PAGE
Fig. 8.14 **A close-up picture of detail from a toy that produces swirl effects in coloured sand.**

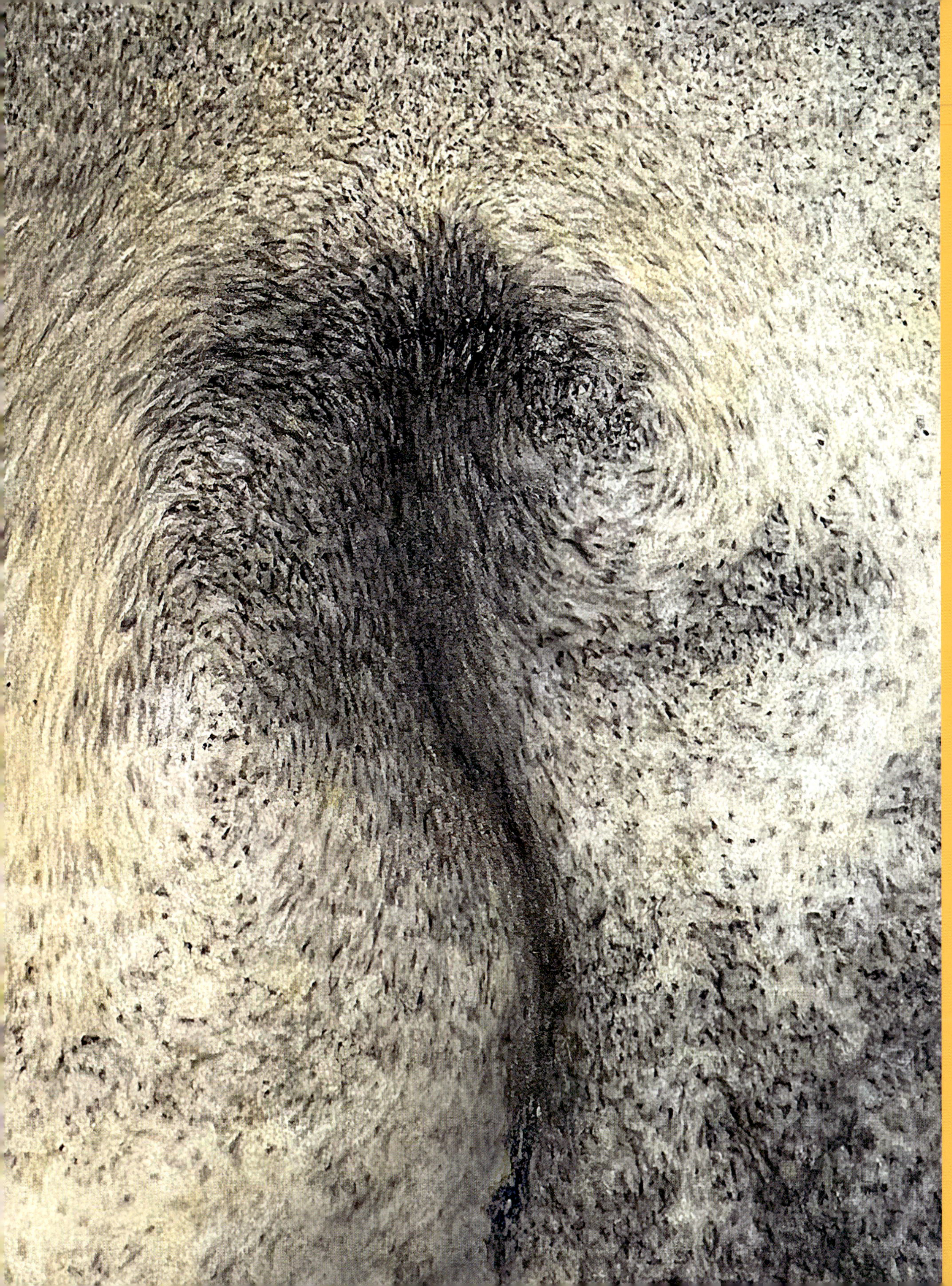

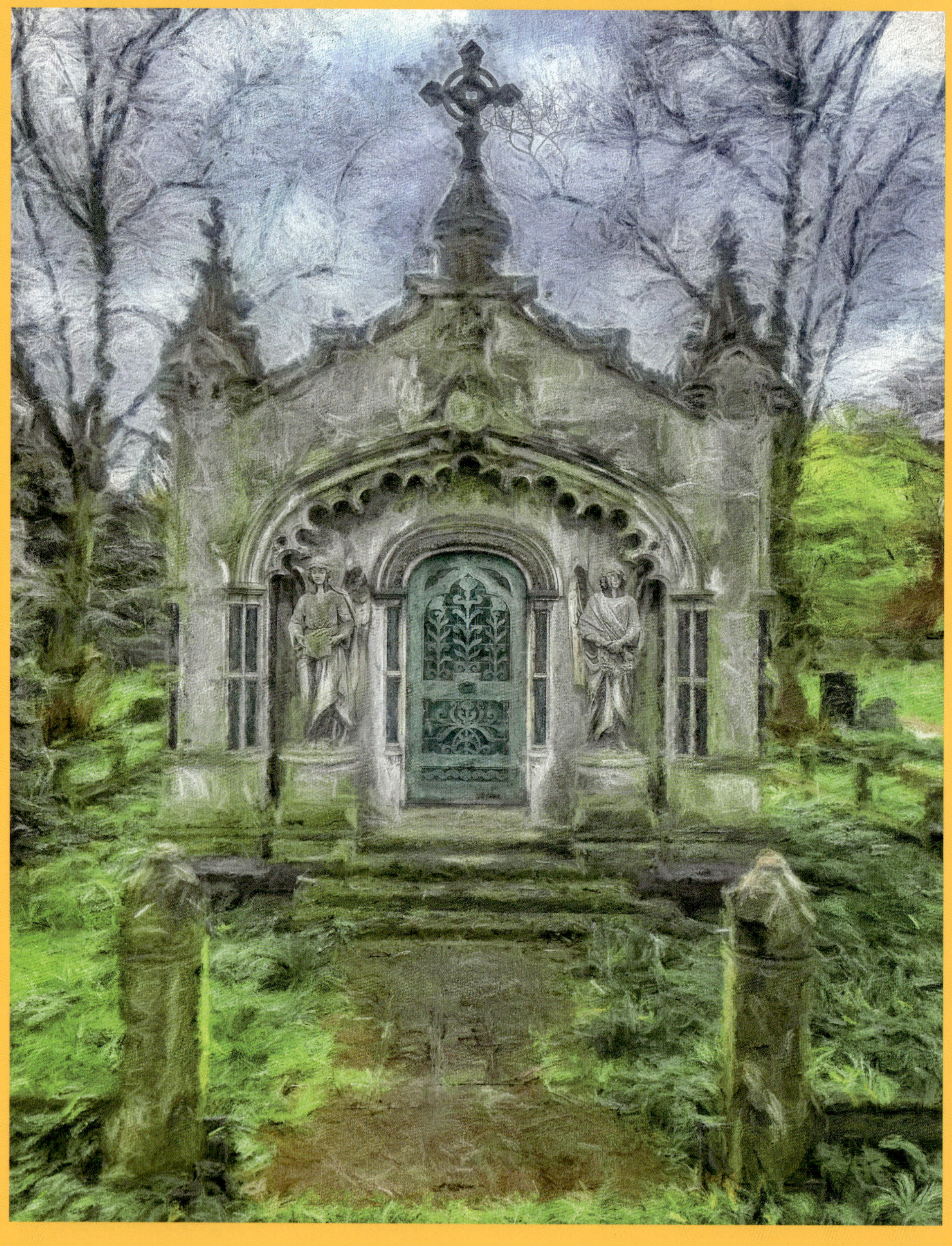

Fig. 9.1 **A picture in Brompton Cemetery, displaced using a texture image of grasses to give a more ethereal appearance.**

LESSON 9

DISPLACING

In Lesson 3, various routes to adding texture to an image were explored. A characteristic of these applications is that the shapes in the subject picture are not changed. Effectively a separate texture image is overlaid on the subject and adds a light-and-shade effect to give the appearance of texture. This Lesson considers a more extreme use of texture in which the pixels of the subject picture are displaced using the tone distribution of the texture (the displacement 'map'). This offers great potential for intriguing effects and for producing dramatic, impressionistic and often abstract results.

In Photoshop, the displacement settings are in the Distort set of filters (Filter > Distort > Displace). This opens a control box in which the level of pixel displacement required on the vertical and horizontal axes can be set. When this is done, click OK and the computer's file structure will open and allow access to PSD files, the required format for displacement in Photoshop. Clicking on a PSD file will then apply the chosen displacement settings.

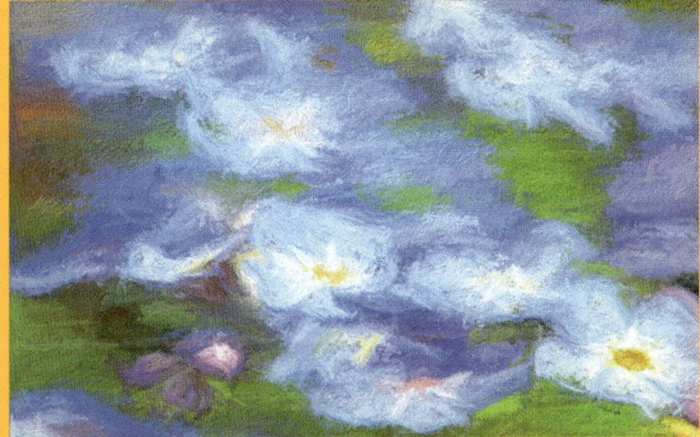

Fig. 9.2 **Forget-me-not flowers displaced with an image of textured rock and adjusted for contrast and saturation.**

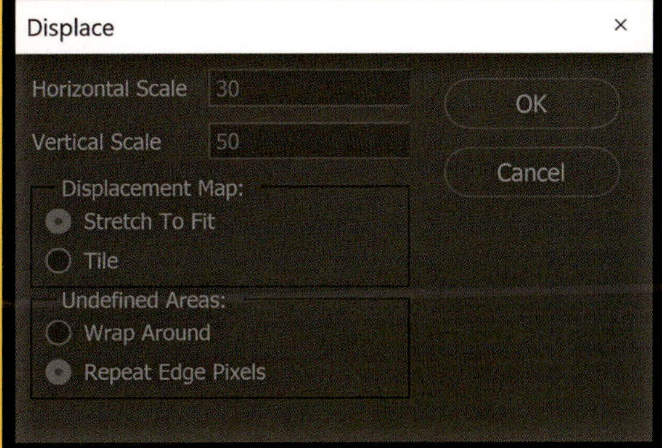

Fig. 9.3 **Photoshop's displacement control box, set for 30 pixels of horizonal displacement and 50 pixels of vertical.**

CONFORMING AN IMAGE TO A BACKGROUND

A widely used application of displacement mapping is to present the appearance of a picture superimposed on a highly textured surface; the subject is made to follow the contours of the texture. To achieve this, start by opening the texture image. The result will be most effective if the texture is quite pronounced, such as a piece of crumpled paper. This image must now be saved as a PSD file (File > Save As; select the PSD option). Save the file with a different name so it will be recognised as the image to choose for the displacement.

Now reopen the original texture file together with the subject picture that is to be displaced. With the Move tool active, drag the subject over the texture so that the subject becomes the top layer with the texture as background. Scale the subject layer so that both layers are aligned (Edit > Transform > Scale). With the subject layer active, go to the Displacement Map controls (Filter > Distort > Displace). This opens the settings box for horizontal and vertical displacement, shown in Figure 9.3. The amount will depend on how displaced the image is to look. Start with 20 pixels on each scale and click OK. The computer folder structure now opens, so locate the PSD displacement image. The subject will now be displaced along the lines of the texture. This process will require some toing and froing to get the levels of displacement just right. The opacity or blend mode of the subject layer will now require adjustment so that it blends comfortably with the textured surface.

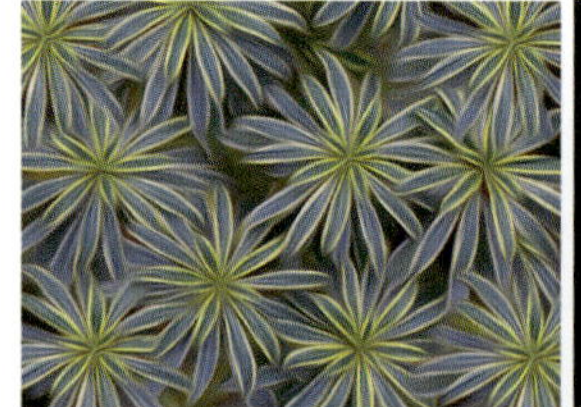

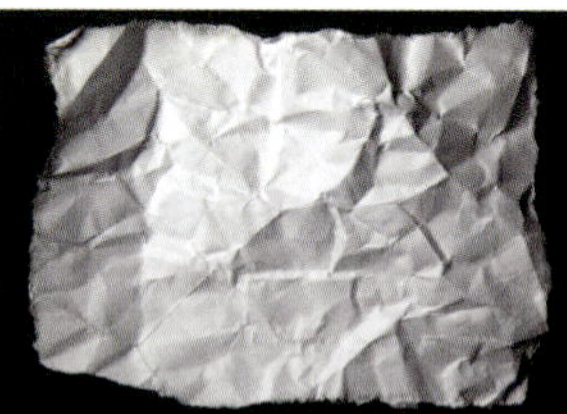

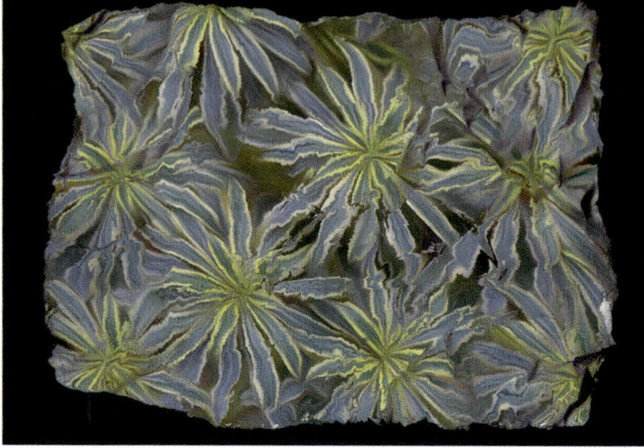

Fig. 9.4 **A picture of euphorbias superimposed on crumpled paper, with the paper image displacing the euphorbias so that the flowers follow the contours of the paper.**

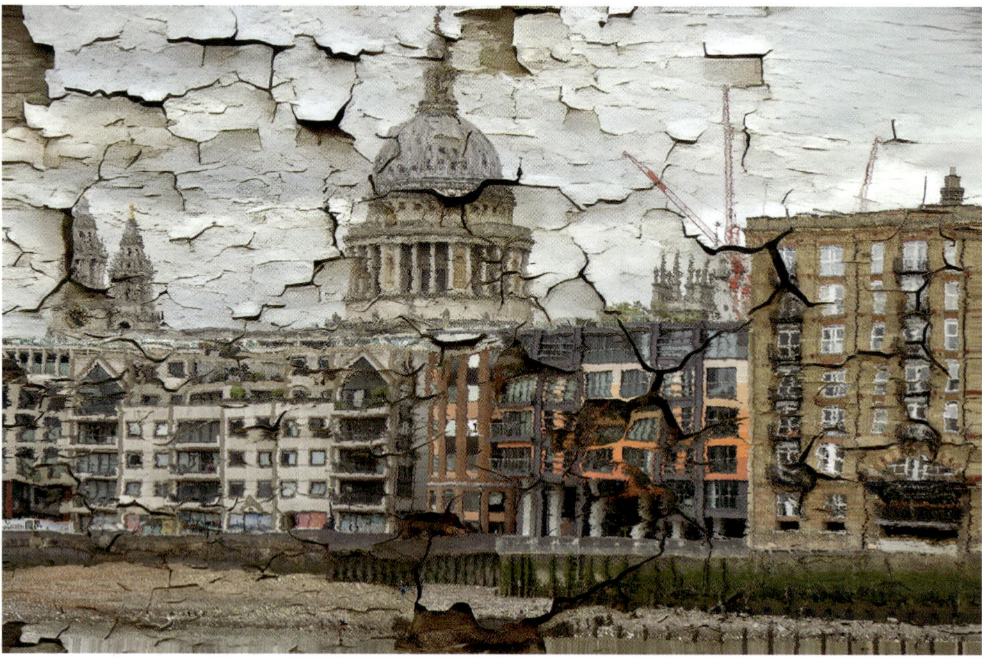

Fig. 9.5 **St Paul's Cathedral combined with a picture of flaking paint. The paint image is used to displace the cathedral picture and the two combined in Photoshop layers using the Darken blend mode on the paint layer.**

ARTISTIC APPLICATION

For more artistic use of displacement mapping there is no need to create the impression of the subject superimposed on the texture. Instead, the change delivered by the displacement can be appreciated in its own right. When pushed to high levels of distortion, the result will be increasingly abstract. Unlike many Photoshop filters it is not usually necessary to reduce image resolution to achieve dramatic results. This is because the range of displacement on the horizontal and vertical axes is from -999 to +999 pixels distortion. Even for very high-resolution starting pictures, it is unlikely that anything approaching these extremes will be needed.

Finding a Subject

The use of displacement as an artistic tool is relatively unusual since it was designed to wrap text round a contoured surface. As a result, there are no prescribed guidelines for purely artistic application. The field is open for experiment and for finding a personal style. Choice of subject is complicated because there are two images involved, the picture to be displaced as well as the texture image that will deliver the displacing. Good starting subjects are often contrasty and colourful. The displacement will then be more striking and more clearly an intentional artistic statement.

Finding a good texture image (the 'map') might involve trying out a few options until the desired result is achieved. It is usually helpful if the texture is quite contrasty. If necessary, a boost to contrast can be made, for example through Photoshop's brightness and contrast settings (Image > Adjustments > Brightness/ Contrast). The texture images can be in colour, but it is the tones, not the colours, that will deliver the displacing, so it is worth converting texture images to black and white (Image > Adjustments > Black & White) so that their effect can be more easily anticipated. Remember that, for use with Photoshop's displacement tool, the texture pictures must be saved as PSD files.

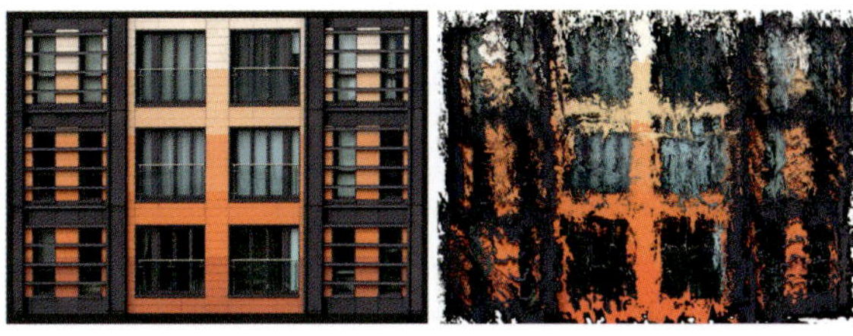

Fig. 9.6 **The London windows, also used in Figure 4.8, displaced using an image of rock formations.**

Fig. 9.7 **Examples of pictures that are suitable for use as displacement maps. They are images of smoke, a stone wall, windscreen frost, a rock face, a wood section and grasses. They must be saved as PSD files, and their effect is most easily visualised when they are converted to black and white.**

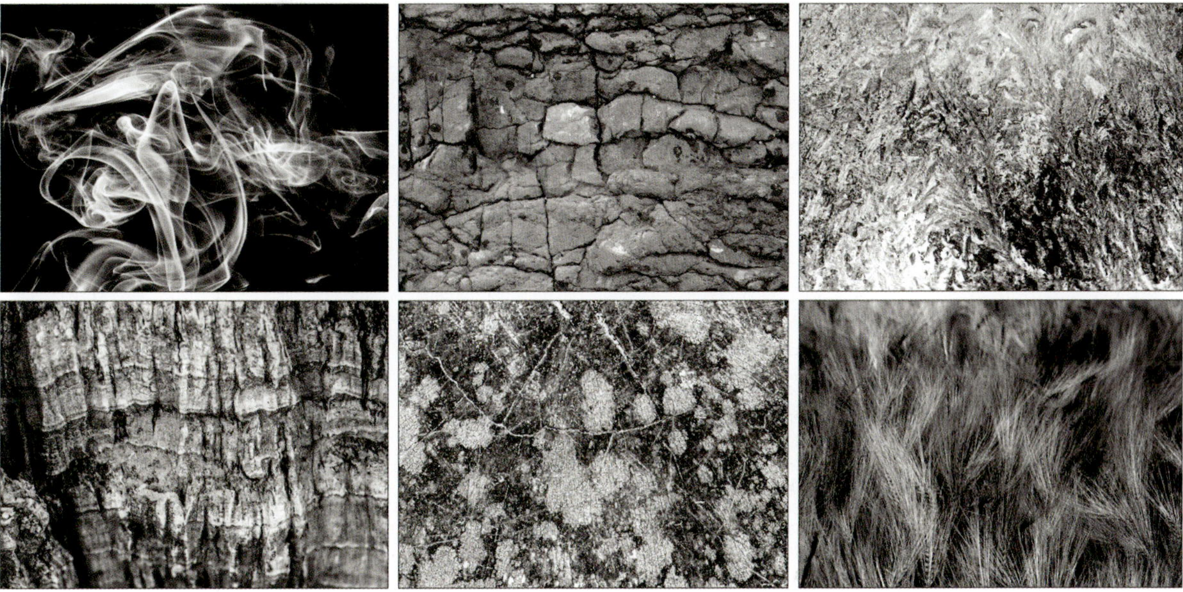

Using a Section

It might seem that there are already too many variables at play here – the selection of the starting picture, the choice of texture, the horizontal and vertical displacement settings. To add a further challenge, it is often the case that only a section of a starting picture lends itself to displacement. An example is in Figure 9.8 where the whole picture did not suit this treatment, but a small section had the right mix of shapes and colours to deliver a striking abstract. The crop required to isolate the chosen section will of course result in much-reduced resolution. However, for the quite abstract results, resolution is often not critical.

Contrast and Saturation

As noted above, it can help to boost the contrast of the texture image in Photoshop's brightness and contrast settings. That same setting can be used to boost the contrast of the newly displaced result. In addition, image saturation can be enhanced in the hue and saturation adjustments (Image > Adjustments > Hue/Saturation). This was pushed to quite an extreme level in Figure 9.8, where precise realism was no longer important.

SELECTIVE DISPLACEMENT

The use of displacement as an artistic tool can be quite radical, resulting in a loss of the identity of the starting subject. As with many digital filtration techniques, it can be helpful to restore some of the original image. There are various ways to do this.

Layer Masking

To restore part of an image that has been displaced, start by making a duplicate copy of the starting picture as a new Photoshop layer (Layer > Duplicate Layer). Now make the displacing adjustments to the top layer. Apply a layer mask to the displaced layer (Layer > Layer Mask > Reveal All). This will appear as a white box alongside the layer. Paint on the mask with a black brush to reveal the sections of the original picture to be restored. It is helpful if the brush is soft (no hard edges), so set a low, possibly zero, level of hardness in the brush settings. This will ensure

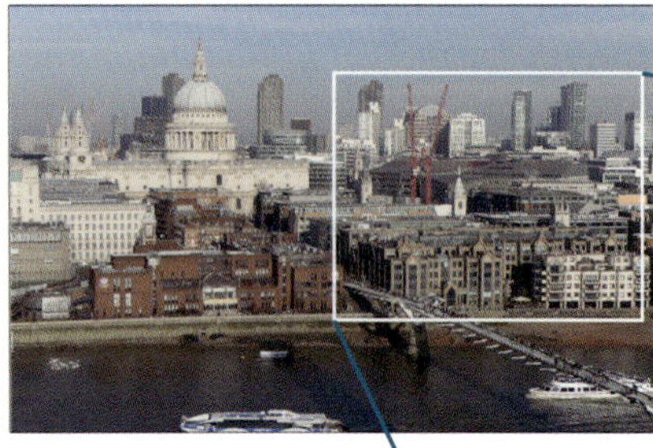

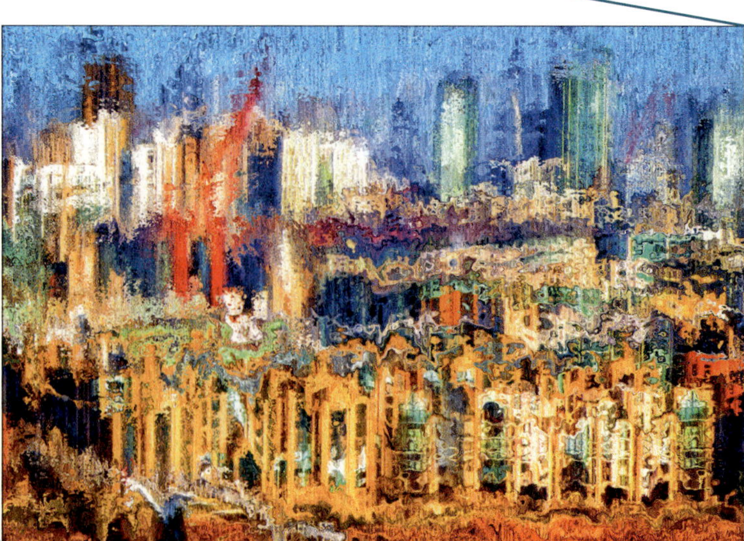

Fig. 9.8 **A picture of the City of London showing a suitable section for displacement treatment, and the resulting abstract image. A high level of increase in colour saturation was used to add drama to the result.**

a gentle transition between the displaced version and the original. Reduce the brush opacity to around 25% so that the transition can be gradually built up and can be concentrated in appropriate areas. This treatment is particularly useful with displaced flower pictures, as in Figure 9.9. where restoration of the centre of the flower establishes a focal point in the image.

Partial Displacement

With any filtration technique, if a selection is made on the starting image, the result will only be applied to content within the selection. This is a useful way to control the area for the displacement. In Photoshop, the selection tools are usually towards the top of the toolbar. They include a Rectangular Marquee tool and an Elliptical Marquee tool. Selection options are reviewed in the Getting Started chapter. They are applied by dragging on screen across the area to be selected. To ensure a smooth gradation from the starting image to the displaced section, the selection should be feathered. The feathering can be set in the box at the top of the screen before making the selection, or after the selection via the Select and Mask box which, when clicked, opens sliders, one of which controls feathering. The displacement is now limited to the selection area. An alternative, offering greater control, is to copy the selection to a new layer (Edit > Copy, followed by Edit > Paste) and to apply the displacement to that layer. This can then be independently adjusted for opacity and blend mode.

Blending Images

Photoshop blend modes enable further creative scope for the use of displacement. Blending the displaced version with the original can result in entirely new pictures. The blend modes merge one layer with the one below based on the qualities of both images. Their names, for example Darken, give an idea of the treatment, but it can be difficult to predict how a blend will appear, so it is best to run through the options to preview the effects. Blend modes are accessed through the drop-down menu at the top of the Layers panel. By default, it is set to Normal, meaning there is no blending. The modes can be viewed by rolling the cursor down the list of options. Since the original and the displaced pictures are different and therefore not

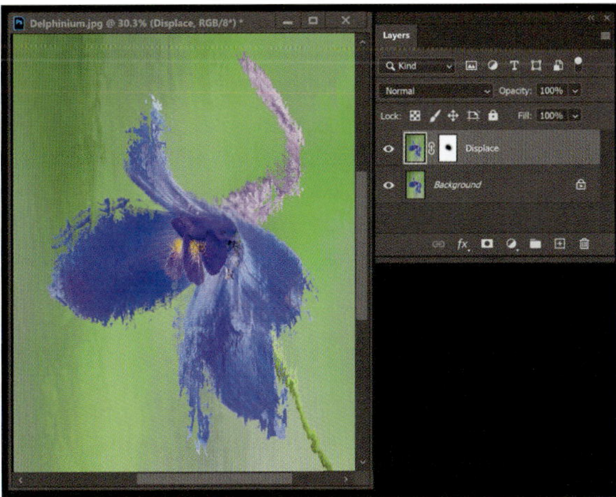

Fig. 9.9 **A delphinium duplicated on Photoshop layers with displacement applied to the top layer. A layer mask is added to the displaced layer and, by painting in black on the mask, definition is restored to the central area of the flower.**

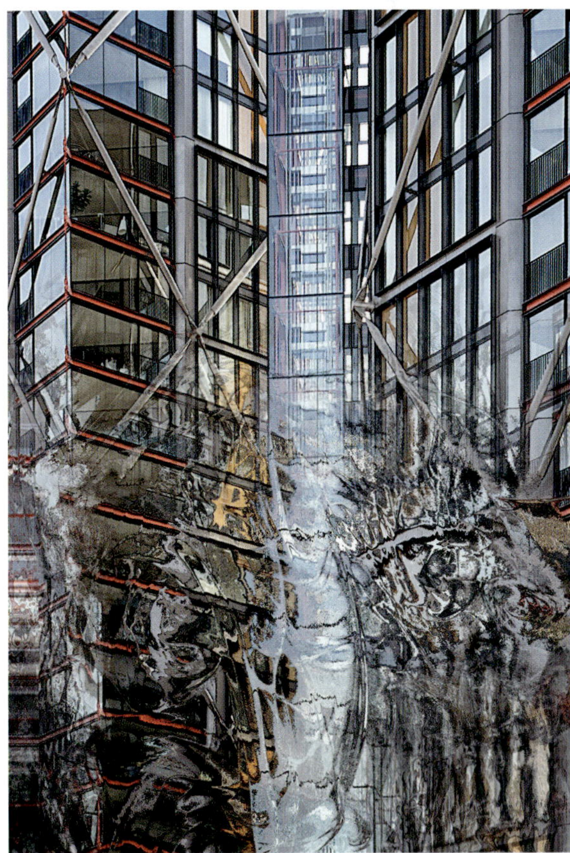
Fig. 9.10 **A building given the appearance of disintegration at the base by making a highly feathered selection of the bottom half of the picture and applying displacement using a picture of waves. The feathering ensures a gradual transition from the original to the displaced image.**

precisely aligned, their combination can produce intriguing effects. For more drama it is interesting to change the hue of one of the layers (Image > Adjustments > Hue/Saturation). The blending of the different colours will create entirely new images.

Fig. 9.11 **A starting picture of trees and water displaced using a high-contrast image of smoke and then combined with the original using Photoshop's Lighten blend mode. The hue of the original picture was adjusted to give a blue colouration so that the blend effect was more pronounced.**

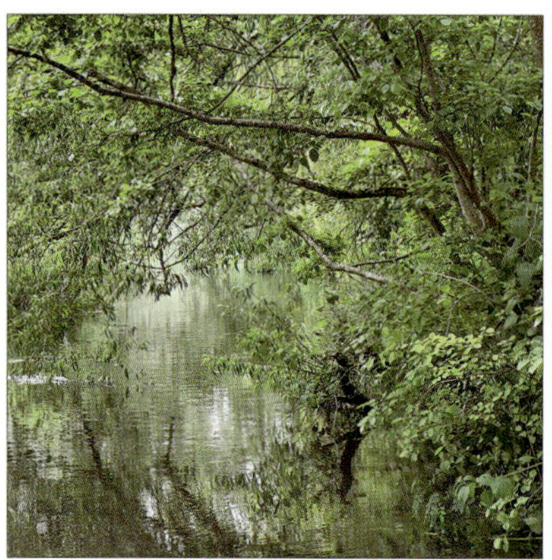

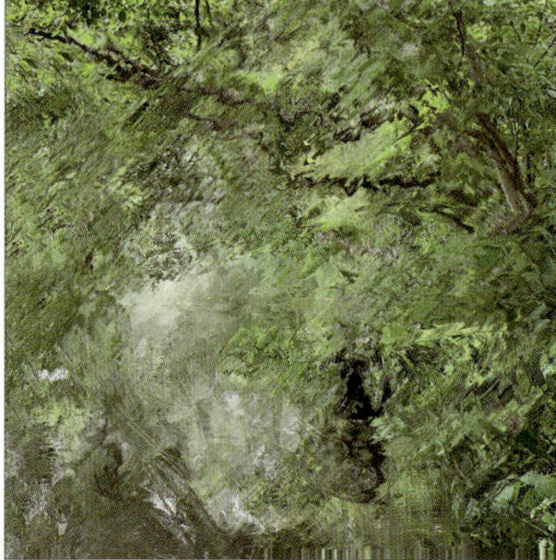

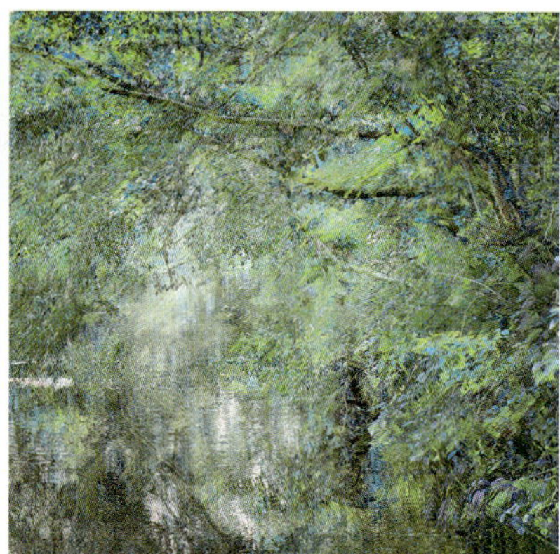

DISPLACING - KEYS

DISPLACEMENT involves nudging the pixels of a digital image using the tonal distribution of another image (the displacement map).

DISPLACEMENT is often used to give the impression that a picture or text follows the contours of an uneven surface.

FOR artistic application of displacement there is no need to match the picture to a texture. Used independently, the results are often abstract in appearance.

THE most effective mapping pictures are high-contrast texture images.

IN Photoshop, the displacing picture must be a PSD file. It can be coloured, but its effect is easier to visualise if converted to black and white.

DISPLACED images can be combined with the starting picture in a variety of ways, including the use of digital blend modes.

FACING PAGE
Fig. 9.12 **A picture of trees displaced using an image of a scratched metal surface and then combined with the original using Photoshop's Multiply blend mode. The colour of the layer with the starting picture was changed to give a blue tone so that new colours were produced. Adjustment was required in Levels to lighten the result.**

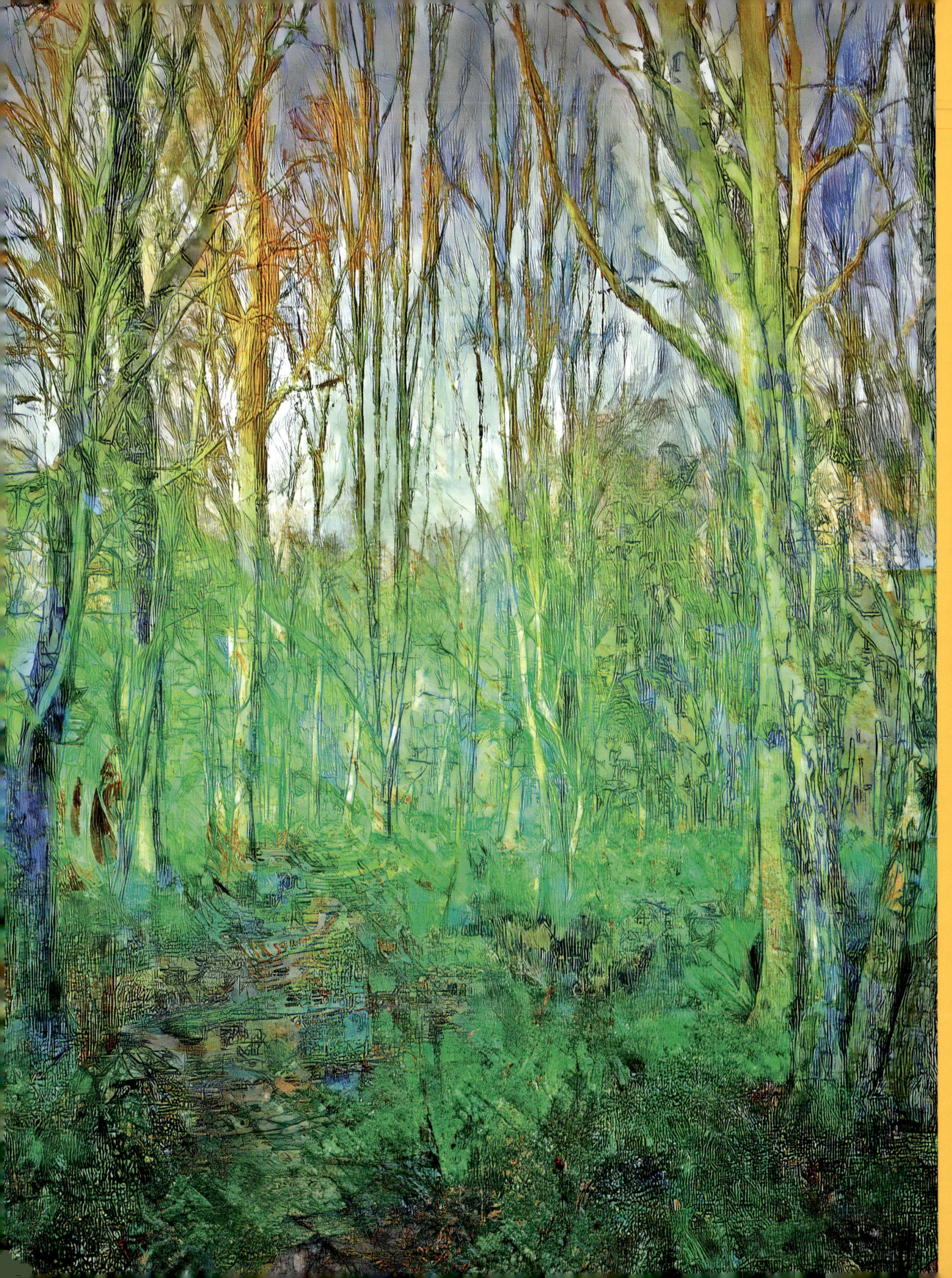

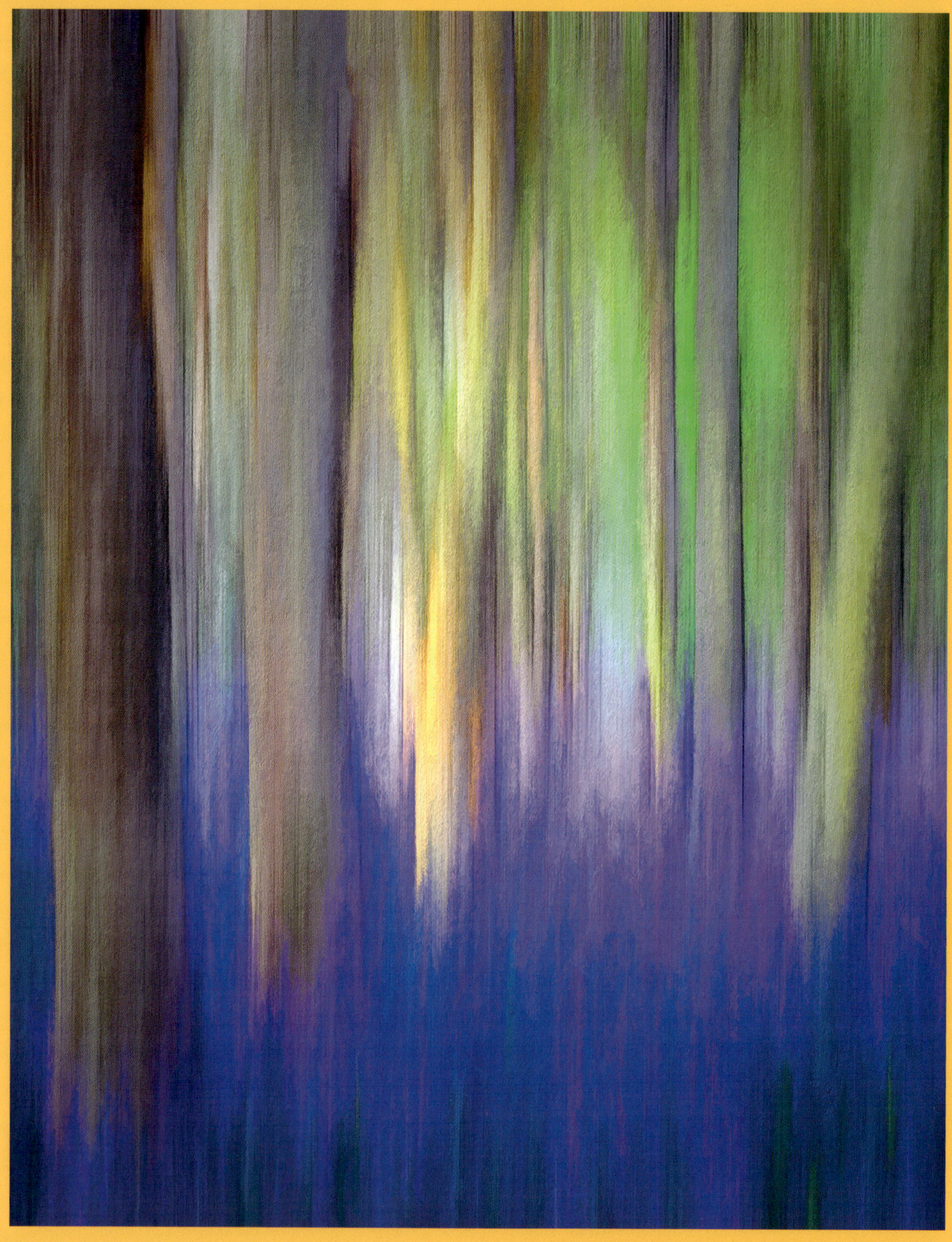

Fig. 10.1 **A bluebell wood directionally blurred using a combination of Photoshop Motion Blur and displacement mapping (Lesson 9) to give a more ethereal appearance.**

LESSON 10

CONTROLLED BLURRING

We usually go to great lengths to avoid blur in our photographs. A blurred photograph lacks detail and simply doesn't look right. Accidental blurring is often caused by movement of the camera or failure to focus on the subject. However, blur in images can also be used to create artistic effects, to highlight aspects of the image and to produce a feeling of depth. This Lesson explores ways in which creative blurring can be achieved, both at the taking stage and in post-processing.

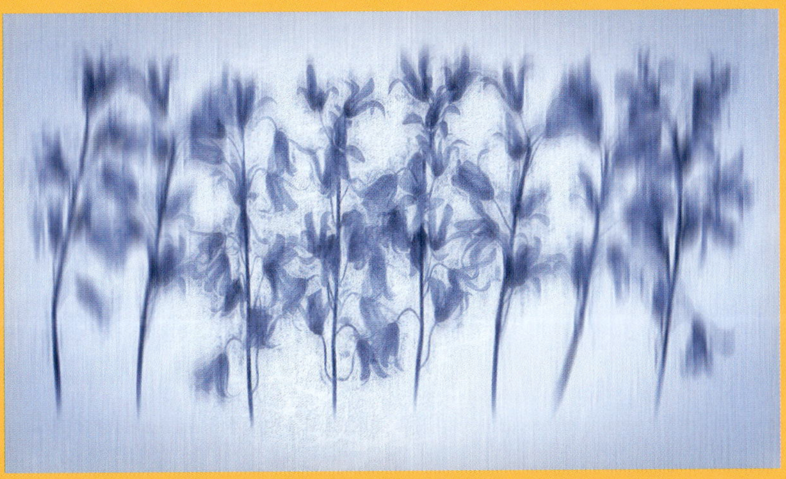

Fig. 10.2 **A picture of bluebell flowers toned as in Lesson 2 and with blurring at the image edges to give emphasis to the centre.**

IN-CAMERA MOVEMENT

In-camera movement, often abbreviated to ICM, is achieved at the taking stage by moving the camera in the direction the blur is to follow. Most commonly ICM is used to emphasise directional lines that already exist in the subject. For example, the vertical lines in rows of trees or buildings, or the horizontal lines in landscapes. Here is the sequence used to add blurring movement to a tree scene:

1. Pre-set the camera's exposure for the trees, bearing in mind that a relatively slow shutter speed will be needed. Some trial and error will be called for but 1/8 second is a good starting point. There is then a need to set the ISO and the aperture to allow for that slow exposure. Because the slow shutter will let in a lot of light, it will probably be possible to have a low ISO, perhaps of 100, and a small aperture, say f16.
2. Turn off the camera's automatic focusing. This will be a setting either on the camera or on the lens. Manually focus on the trees. You will be sweeping the camera from the ground upwards and auto focusing would result in the focus being on your feet rather than the trees.
3. Starting with the camera pointing down, smoothly sweep the camera upwards following the line of the trees. When the camera reaches the trees, press the shutter button. Keep moving and do not stop until the shutter closes.
4. Experiment with this movement until you are confident that the sweep of the camera encompasses mainly the body of the trees and not too much ground or sky.

Be ready for a good deal of trial and error to get this right and experiment with a range of shutter speeds. Often dozens of pictures are needed to get one good result. The most common failures result from inclusion of more than just the trees in the picture, or from the movement of the camera not following the same lines as the trees. This is one of the great advantages of digital photography – lots of failed pictures on film would be very expensive.

Any scene that has directional lines will lend itself to this treatment. Vertical lines are often found in flowers and grasses as well as in many buildings. Where the lines are horizonal, as in many landscapes and seascapes, the process is the same except of course that the camera sweep will be horizontal.

For brightly lit subjects it might be impossible to obtain a sufficiently slow shutter speed for the desired effect even at low ISO and a small aperture. An option is to use a neutral density (ND) filter on the front of the lens. These are neutral grey filters that cut the light into the camera and allow for long exposures. They are available in a variety of strengths that reduce the exposure by anything up to ten stops.

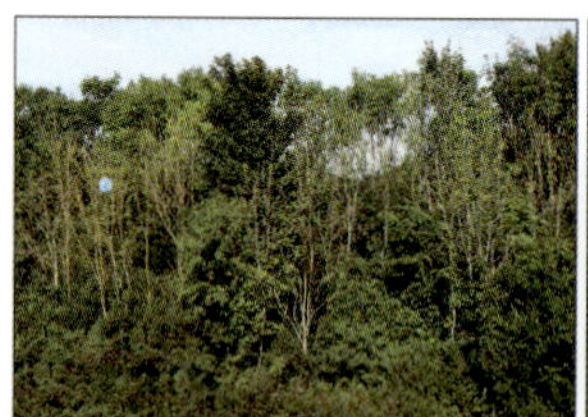
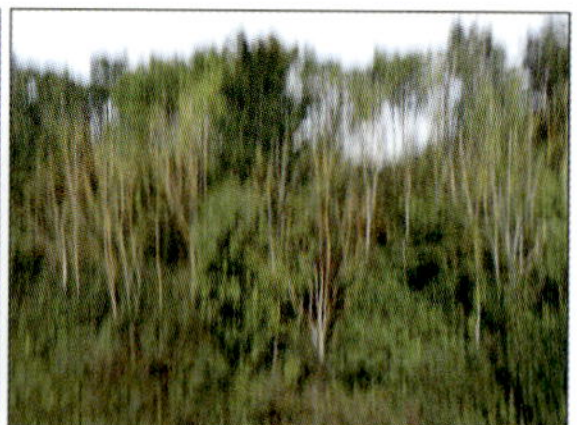

Fig. 10.2 **A picture of roadside trees together with the same scene vertically blurred by panning the camera along the lines of the trees during the exposure. The camera shutter speed was 1/15 second. The ragged appearance of the sky shows the challenge of managing highlights when using camera movement.**

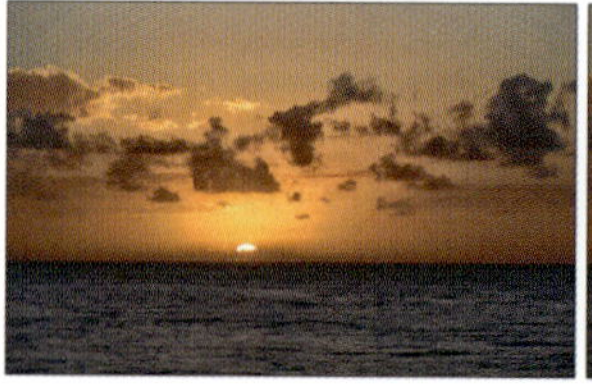
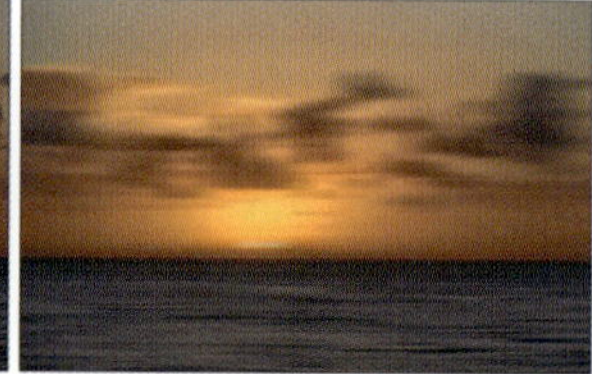

Fig. 10.3 **A sunset seascape with and without blurring following the line of the horizon. The simple starting picture with strong horizontal composition is suited to further artistic simplification by blurring. With intentional camera movement, the challenge is to maintain smooth and accurate horizonal movement and this can be aided by mounting the camera on a tripod.**

TAKING PICTURES THROUGH A DISTORTING FILTER

Artistic blurring can often be added to an otherwise mundane subject by taking the picture through a textured translucent filter. Many commonly available objects such as paperweights, textured or cut glass, and crumpled clingfilm can become distorting filters. The challenge is often not so much the taking of the picture as holding everything in place. In the absence of three hands, some DIY ingenuity will be called for to position the filter in front of the subject. For indoor photography, laboratory clamp systems can be purchased, which are ideal for the purpose.

Beautiful, creative results can be obtained by taking pictures through a surface smeared with a translucent grease such as Vaseline. When used directionally, this produces results rather like the camera-movement technique but gives greater control since the image can be composed and controlled through the viewfinder. The images are generally smoother than those from camera movement. It is of course advisable not to smear the Vaseline directly on the lens. Once on, it is impossible to remove. A good option is a plain glass filter such as a skylight or UV filter kept specially for the purpose. A square filter mounts into a holder that screws into the lens filter thread. The filter can then be rotated to adjust the exact direction of the blurring effect.

Any gel-like substance such as hair cream will do the job. Some of these have the additional advantage of being water soluble, making the smeared filter much easier to clean.

Sometimes distorting filters just 'turn up'. It is worth being on the lookout for subjects viewed through distorting surfaces, in particular rain or snow on windows. The best images are generally produced when the camera is focused on the window rather than the subject.

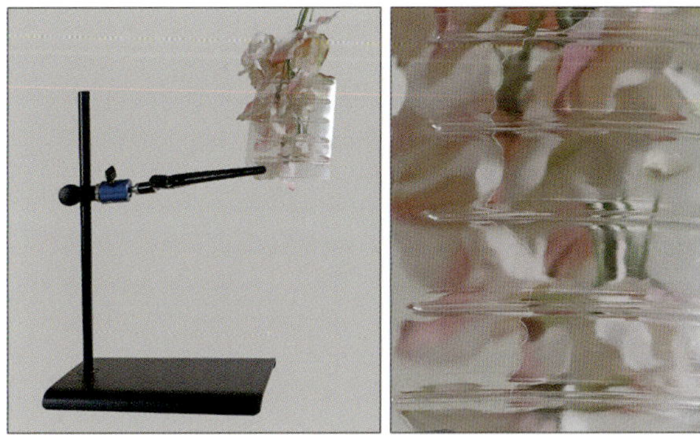

Fig. 10.4 **An adjustable stand used to hold a distorting filter through which suitable subjects can be photographed. The filter here is a section of a discarded plastic bottle positioned in front of an artificial flower. The resulting abstract image is shown alongside.**

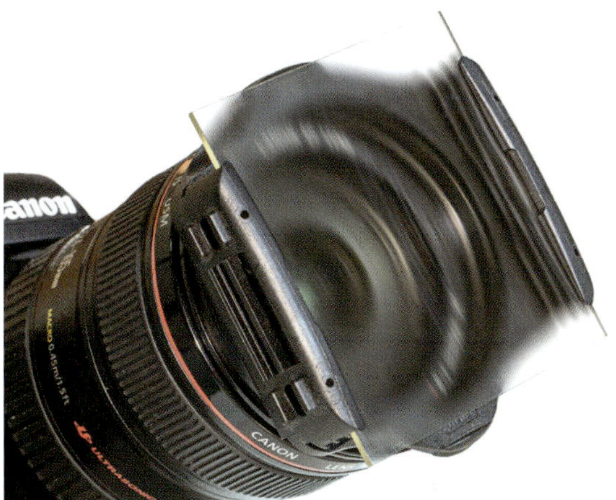

Fig. 10.5 **A square skylight filter in a lens-mounted filter holder, smeared with Vaseline to produce directional blurring effects.**

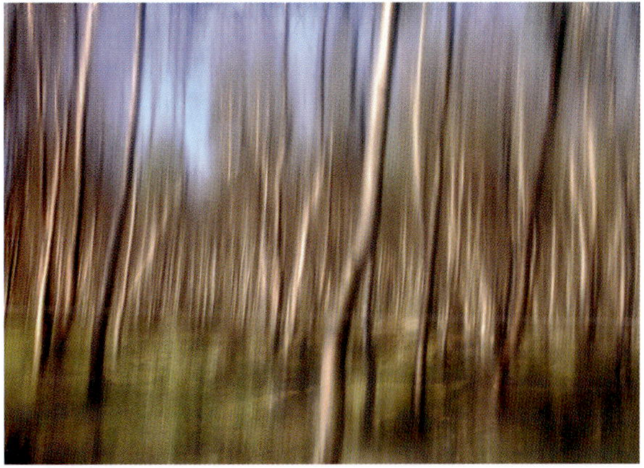

Fig. 10.6 **Woodland trees vertically blurred by photographing through a Vaseline-smeared filter. This generally produces smoother blur lines than the camera-movement technique and the shorter exposure is better for highlights such as sky.**

DIGITAL BLURRING

There are countless ways to blur an image using software such as Photoshop. Here are some of the tools available in most programs.

Gaussian Blur

Gaussian blurring removes fine detail, and the visual effect is a smooth blur similar to viewing the image through a translucent screen. The strength of Gaussian blurring can be controlled in the settings (Filter > Blur > Gaussian Blur), where the blur radius can be set on a scale from 0 to 1,000 pixels. Like all blurring tools, its creative value is often with the selective application of blurring in part of an image.

Motion Blur

Motion blur (Filter > Blur > Motion Blur) creates a sense of speed by adding a blur that flows in one direction. There are two adjustments to make. The first sets the angle of direction of the subject's motion. Then the distance setting controls the amount of blur. Motion blur will digitally replicate the directional blurring achieved using the panning technique and the smeared filter method already described.

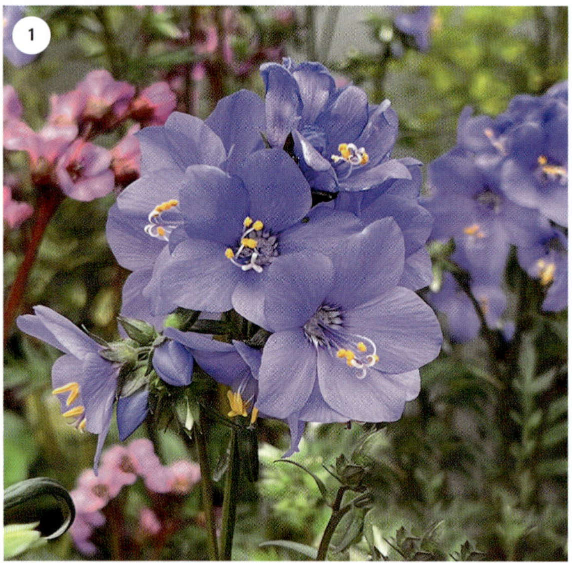

Fig. 10.7 **A polemonium flower photographed amongst other garden plants alongside the picture treated with Gaussian blur. The Blur was set at 50 pixels but will vary according to the effect required and the resolution of the starting image. The final image has sharpness restored to the flower to leave blur only in the surroundings. This is achieved by placing the blurred image above the original in Photoshop layers, placing a layer mask on the blurred image and painting with a black brush on the mask to reveal sharpness where required.**

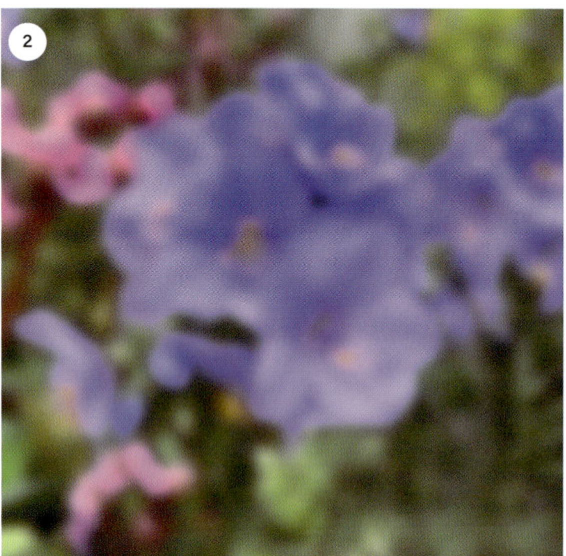

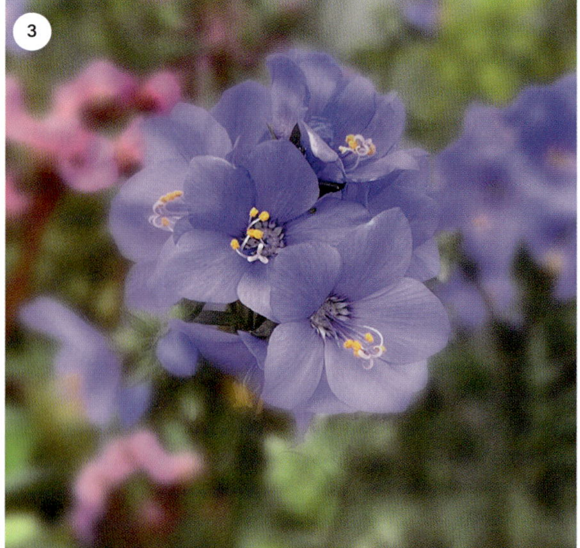

Path Blur

Creative effects can often be produced by directional blurring in which the direction is not linear as in motion blur but follows the curved lines of part of the image. Path blurring (Filter > Blur Gallery > Path Blur) is a valuable creative tool for this effect. It is a little more complicated than motion blur and can take a while to get used to. Drag the controls to set the contours of the blur lines and create a blur in the direction of the arrow. Then click and drag in other areas to create blur paths in other directions.

The Speed slider in the path blur control box specifies the amount of blur to be applied. The speed setting is applied to all the path blurs in the image. The Taper slider specifies the extent to which the blur tapers off gradually.

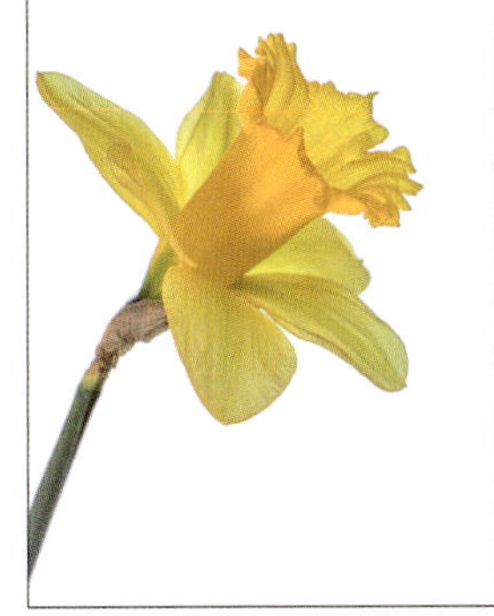

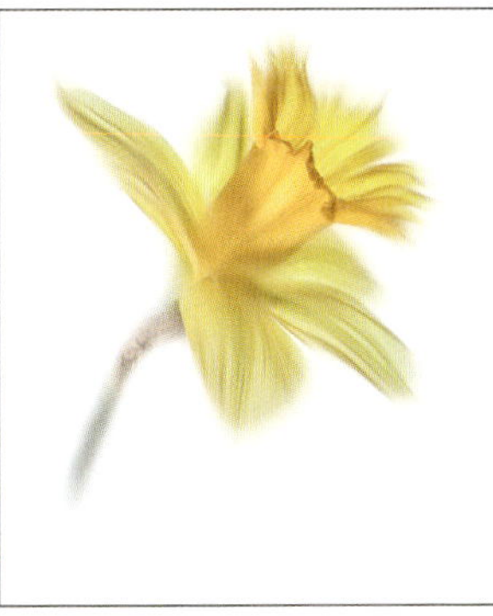

Fig. 10.8 **A daffodil photographed against a white background using a small aperture of f16 to give sharpness throughout. In the adjacent picture the daffodil has path blur applied to the petals to emphasise their directional lines. Sharpness has been restored to the leading edge of the flower to give a clear focal point.**

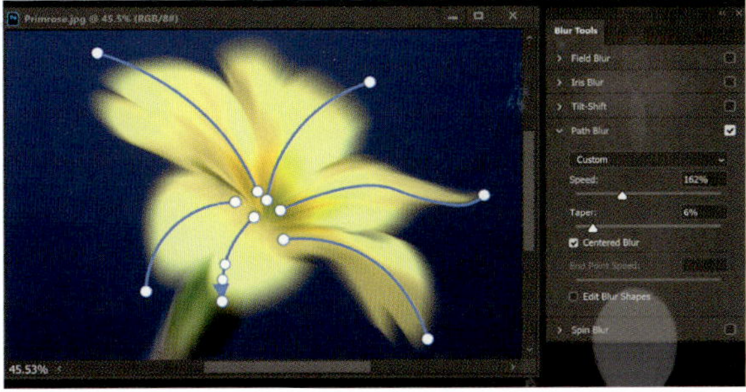

Fig. 10.9 **A primrose picture with Photoshop Path Blur lines drawn in on each petal. The Photoshop panel alongside shows the settings that are about to be applied.**

Radial Blur

The Radial Blur filter offers two types of blurring. Zoom (Filter > Blur > Radial Blur > Zoom) produces a blurring effect that radiates out from a selected point. The Photoshop setting allows the starting point of the blur to be set as well as the quality and level of the blurring. Zoom blur is like the effect of zooming a lens during exposure.

The second option in the Radial Blur filter is Spin (Filter > Blur > Radial Blur > Spin). This creates a circular motion effect that emulates an object's rotation. This tool can be used to give the appearance of rotation to parts of an image, such as the wheels of a moving car.

Fig. 10.10 **Close-up detail of an orchid flower alongside the image treated with the Radial Blur filter, firstly using its Zoom setting. The blur is set at best quality and a blur amount of 30. In the third picture radial blur is applied using the Spin setting with the blur set at best quality and a blur amount of 15.**

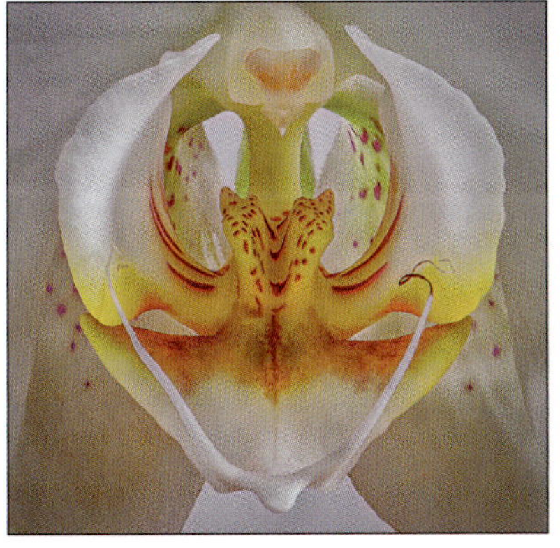

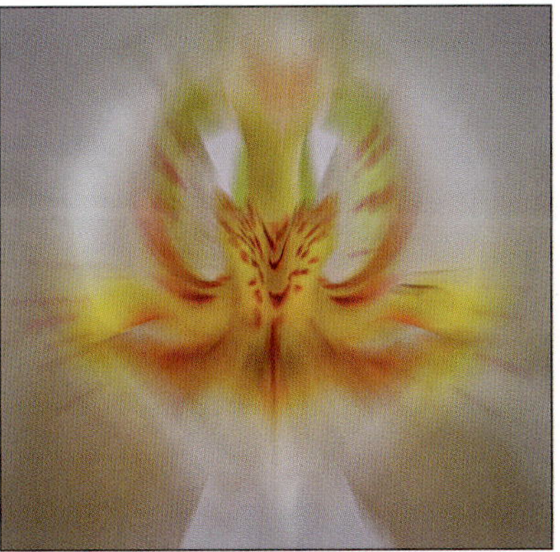

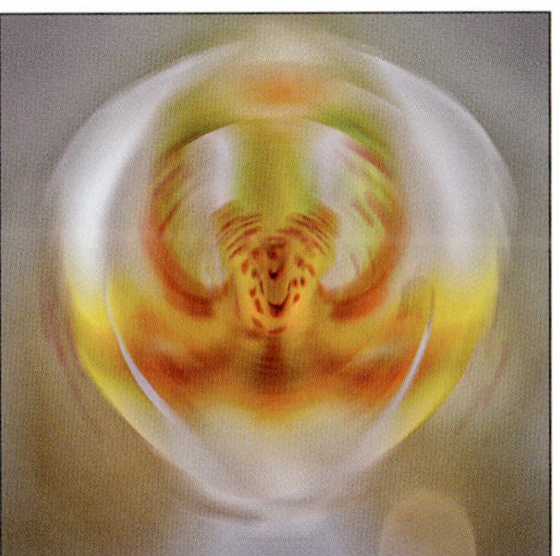

Replicating a Distorting Filter in Software

The in-camera technique described above to blur a subject by photographing it through a distorting filter can, to some extent, be mimicked in software. In Photoshop the tool is in the Filter Gallery (Filter > Filter Gallery). In the Gallery there is a set of tools labelled Distort, one of which is the Glass filter. When Glass is selected the type of 'glass' can be chosen in the Texture setting. Photoshop offers a limited set of textures but the box next to the Texture setting allows you to load your own distorting images. In Photoshop these must be PSD files, so if you have glassy pictures but in some other format such as JPEG, save them in PSD format (File > Save As; select PSD). The magnitude and smoothness of the distortion can be set in the Filter Gallery using the displayed sliders.

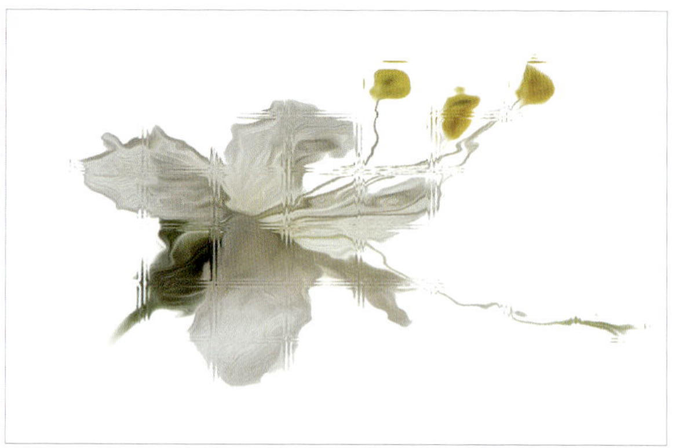

Fig. 10.11 **A lily with the Glass filter applied in Photoshop's Filter Gallery. One of Photoshop's pre-set filters is used here, the Blocks texture. The settings are Distortion 10, Smoothness 8, Scaling 175. However, these need to be adjusted to achieve the desired result and to suit the starting resolution.**

BLURRING - KEYS

BLURRING an image can create artistic effects with a sense of movement and depth.

BLURRING can be achieved by in-camera techniques as well as software manipulation.

IN-CAMERA methods include panning the camera during taking a photo, following the natural lines in the subject.

ARTISTIC blurring can be achieved by photographing a subject through a translucent distorting filter such as textured glass or a smeared filter.

MANY software tools deliver image blurring and offer high levels of control.

THE most creative use of blurring may require treatment to only selected parts of the image.

FACING PAGE
Fig. 10.12 **A tulip with some petals removed to reveal the stamens, converted to black and white (Lesson 1) with path blur applied individually to each of the petals.**

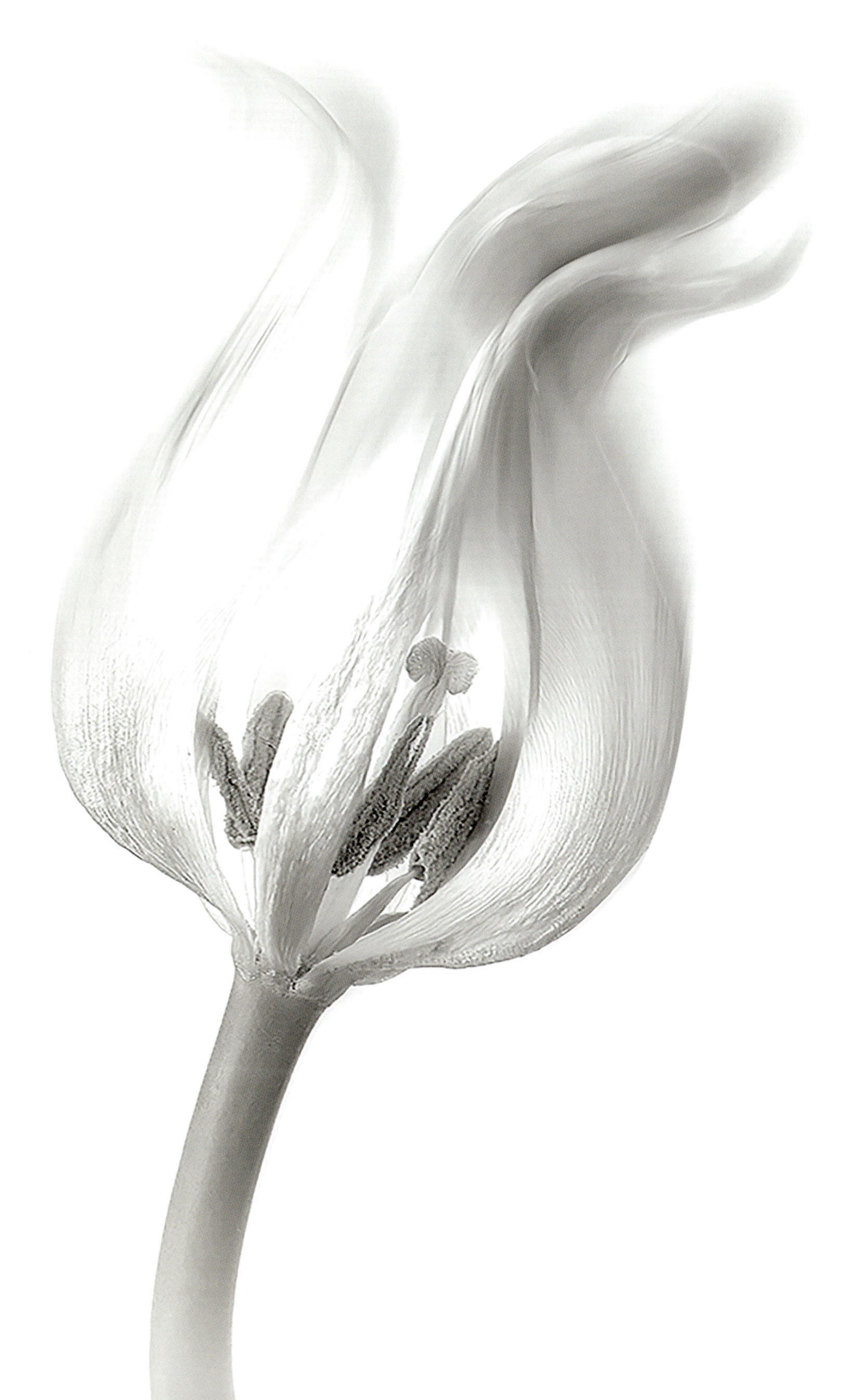

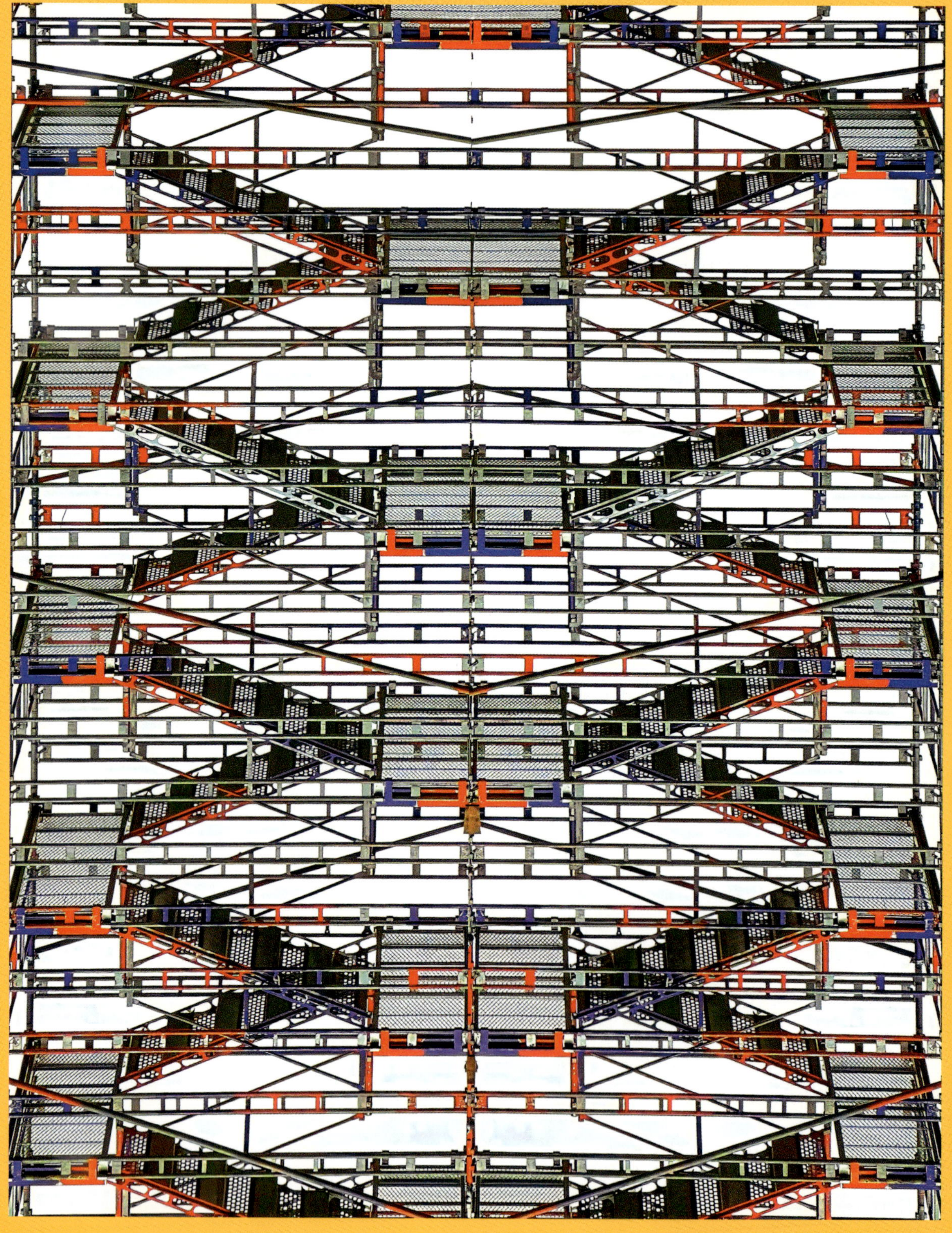

Fig. 11.1 **A section of scaffolding copied and mirrored horizontally. Contrast and saturation were increased for greater impact.**

LESSON 11
MIRRORING

Interesting and decorative pictures can often be produced by copying all or part of an image, flipping it horizontally or vertically and aligning the two sections. The resulting symmetry appeals to a love of uniformity and pattern and will often transform a picture that initially didn't quite make it. Before embarking on the digital routes to mirrored pictures, it is worth noting the 'straight' photography option – namely to photograph something on a mirror or other reflective surface. An interesting surface to use is a sheet of black Perspex which, since reflections on black are unusual, can deliver striking results.

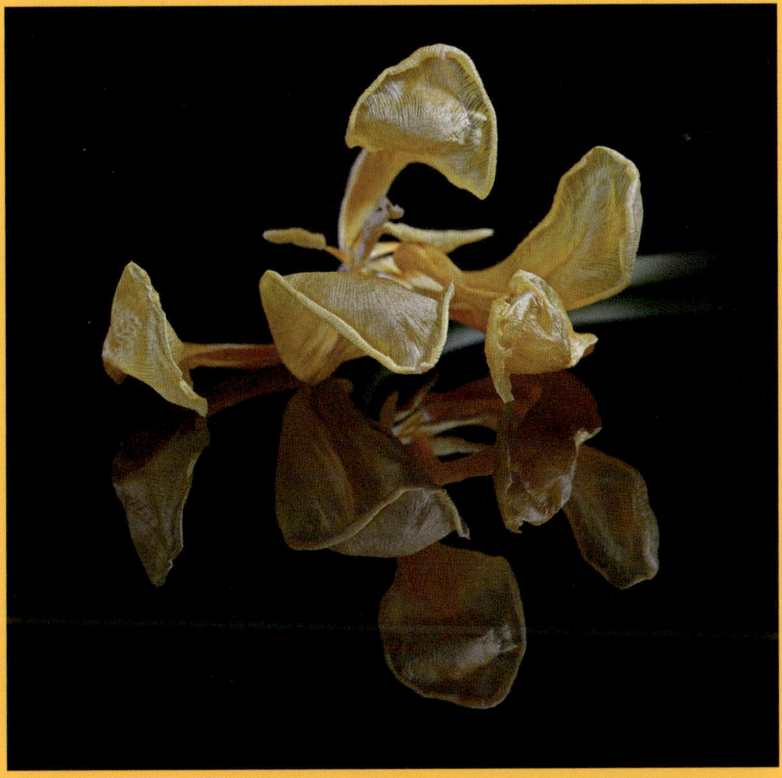

Fig. 11.2 **A dry tulip reflected on a black Perspex surface. Shiny Perspex gives interesting reflections on black but tends to build up a static charge that attracts dust.**

DIGITAL MIRRORING

Using software to produce mirrored pictures enables creative experimentation and can deliver results that would have been extremely difficult, perhaps impossible, with the restrictions of film.

Horizontal Flipping

Several subjects are suited to the panoramic type of effect produced when they are copied and flipped horizontally. Natural subjects are landscapes and rows of buildings, where there is already a horizontal direction in the composition. Once a suitable picture is identified, the first step is to create sufficient space for the mirrored section. This is most easily achieved by increasing the canvas size of the starting image.

The canvas-size settings (Image > Canvas Size) enable more space to be added around the starting picture. New width and height dimensions can be entered here. If the box marked Relative is ticked, the dimensions are presented as zeros and any dimensions now entered are added to the overall image size. Arrow boxes marked Anchor enable the new size to be uniformly added around the image (the default) or to be set to position the increase for addition to the top, bottom or either side. Since the mirroring for a horizontal landscape is going to be only to one side, the width increase will be entered to match the starting image size and the Anchor arrow will be set to point left or right, depending on what side the flipped image is to be positioned. The colour of the canvas increase can be set here but, since the space is going to be filled with the flipped image, the colour is not important. Select the subject image using the Rectangular Marquee tool and copy the content to the clipboard (Edit > Copy), then paste the copied image onto a new layer (Edit > Paste). Flip the new layer horizontally (Edit > Transform > Flip Horizontal). Make sure this flipping is achieved via the Edit set of controls and not the Image controls since the Image options would flip the whole canvas. Make the Move tool active (the top of the toolbar) and drag the flipped image to align with the original. The image can now be flattened (Layer > Flatten Image) and adjustments made to Levels, and so on, as required. The resulting picture will not of course be a true representation of its subject and may

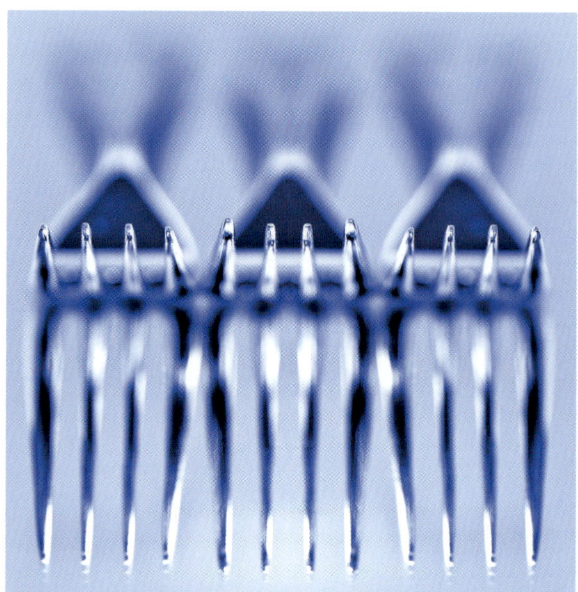

Fig. 11.3 **The image of three forks uses both in-camera and digital mirroring. The initial photograph of forks on a mirror was not sufficiently symmetrical so one half was copied and flipped horizontally. The image was given a blue tone as described in Lesson 2.**

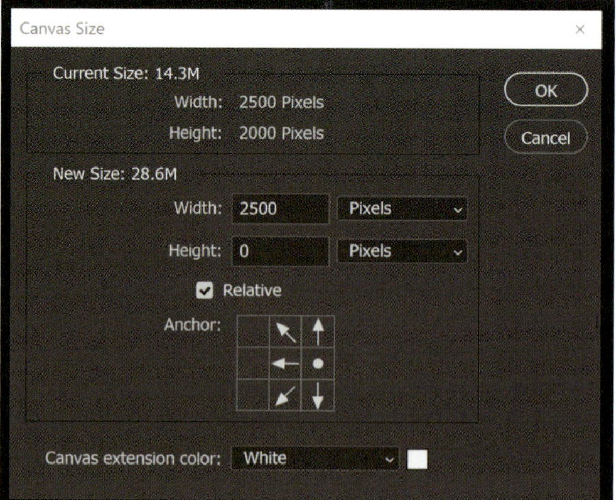

Fig. 11.4 **Photoshop's canvas-size settings box. Here it is set to double the canvas width by adding a further 2,500 pixels to the left of the main image. The zero entry in the height setting means that the size increase will only apply to the width.**

well be an obviously mirrored picture. However, the stretched symmetry will be a new, harmonious composition.

Vertical Flipping

Vertical flipping can add symmetry and depth to pictures with natural vertical lines, add completeness to curves and add detail and intrigue to otherwise unexciting images. The process is identical to that for horizontal mirroring except that here the height dimension is changed in the canvas-size settings and the up or down Anchor arrow is clicked depending on whether the copied image is to be placed on the top or bottom of the starting picture.

Two-Way Flipping

Effective mirrored images result from flipping a starting picture both horizontally and vertically. This delivers a uniformity radiating from a central point and is suited to many types of pictures. In this case the first decision is to choose in which corner of the new composite the starting picture will fit. Click that corner in the Canvas Size Anchor box. Add the starting picture's dimensions in both the width and height settings. Select and copy the starting picture as before and paste onto a new layer as above. Copy that layer twice (Layer > Duplicate Layer) so that there are three identical layers above the background. Click on each layer in turn and, using the flipping tool in the Transform menu, flip one layer horizontally, one vertically and one both horizontally and vertically. With the Move tool active, drag the new layers into the corners so that the new image radiates from the centre. An example of the result is illustrated in Figure 11.7.

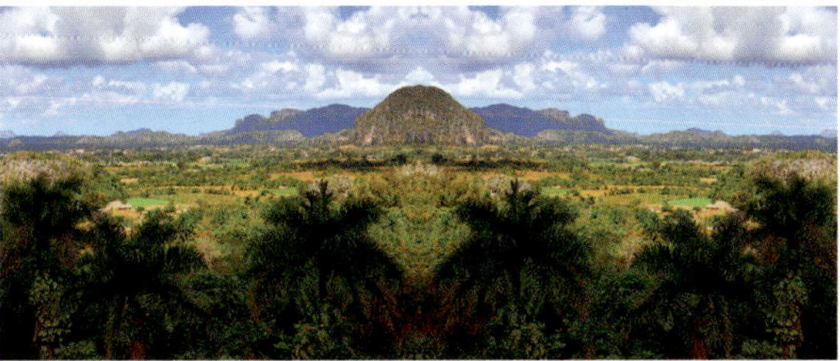

Fig. 11.5 **A Cuban landscape mirrored horizontally. The intersection line must be selected to deliver a smooth transition.**

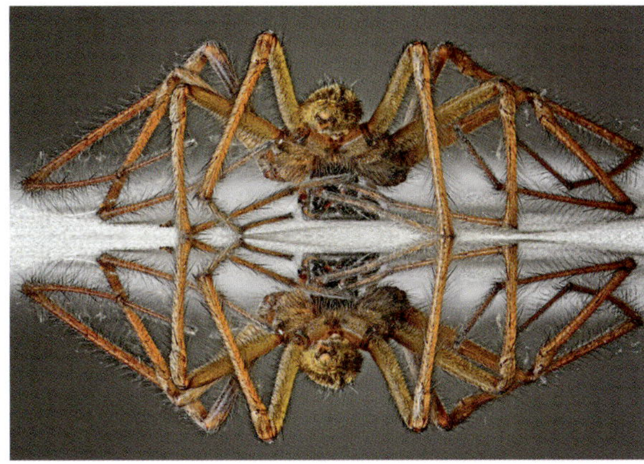

Fig. 11.6 **A picture of a deceased spider takes on symmetry and menace when mirrored and flipped vertically.**

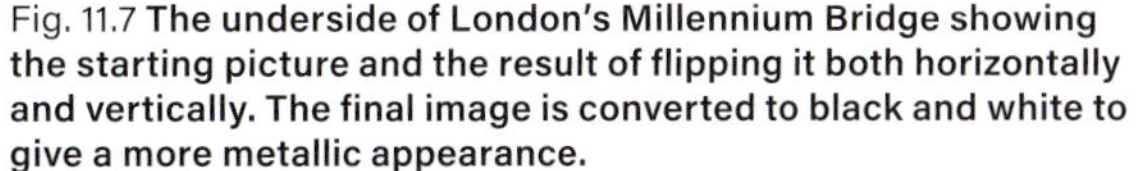

Fig. 11.7 **The underside of London's Millennium Bridge showing the starting picture and the result of flipping it both horizontally and vertically. The final image is converted to black and white to give a more metallic appearance.**

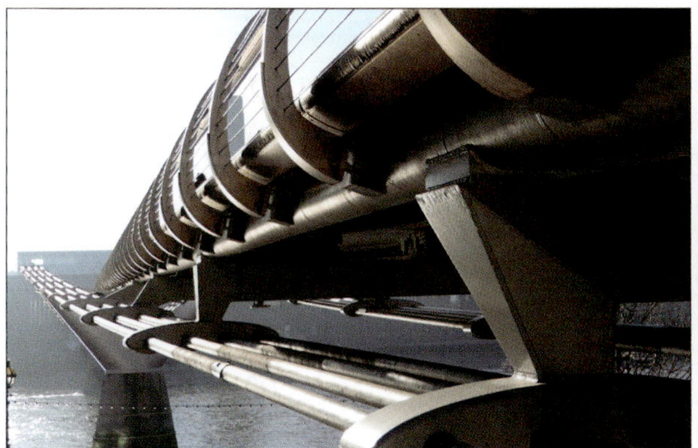

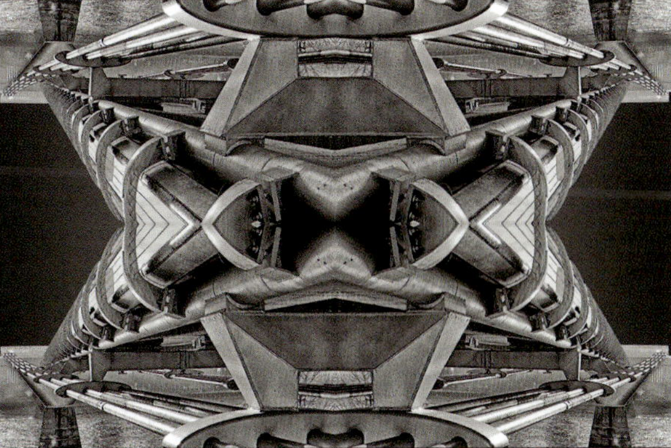

Aspect Ratio

Mirrored images can become quite abstract, with their appeal being their symmetry. This might be enhanced by revisiting the aspect ratio of the picture (the ratio of its width to its height). The greatest symmetry is often achieved by making the image square. Visit the image-size setting (Image > Image Size), unclick the link between Width and Height and enter the same number in each.

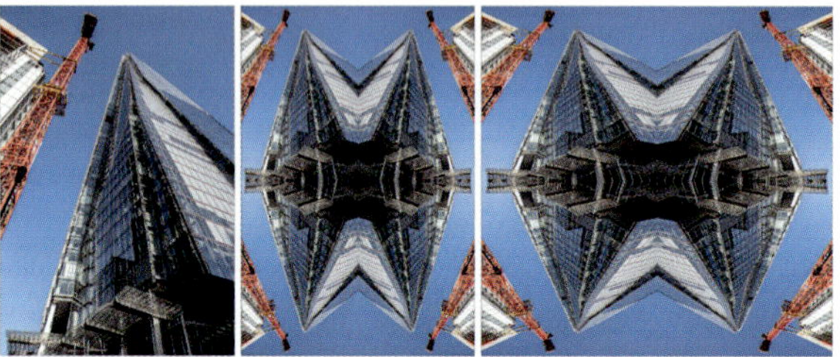

Fig. 11.8 **A picture from the base of The Shard in London showing the result of flipping both horizontally and vertically, and the effect of changing the aspect ratio to square format to emphasise the symmetry of the composition.**

MIRRORING SELECTIONS

Examination of relatively unexciting pictures will often reveal areas that will lend themselves to the mirroring treatment. Once a section is identified, select it with the Rectangular Marquee tool and, as above, copy it to a new layer. Make additional copies of that layer and flip them horizontally, vertically or both, then align them with the starting selection. If the starting picture is sufficiently large, there may be no need to increase the canvas size since all the flipped sections fit on the original. If there is surplus space, the result will require cropping. If there is not enough space, increase the canvas size sufficiently to accommodate the selections. A selection of a starting picture and the resulting four-way mirror is shown in Figure 11.9.

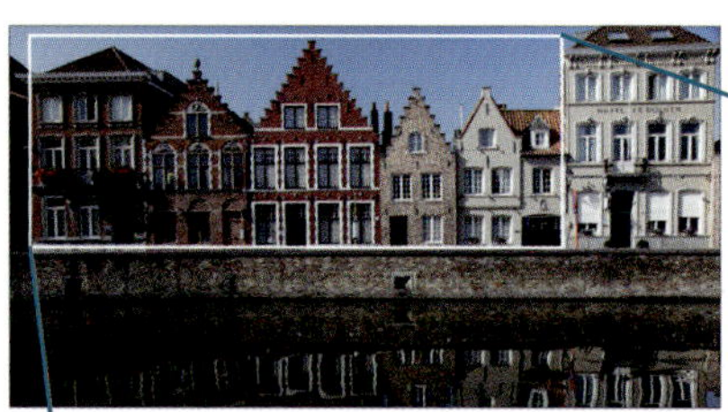

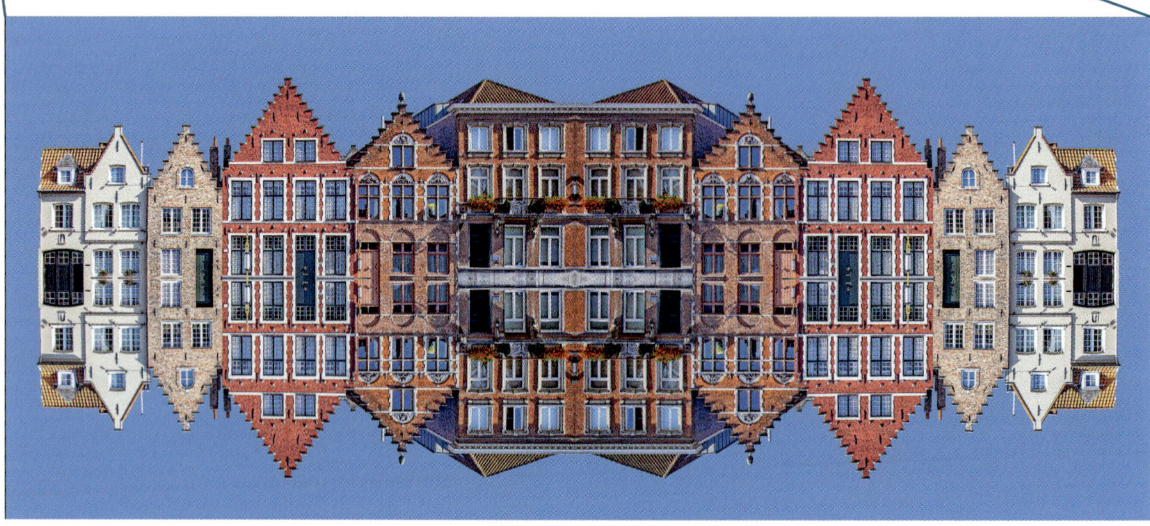

Fig. 11.9 **A picture of buildings alongside the canal in Bruges. The marked selection has been mirrored both horizontally and vertically. The saturation of the final image is increased to emphasise the colourful contrast of the red buildings and blue sky.**

Kaleidoscope

If even more copied selections are brought into play, they can be built up to make a kaleidoscope image. Start by making a slim triangular selection from a picture that has a promising range of shapes and colours. Copy the selection onto a new layer and drag it so that the corner of the triangle is roughly in the centre. Increase the canvas size if needed and fill the background layer (the original picture) with a single colour (Edit > Fill > Color). Make a copy of the triangle layer (Layer > Duplicate Layer) and drag and rotate it (Edit > Transform > Rotate) so that it fits alongside the first triangle with the same centre point. This process is repeated until a full circle of the triangles is assembled. It is possible to speed things up by merging some of the triangle layers and using duplicates of these merged layers to continue with the circle build-up. When the circle is completed, unless the angle of the starting triangle was a convenient fraction of 360°, there may be a gap in the new kaleidoscope. Filling this by selecting it and using content-aware fill (Edit > Fill > Content-Aware) will usually make the gap unnoticeable. Now make a circular selection of the kaleidoscope using the Elliptical Marquee tool (keep the Shift and Alt/Option key pressed to make a perfect circle from the centre) and adjust the image for saturation and contrast. Now invert the selection (Select > Inverse) and fill the surroundings with a suitable colour.

ARTIFICIAL REFLECTIONS

An intriguing application of mirroring is the creation of artificial reflections in water, as in Figures 11.11 and 11.12. The technique is to pick a suitable scene, such as a landscape or cityscape beside water, to select the section to be reflected and to apply vertical flipping as described above. With the flipped section on a new layer, drag it down to where the reflection is to appear. Increase the canvas size as described above to accommodate the reflection if needed. Now modify the selection so that it is a more convincing reflection. Don't slant it to the right or left, as is sometimes tempting; reflections are always perpendicular to their subject. However, they can be stretched, rippled and toned to better suit the composition. A good option is to stretch the selection vertically by resizing (Edit > Transform > Scale; keep the Shift key pressed so that the width of the selection is not linked to the height). Add vertical motion blur (Filter > Blur > Motion Blur, set vertically) and possibly some ripple effect (Filter > Distort > Ripple). Adjust the colour or saturation to deliver

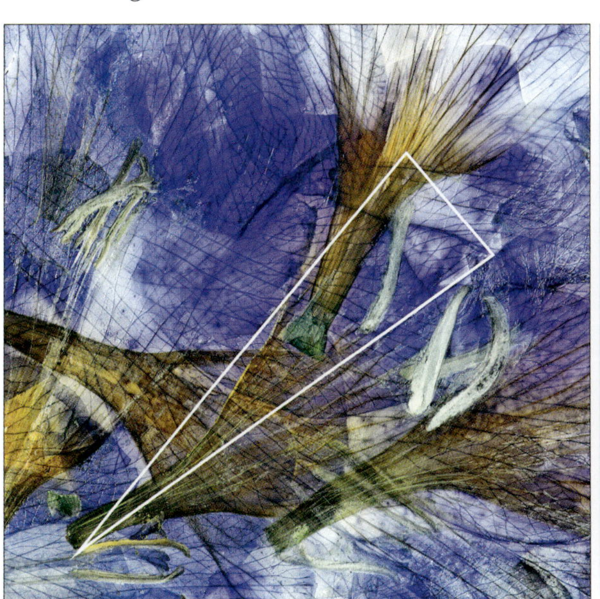

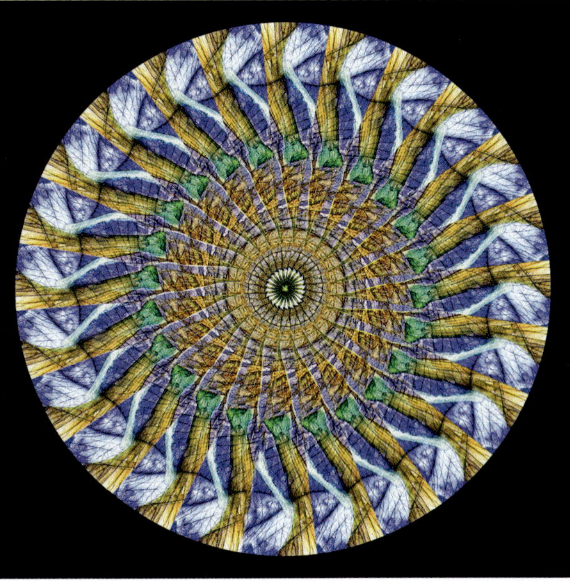

Fig. 11.10 **A slim triangular section of a pressed freesia flower repeatedly copied and rotated around a centre point to produce a kaleidoscopic image.**

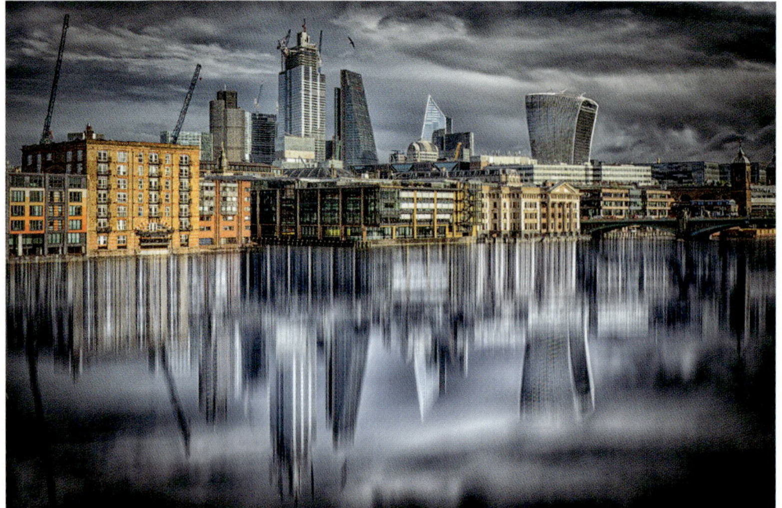

Fig. 11.11 **A picture of the City of London across the River Thames, with an artificial reflection produced by copying the buildings and flipping them vertically. Motion blur and blue toning have been added to give a more convincing reflection effect. Masking on the reflection layer was used to adjust the join between the buildings and the water.**

the desired effect. If the subject is not above a continuous horizontal line, as in Figure 11.11, it will be necessary to apply a layer mask and conceal parts of the reflection so that there is clean join between the subject and its reflection.

MIRRORING - KEYS

MIRRORING an image involves copying all or part of a picture, flipping it horizontally, vertically or both, then aligning the flipped sections with the original.

MIRRORED pictures can be achieved in camera by photographing a subject on a reflective surface.

DIGITAL mirroring can transform an otherwise ordinary photograph and produce an image with appealing symmetry.

THE symmetry can often be emphasised by making the resulting picture square.

ALIGNMENT of multiple triangular selections will result in a kaleidoscopic picture.

ARTIFICIAL reflections can be created by mirroring a subject vertically and applying blurring and toning.

FACING PAGE
Fig. 11.12 **A picture of the Canary Wharf area of London with a vertically flipped artificial reflection. The reflection was stretched by resizing the flipped layer and motion blur added to enhance the reflection appearance.**

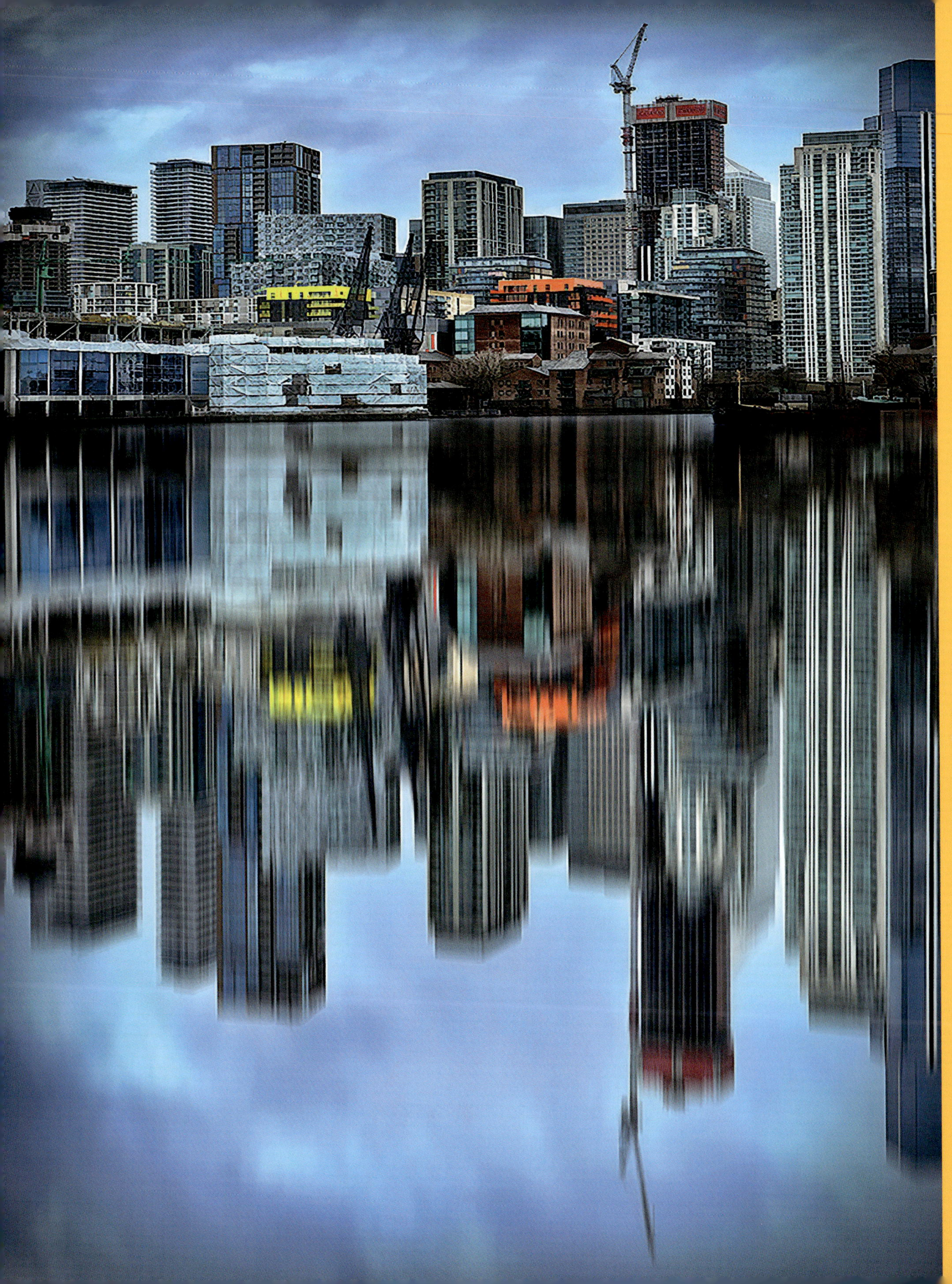

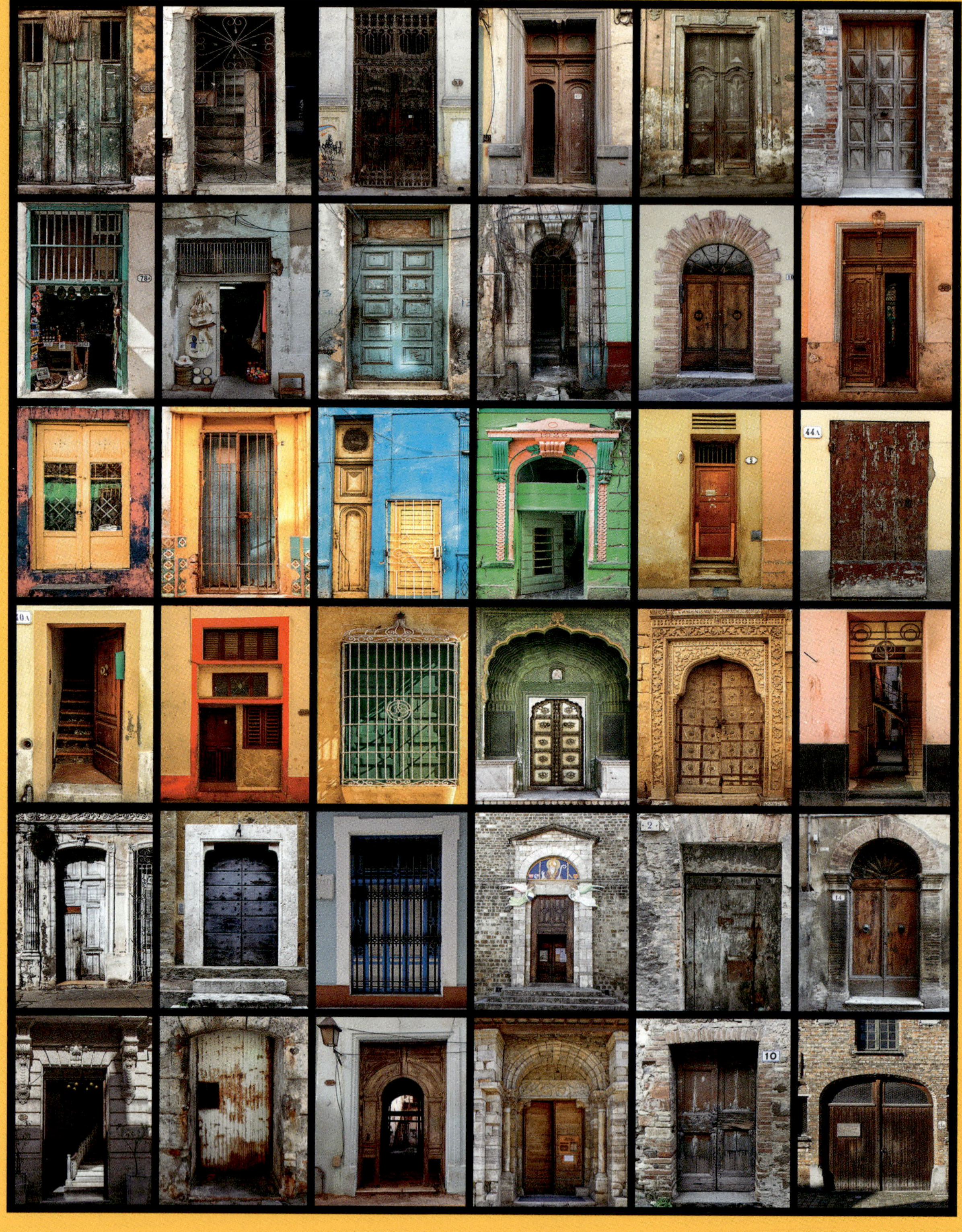

Fig. 12.1 **A collection of 36 doors. None of the individual pictures would be impressive, but they gain pictorial strength as a set. A black grid has been added to separate the doors and add contrast.**

LESSON 12

PAIRS, SETS AND COLLECTIONS

Photographs often gather meaning and impact when presented in combination with others. Displaying several pictures together can demonstrate intent, tell a story or be more artistically satisfying. Sometimes a picture that struggles to stand alone will come into its own as part of a set. On a large scale this can be achieved through display in a gallery or exhibition. However, without that luxury, digital presentations offer creative ways of assembling photographic sets and collections.

Sets and collections have different meanings in different contexts. Here a collection will be taken to be images that are not necessarily connected, such as in an album or portfolio. A set is a structured combination of images that relate to each other. A pair is a set of just two pictures.

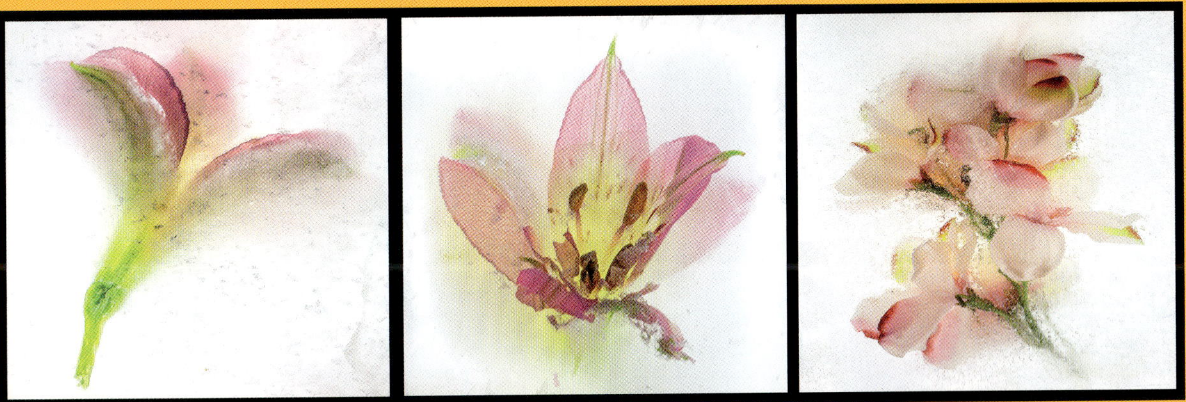

Fig. 12.2 **A set of three pictures of frozen flowers. They are connected both by the nature of the subject and the similar colouration.**

TECHNIQUES

Pictures can be grouped together physically, for instance by printing, framing and hanging on a wall. Digital programs offer many alternative routes, and it is common to view photo collections on social media and websites. However, the ease of downloading pictures presents a real risk of overkill, with the viewer expected to look at possibly hundreds of photographs. Much more impact will be made if only a small selection of our best pictures is on display.

Dragging on a Digital Space

When a group of pictures has been earmarked for presentation as a set, they can be dragged into position on a blank digital canvas. The first decision to be made is on the size of the display. If the images are for viewing on a computer monitor then a panoramic display with a ratio of 16:9 is likely to be appropriate. Pixel dimensions of 1,920 wide by 1,080 high will deliver this for screen viewing. A digital space of this size can be generated by opening a new file in Photoshop. This is accessed through a button at the top of the Photoshop screen titled New file, or through the menu (File > New). The dimensions of the file can be entered with a choice of units, pixels, centimetres and so on, and the image resolution set. Photoshop includes many file size presets, including 1,920 × 1,080 pixels at 72 pixels per inch, the conventional resolution for screen viewing. The colour of this empty space can also be set here, with a default of white.

For other forms of display, the size and resolution will have to be set appropriately. For example, if the result is to be printed on A3-size paper, the dimensions will be 42 × 29.7cm (16.5 × 11.7in), ideally at a good printing resolution of 300 pixels per inch. This, together with all the A series of paper sizes, is another Photoshop preset under the Print heading.

With the digital space open, the set of pictures can now be added. Once again, image sizes and dimensions are the consideration, and some calculation may be called for. If, for example, six pictures are to be added to an A3 canvas, dimensions for each picture of 12 × 12cm (4.7 × 4.7in) will be a comfortable fit with reasonable separation between the pictures.

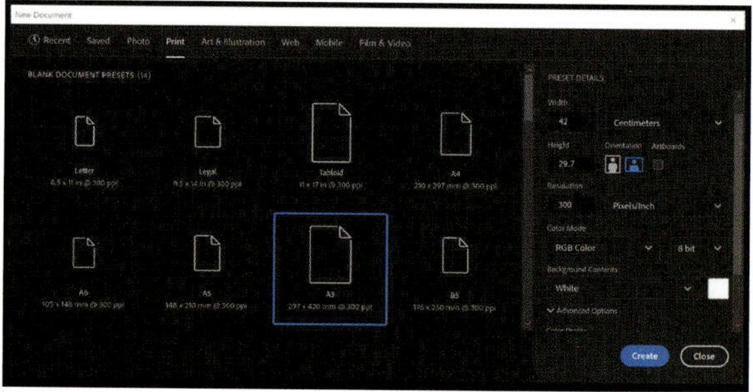

Fig. 12.3 **Photoshop's New Document settings by which a blank digital canvas can be created at any size. In this case a preset is used, giving dimensions and resolution for an A3 image at 300 pixels/inch with a white background.**

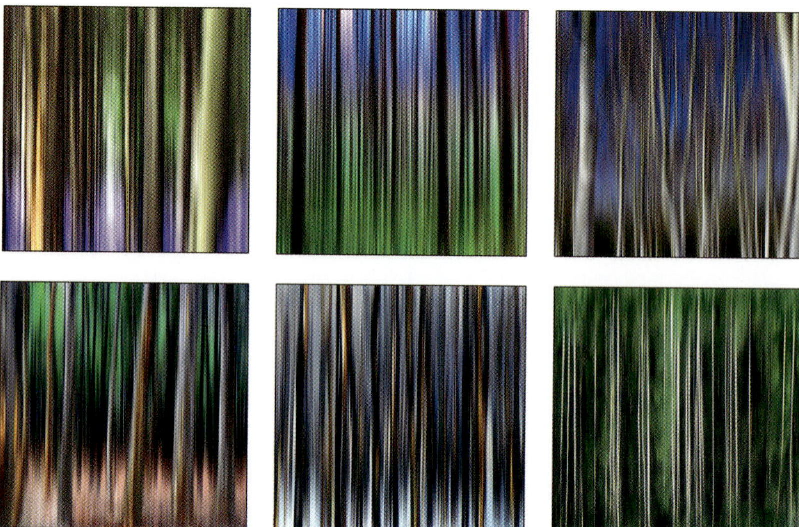

Fig. 12.4 **A set of six directionally blurred tree pictures presented in a symmetrical grid of two rows and three columns.**

Once the size decisions are made and the individual pictures sized for the purpose either by cropping to the appropriate dimensions or by resizing (Image > Image Size), make the Move tool active (the top of the toolbar) and drag the pictures onto the blank canvas. Some Photoshop settings can make life easier here by displaying a screen grid and by showing guidelines as the individual images are moved around (go to the View drop-down options, set Show > Grid and ensure that Snap is ticked). This will ensure that the pictures can be easily aligned and evenly spaced.

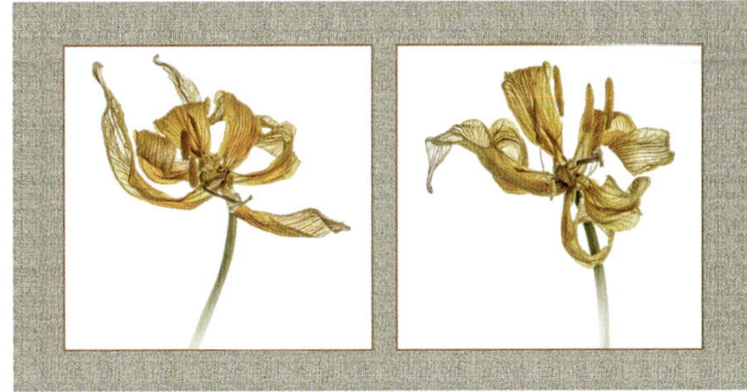

Fig. 12.5 **Two dry-daffodil pictures with texture added to the background. The texture colour is a tone from the flowers, and a darker tone of a similar colour is used as a stroke around each image.**

Adjusting Appearance

With the pictures grouped for display, adjustments can now be made to create a more artistic or striking appearance. A straightforward option is to visit the background. A colour might have been chosen when the canvas size was set, rather than the white default. However, with the pictures in place, a colour taken from one of the subjects might be more suitable. To change the background colour, make the background layer active by clicking on it in the Layers panel. Go to Edit > Fill, and select Color; this will open the Color Picker. Click in one of the pictures that has a suitable colour for the background, and this will be displayed in the Picker box. If the colour is too intense for the background, move the cursor around in the box to select a lighter or more muted shade of that colour. Click OK and the background will be filled with the new colour.

A further adjustment might be to add texture to the background using one of the techniques from Lesson 3. It is also worth considering giving a clear demarcation to the edges of the individual pictures by adding a stroke. This requires that each image is separately selected. The selection can be made using the Rectangular Marquee selection tool, or by clicking in the space around an image in the Layers panel with the Control key pressed. A stroke can then be added in the stroke selection box (Edit > Stroke). The width and colour of the stroke can be selected here as well as whether the stroke should appear inside or outside the selection or fit across the centre. The cleanest strokes are those when inside is chosen.

One further adjustment, which will add a three-dimensional depth to the collection of pictures, is to add drop shadows. This will give the appearance of each picture standing proud of the background. Drop shadows can be added using a Photoshop Layer Style. Click on the image layer to make it active and open the layer style options (Layer > Layer Style, or use the drop-down options at the bottom of the Layers panel). Select Drop Shadow and set the position, colour, size and intensity of the shadow using the control sliders. The shadow can also be dragged into position with the cursor.

The adjustments described so far have assumed that the individual pictures in a set will be arranged uniformly in straight rows or columns. This does not have to be the case and there is creative scope for changing the arrangement to something more dynamic, including rotation and overlapping of images. When the cursor is moved around the edges of an individual picture on a

Fig. 12.6 **A pair of pictures of a bee on an allium flower. The background is coloured using a hue from the flower and a drop shadow added to each picture to give an impression of depth.**

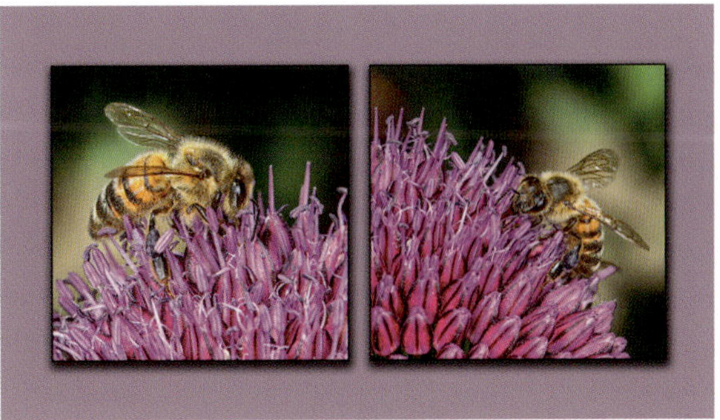

Photoshop layer, options for resizing and rotating the image are displayed. An alternative route is to visit the options in the Transform tools (Edit > Transform), where there are also size and rotation controls.

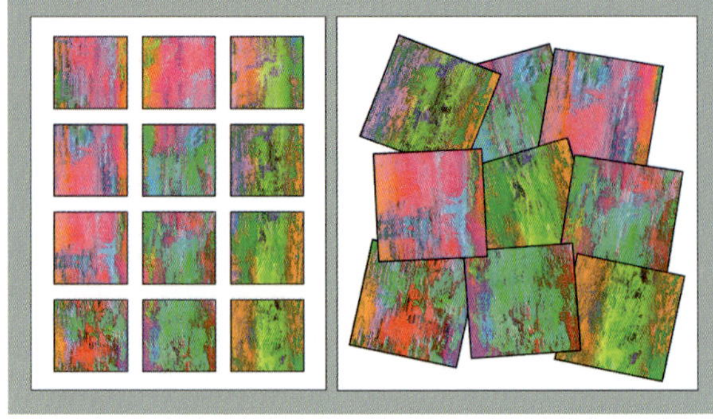

Fig. 12.7 **Two presentations of a set of abstract pictures. The first is a symmetrical grid and the second a more random presentation using position and rotation tools in Photoshop.**

SUBJECTS

As noted, the subjects in a collection of photographs might have no connection. They might be together for historical reasons, or to assemble the work or interests of the collector. Here however, the focus is on a set of images with a related style or theme.

Telling a Story

A set of images, more readily than a single picture, can tell a story. It can show the viewer around a town or country, give an account of a holiday from airport to destination or show a child's development. One interesting project, time and patience permitting, is to photograph a flower as it emerges from bud to blossom. The flower should be photographed with similar lighting each time, and against a background from which it can be digitally isolated. Each stage of development can then be placed on a single continuous background.

Fig. 12.8 **Two sets of pictures showing the emergence of a chrysanthemum and a clematis from bud to flower. They have been positioned on graduated backgrounds using Photoshop's Gradient tool, with colours suited to the flowers.**

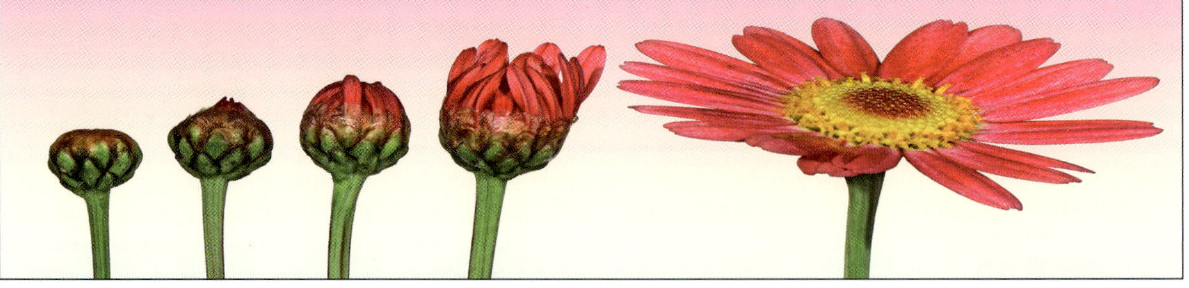

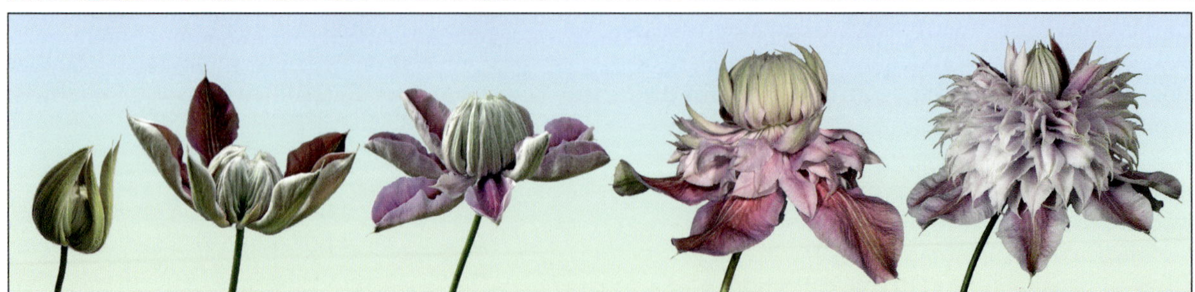

Repeat Images

If no suitable subjects for a set come to hand, all is not necessarily lost. Effective pictures, often with appealing symmetry, can be produced by copying a single image. With some adjustments to colour or orientation the result can have complexity and variation. Start with the end in mind and map out a structure that will be a guide to the position and size of each element. As above, create a blank file and drag the individual images into position. They can be recoloured using hue and saturation (Image > Adjustments > Hue/Saturation) and rotated or flipped via the Transform tools (Edit > Transform).

Still Life

Whilst anything at all can be the basis for a photographic set, the treatment particularly suits subjects that are either mundane in isolation, or that are quirky and look rather odd by themselves. An example is single still-life objects such as pictures of kitchen cutlery or glassware. When they are partnered with other similar images, they gain interest and become an artistic statement.

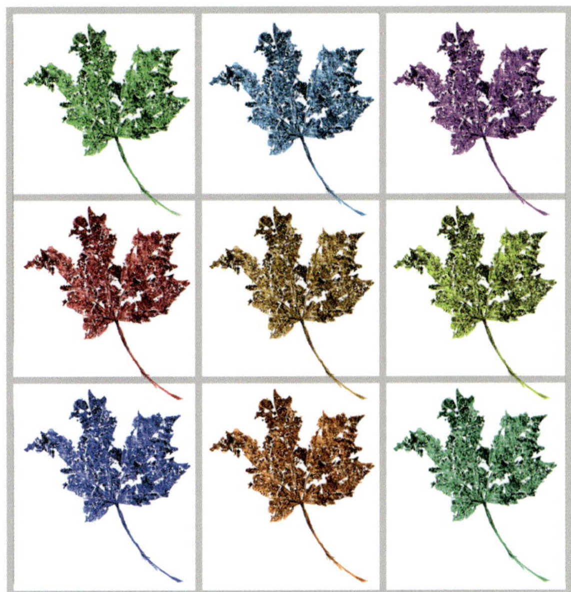

Fig. 12.9 **A single dry leaf presented as a set of nine pictures by recolouring each copied image and superimposing on a grid to give structure and separation.**

Fig. 12.10 **Two quirky pictures of glasses of water against high-contrast backgrounds. Presentation as a pair adds symmetry and is a more deliberate artistic statement.**

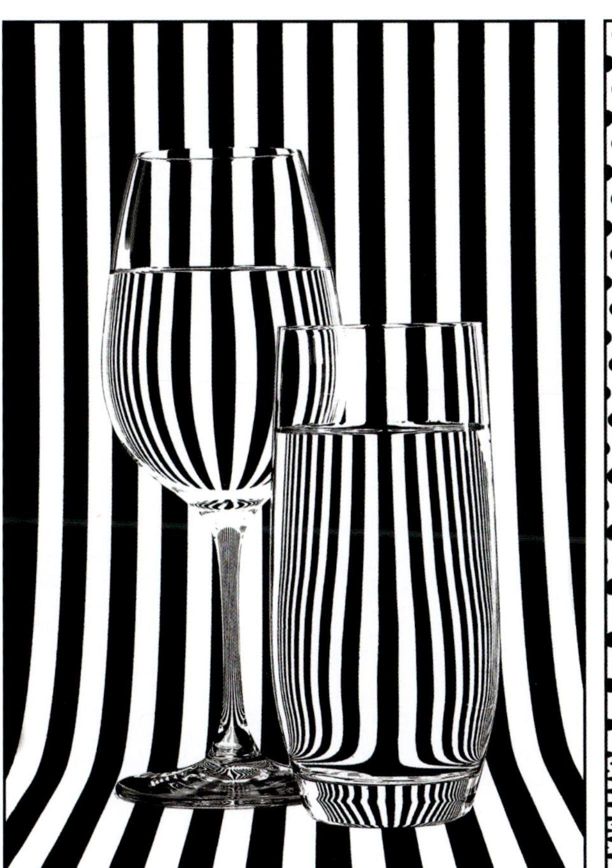

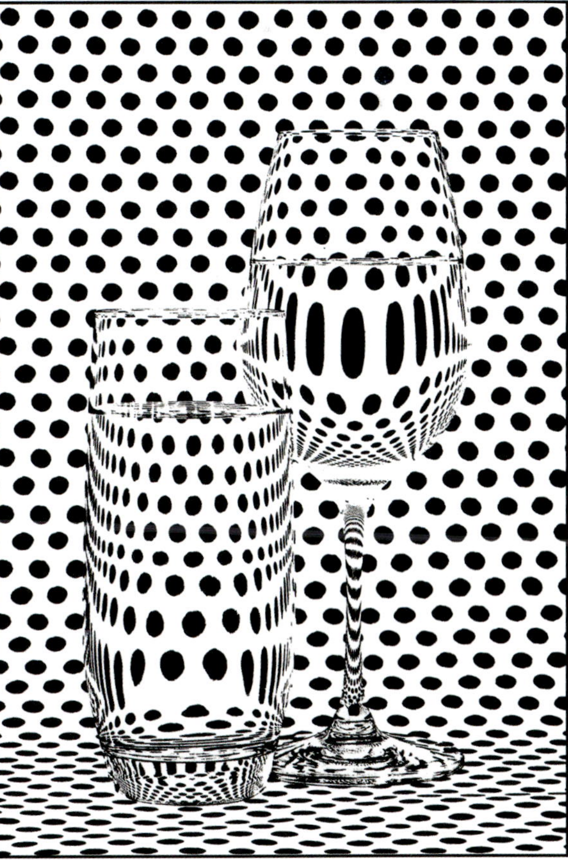

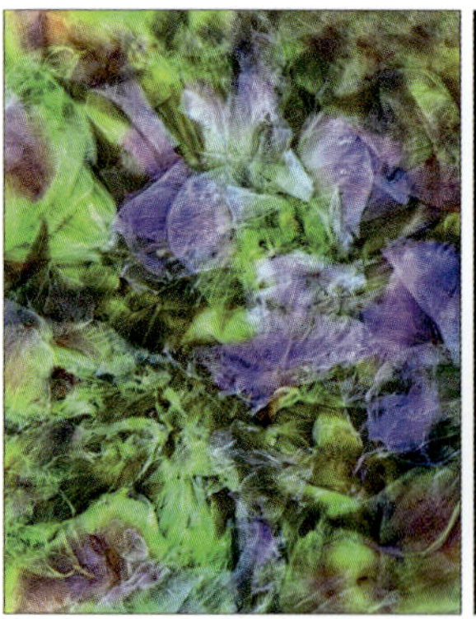
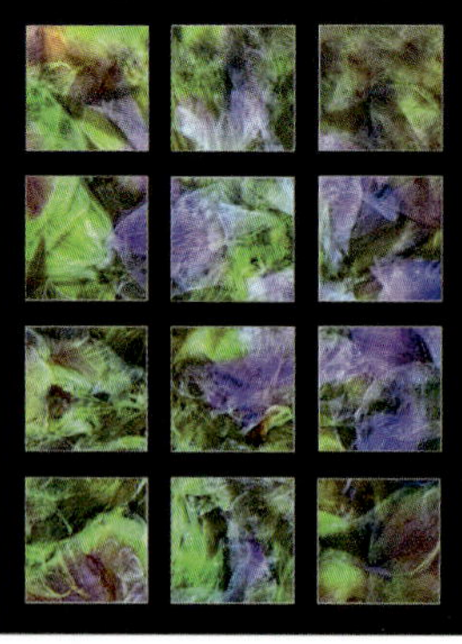

Fig. 12.11 **A starting picture of a pressed delphinium presented as a set of abstracts by superimposing a black grid with white squares over the original and using Photoshop's Darken blend mode. A white stroke has been placed around each square to give clear separation.**

FAKING IT

An intriguing digital treatment is to take a single picture and convert it to the appearance of a set by breaking it into sections. This can be achieved by selecting areas of the starting image and copying them (Edit > Copy). Then open a new file at a suitable size and paste in each copied section (Edit > Paste). Once a suitable number of sections have been pasted, they can be moved around to create a composition. An alternative is to create a grid image in Photoshop by making white rectangles on a black background, or black on white. Drag the grid over the starting picture and apply a blend mode so that the grid remains visible, but the image shows through the rectangles (the Lighten blend for a white grid, Darken blend for a black grid). This is especially effective for relatively abstract pictures and gives the illusion of a set of miniature abstracts.

SETS AND COLLECTIONS - KEYS

SETS of pictures with a shared theme or style can make more impact than a single isolated image.

PICTURE collections, such as portfolios and social media entries, do not necessarily have a shared subject and run the risk of displaying too many images.

SETS can be presented digitally by creating a blank space and dragging images into position.

IMAGES in sets can be enhanced by adjustments such as the addition of strokes and drop shadows.

THE appearance of a set can be achieved by replicating a single image, or by breaking up sections of a starting picture.

FACING PAGE
Fig. 12.12 **A set of abstract pictures using blends of sections of wall and ceiling as described in Lesson 4 and illustrated in Figure 4.11. Each image has been recoloured and reorientated and placed in a grid of twelve squares. Drop shadows have been added for an illusion of depth.**

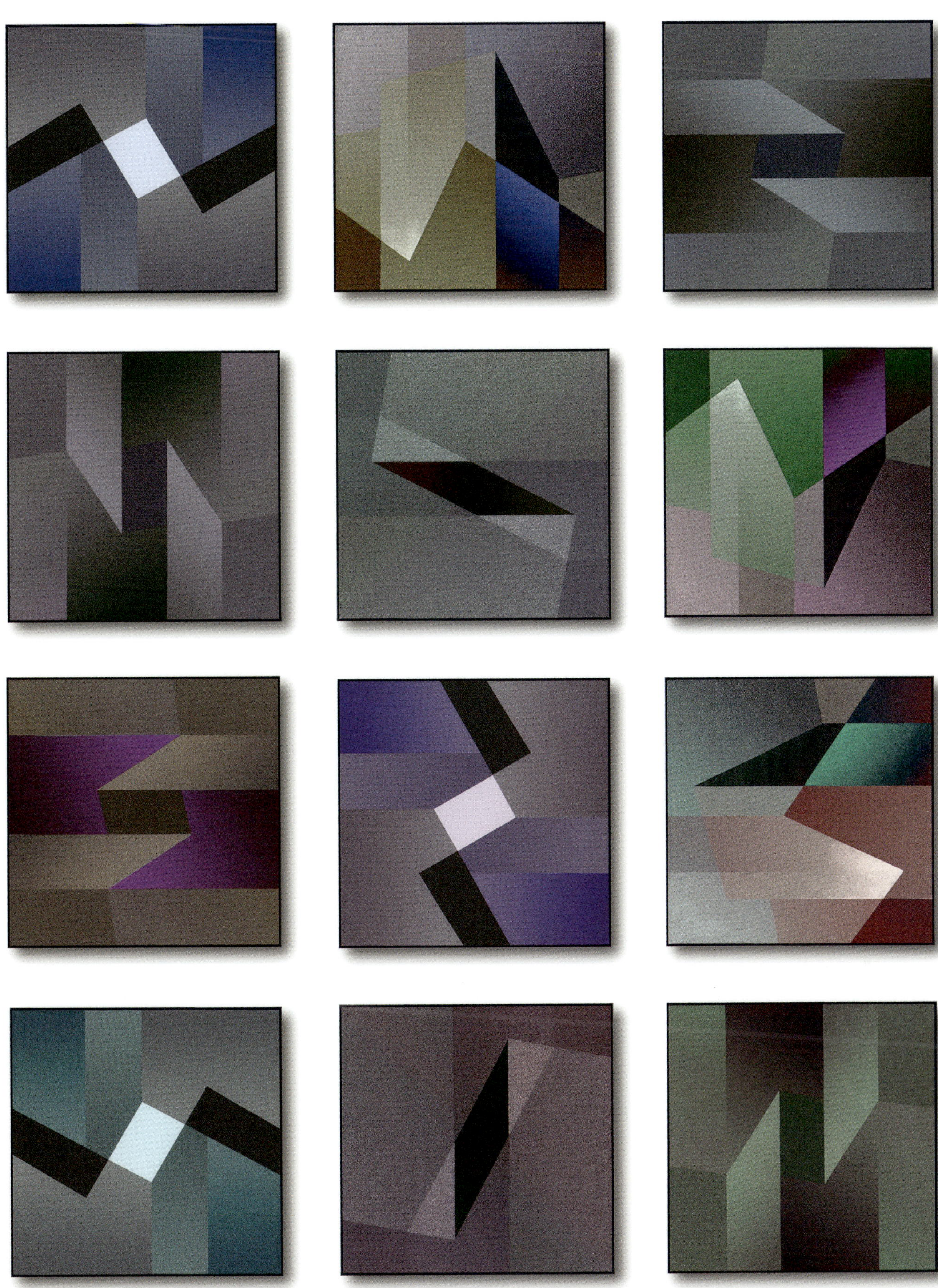

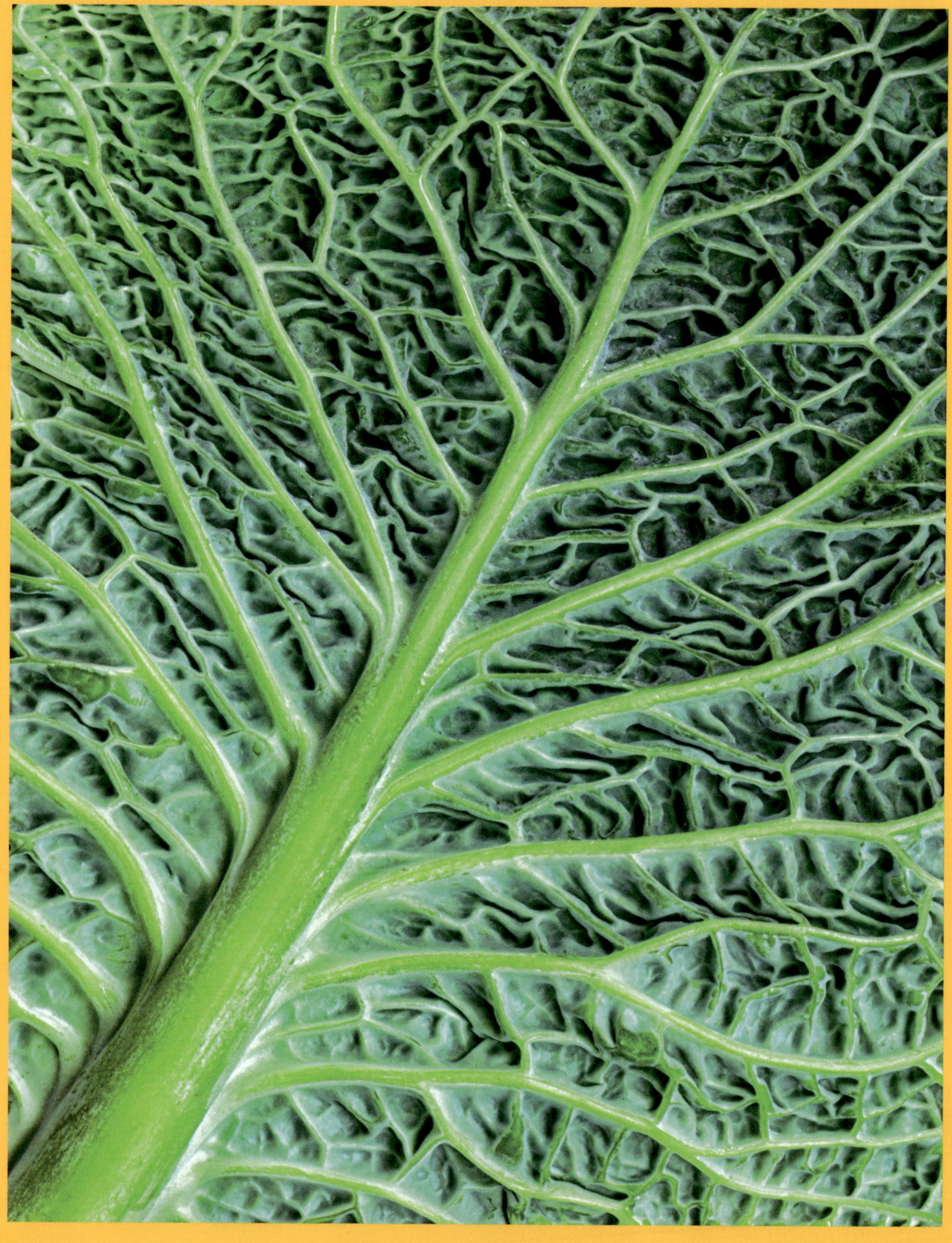

Fig. 13.1 **Detail of a cabbage leaf with strong directional lighting to emphasise the texture and positioned to give a flowing composition.**

LESSON 13

DETAIL

Many photographs, when inspected closely, reveal interesting detail. However, isolating the detail can present challenges resulting from lack of image resolution. This Lesson looks at ways of restoring resolution or using the lack of definition for artistic effect. It is also possible to home in on detail at the taking stage and to find pictorial detail in otherwise mundane subjects.

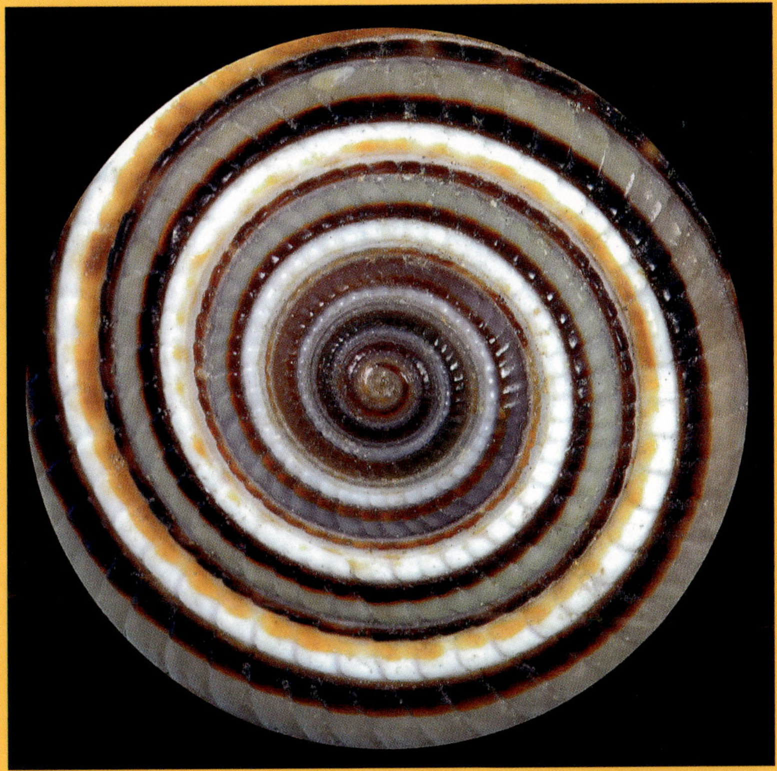

Fig. 13.2 **Detail from the surface of a small snail shell with a circular section placed on a black background. The photograph was taken with a macro close-up lens, the original subject being about 1cm wide. The pattern shows the Fibonacci spirals often found in nature.**

CROPPING

It can be a rewarding experience to browse through old photographs and to identify sections that would be good images in their own right. A single starting picture might turn out to have several embedded images, each more effective than the original. The problem with this approach is the sacrifice of pixels resulting from an extreme crop. If, for example, the starting picture is A4 size (29.7 × 21cm or 11.7 × 8.3in) with a resolution of 300 pixels per inch (ppi) and the crop is a quarter of the original, the picture will now be A6 in size (14.8 × 10.5cm or 5.8 × 4.1in). The pixel count will have been reduced from about eight million to two million. This is likely to be fine for applications such as screen display or social media, but not if the intention is to restore the original A4 size so that the picture can be printed. Fortunately, software will come to the rescue. Photoshop will resize the picture to any chosen dimensions through its image-sizing settings (Image > Image Size). This often works surprisingly well but of course will not create additional detail, so the result may lack precision and sharpness. Imaging software is available that aims to fill the gaps and add that detail, often utilising artificial intelligence, giving a high-resolution result without apparent loss of quality. There is a range of specialist software for this purpose, for example Topaz Gigapixel AI. The result is not guaranteed to deliver perfection and is sometimes described as 'plasticky'. Its effectiveness can depend on the type of detail in the starting picture, but high-resolution results can be delivered that would previously not have been possible.

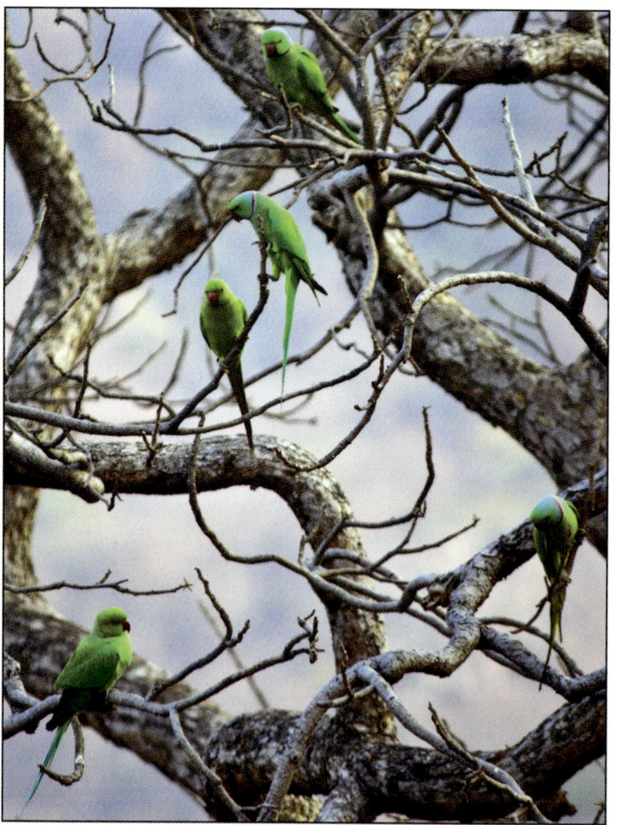

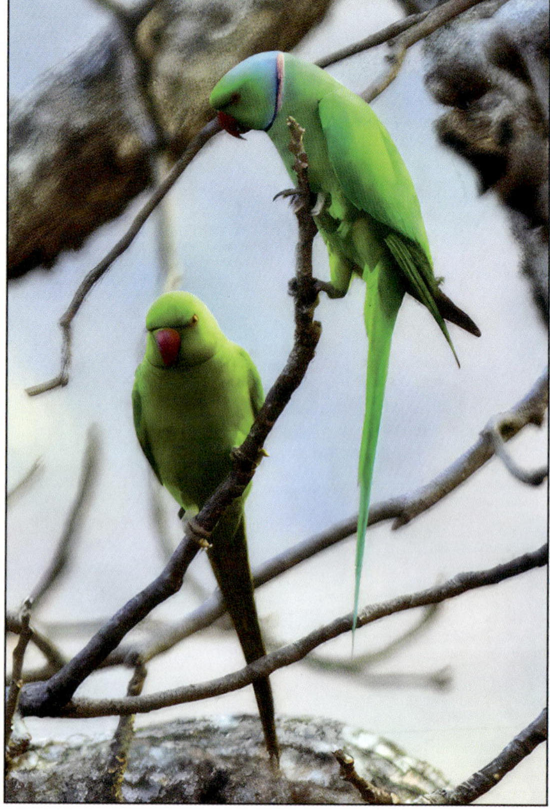

Fig. 13.3 **The crop of the resting parakeets gave a more successful composition but involved sacrificing 90% of the pixels. AI enlargement software was used to restore the crop to the original image size. The result is a little 'plasticky' but has acceptable detail and sharpness.**

Abstract Crops

Abstract pictures, described in Lesson 4, can be found in the detail of many photographs. In these cases, the lack of image resolution may not be a problem since their impact is based mostly on the distribution of shapes and colours. When a section is identified that has compositional appeal, it can be upsized as required without the usual concerns over sharpness and detail. Since the result is abstract there can be considerable flexibility in adjusting contrast, colour and saturation.

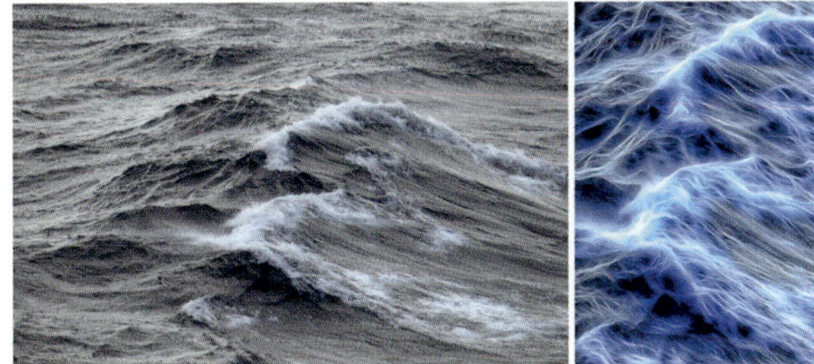

Fig. 13.4 **A crop from a picture of waves gives an abstract composition. Sharpness, contrast and saturation were increased to add impact to the result.**

UTILISING LOW RESOLUTION

Lesson 6 explores the subject of image resolution and notes that the impact of most digital filters is greater on images with a low starting resolution. This suggests an alternative approach to using cropped photographs, namely to capitalise on their low resolution and take advantage of artistic filter treatments. With fewer pixels to adjust, treatments such as Photoshop's Oil Paint filter will have more dramatic effects, often delivering abstract or semi-abstract pictures.

Occasionally a very extreme crop will create an interesting picture without any further treatment. In this case the individual square pixels make up a grid-structured pattern. These pictures resemble puzzle pictures in which the subject cannot be identified without being viewed from a distance or with eyes half closed. For enlargement to a size suitable for printing, the Nearest Neighbor (hard edges) setting must be used in Photoshop's image-size settings, otherwise the crisp pixel edges will be lost. This is described in Lesson 6.

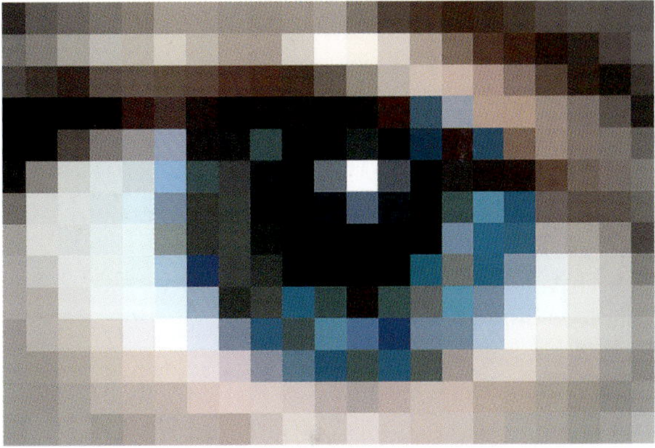

Fig. 13.6 **A radical crop of the eye from a portrait resulted in an image only 21 pixels wide. The result is an abstract pattern that can only be recognised as an eye by viewing from a distance. If the intention is to maintain the appearance of the solid square blocks of the original pixels when enlarging to a printable size, the resizing software must be set to preserve hard edges.**

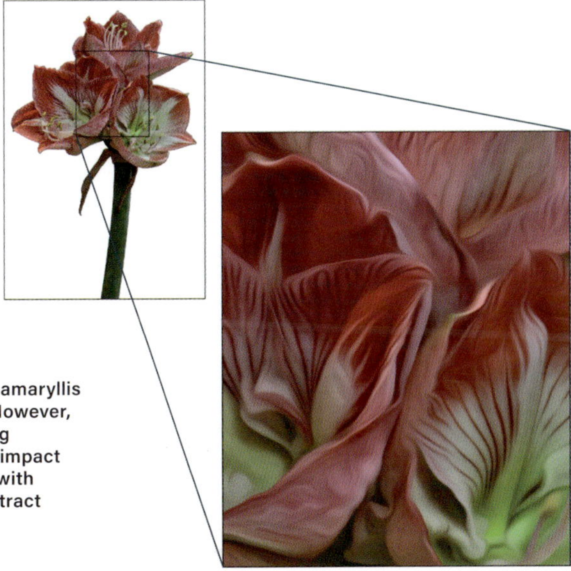

Fig. 13.5 **The crop of the centre of the amaryllis flower gave a low-resolution result. However, this was advantageous when applying Photoshop's Oil Paint filter since the impact of the filter is much more significant with fewer pixels. The result is a semi-abstract interpretation of the flower.**

PHOTOGRAPHING DETAIL

Photographers spot interest and beauty in things that often go unnoticed. Objects that seem mundane or utilitarian have shapes and colours that, when examined closely, provide perfect material for pictorial compositions. A wide range of equipment is available for close-up photography. More important, however, is the habit of close observation and the recognition that we are always surrounded by photographic potential.

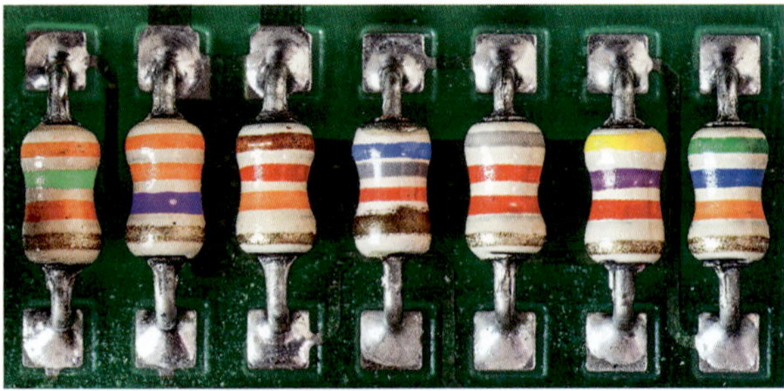

Fig. 13.7 **A colourful close-up section of a discarded printed circuit board. By focusing on detail, photographic images can be found in unlikely places.**

Equipment

All cameras, including those in smartphones, have a minimum distance between subject and lens closer than which they will not focus. It may well be that this gives enough scope for detail photography. If not, the options are to crop the images as described above, or to invest in additional equipment.

If the camera has a removable lens, as with a single lens reflex (SLR) or interchangeable-lens mirrorless camera, then an ideal option is to use a macro lens, specifically designed for close focusing. Macro lenses have the merit of maintaining the camera's automatic focus and exposure facilities but do require additional investment.

There is no shortage of further routes into close-up and detail photography. Detailed explanation is outside the scope of this book but options worth exploring include:

- *Supplementary lenses*. These are magnifying lenses that screw onto a standard lens and enable closer focusing. They are low cost but result in some loss of image quality.
- *Extension tubes*. These are empty tubes that fit between the camera body and the lens. The increased camera-to-lens distance allows close focusing without loss of quality but with some loss of light, so there will be a need to increase exposure or raise the sensitivity of the camera sensor (the ISO).
- *Reversing rings*. These have a camera-body coupling on one side, and a male filter screw thread on the other. When mounted on the camera body, a lens can be mounted back to front. This enables high magnifications to be achieved, especially from relatively wide lenses.
- *Coupling rings.* These have a male filter screw thread on both sides and enable two lenses to be 'stacked' together. One lens is mounted normally on the camera body, and the other is reversed on the front of the first lens. The resulting assembly can be a little unwieldy but can deliver high magnification at high quality for very little cost (assuming you already have two lenses).

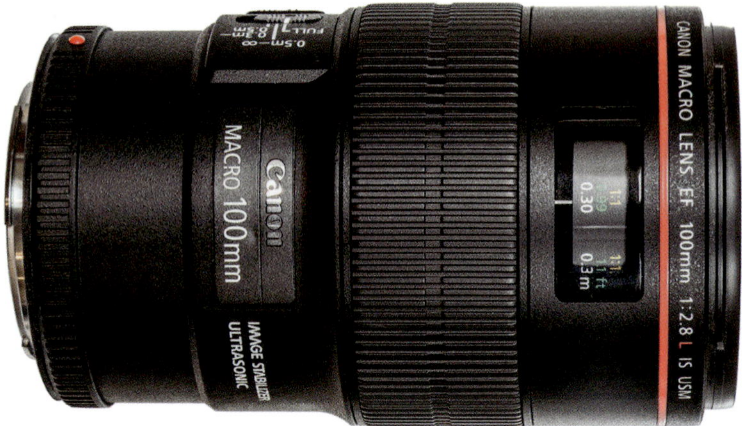

Fig. 13.8 **A dedicated macro lens, which can be fitted to interchangeable-lens cameras. The macro lens enables the detail in small objects to be captured at full size on the film or image sensor.**

Subjects

Interesting and photogenic detail can be found everywhere, and a list of potential subjects would be endless. The following are starter suggestions using everyday items.

Flowers are the most photographed of all subjects. This is not surprising since they are inherently beautiful and offer endless variety of shape, colour and texture. However, it can be difficult to find ways to portray flowers that are different from the countless existing images. Homing in on detail will reveal new compositions with an emphasis on lines and colours. The results are often quite abstract.

Utensils such as the forks in Figure 11.3 are often neglected photographic subjects. They have distinctive curves and edges which, when examined closely, lend themselves to perfect photographic compositions. Their shininess can become a challenge since they will reflect nearby objects and lights, so it is often best to photograph them in dull conditions. They aren't moving, so long exposures won't be a problem. Photographing with a shallow depth of field (large apertures, small f numbers) will create a sense of depth and emphasise prominent lines.

Fruit and vegetables deliver drama and pattern when closely inspected. The tomato close-up in Figure 7.4 was used for colour impact, but often the detail of sliced sections offers the greatest photographic potential. Thin slices are quite translucent and can be effectively backlit, for example by placing them on a lightbox, to reveal their colourful structure.

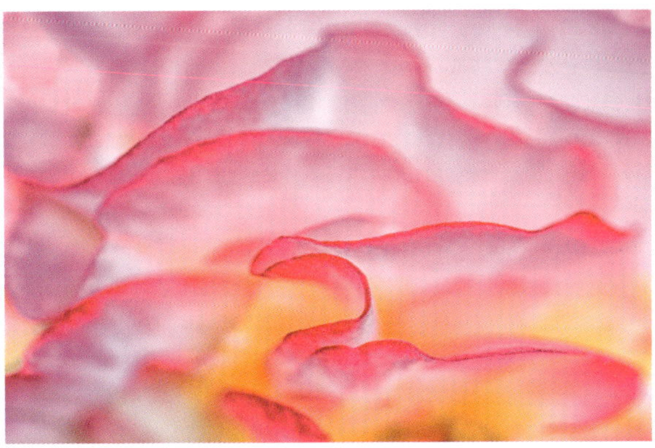

Fig. 13.9 **A close-up section of the petals in a begonia flower. A shallow depth of field was achieved by setting a wide aperture on the camera, creating a sense of depth.**

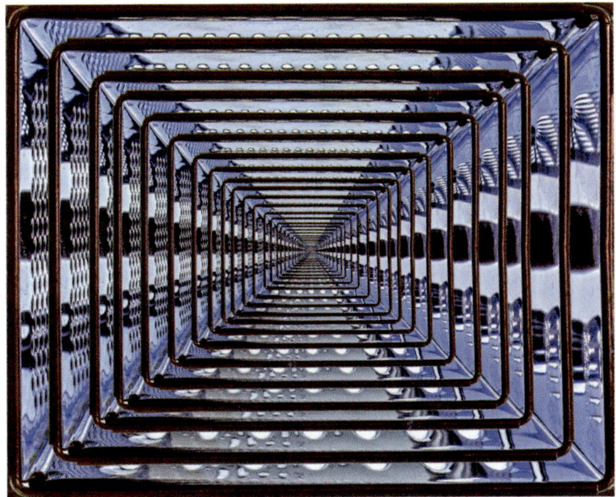

Fig. 13.10 **A picture of a kitchen cheese grater repeatedly copied and reduced in size to create a continuous-regression image as explained in Lesson 14.**

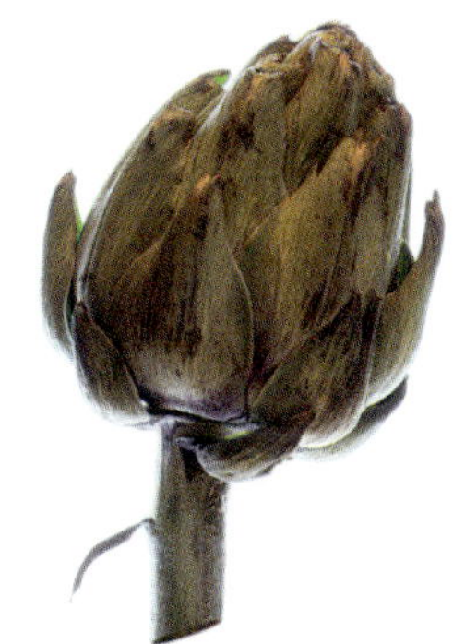

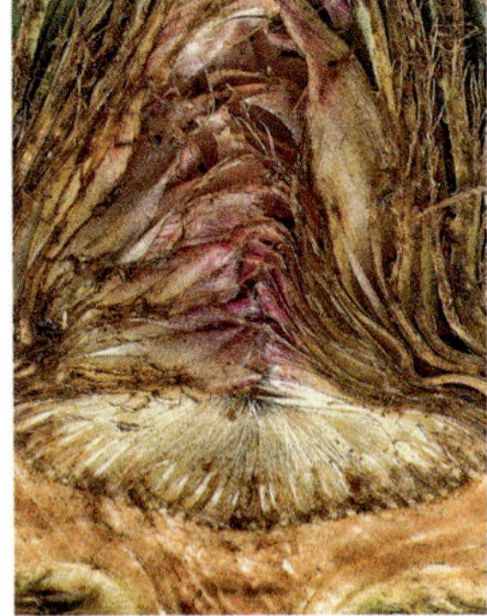

Fig. 13.11 **The outside of an artichoke is pictorially unexciting. However, like many vegetables, it reveals interesting detail when sliced in half.**

Rust and decay on objects that are past their best for practical purposes come into their own for photography. Detail photographers are always on the lookout for rusty hinges and peeling painted doors. Ideal circumstances are when the decay reveals contrasting colours, and these can often be accentuated by wetting the surface.

Landscape is usually thought of in terms of sweeping panoramas, not a subject for detail. However, the detail in landscape has great photographic potential. Zooming in can produce distinctive images, sometimes referred to as intimate landscapes. Without the usual markers of buildings, trees and so on, the pictures lose a sense of scale and present as mysterious new worlds.

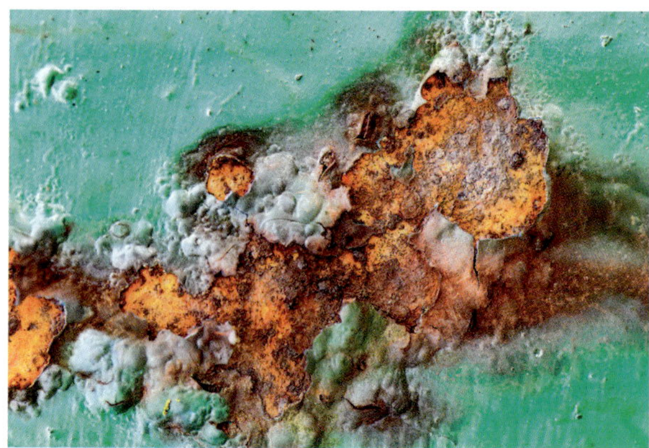

Fig. 13.12 **Peeling paint on a rusty surface. This had the ideal combination of complementary colours for an abstract composition.**

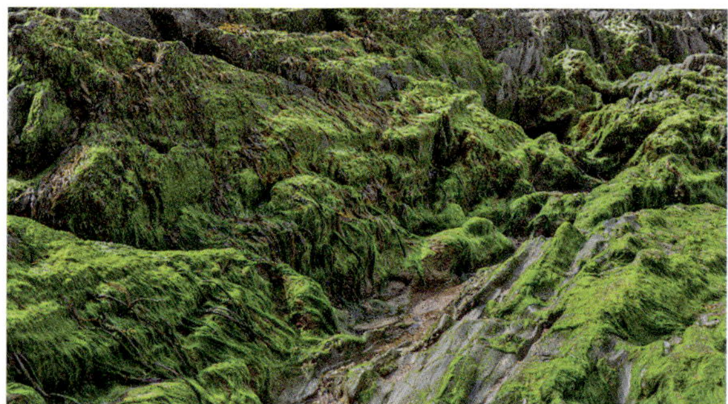

Fig. 13.13 **An 'intimate landscape' from a small part of a seaside rock pool. By excluding the surroundings, the resulting picture has no obvious scale, adding a sense of intrigue and mystery.**

DETAIL – KEYS

THE detail in sections of photographs and in close-up pictures of everyday objects can be used to make striking pictorial compositions.

CROPPING a picture to isolate detail reduces image resolution. However, AI software can often be used to restore the image to the desired size.

THE low resolution of cropped sections can be used to advantage by applying digital filters. In some cases, the low-resolution picture will have its own pictorial merit without further treatment.

MANY everyday objects have interesting shapes, textures and colours in their detail.

EQUIPMENT is available that reduces the minimum focusing distance of cameras and enables them to be used to take close-up photographs of fine detail.

FACING PAGE
Fig. 13.14 **A section of frost on a car windscreen. The picture has been split toned using the techniques described in Lesson 2.**

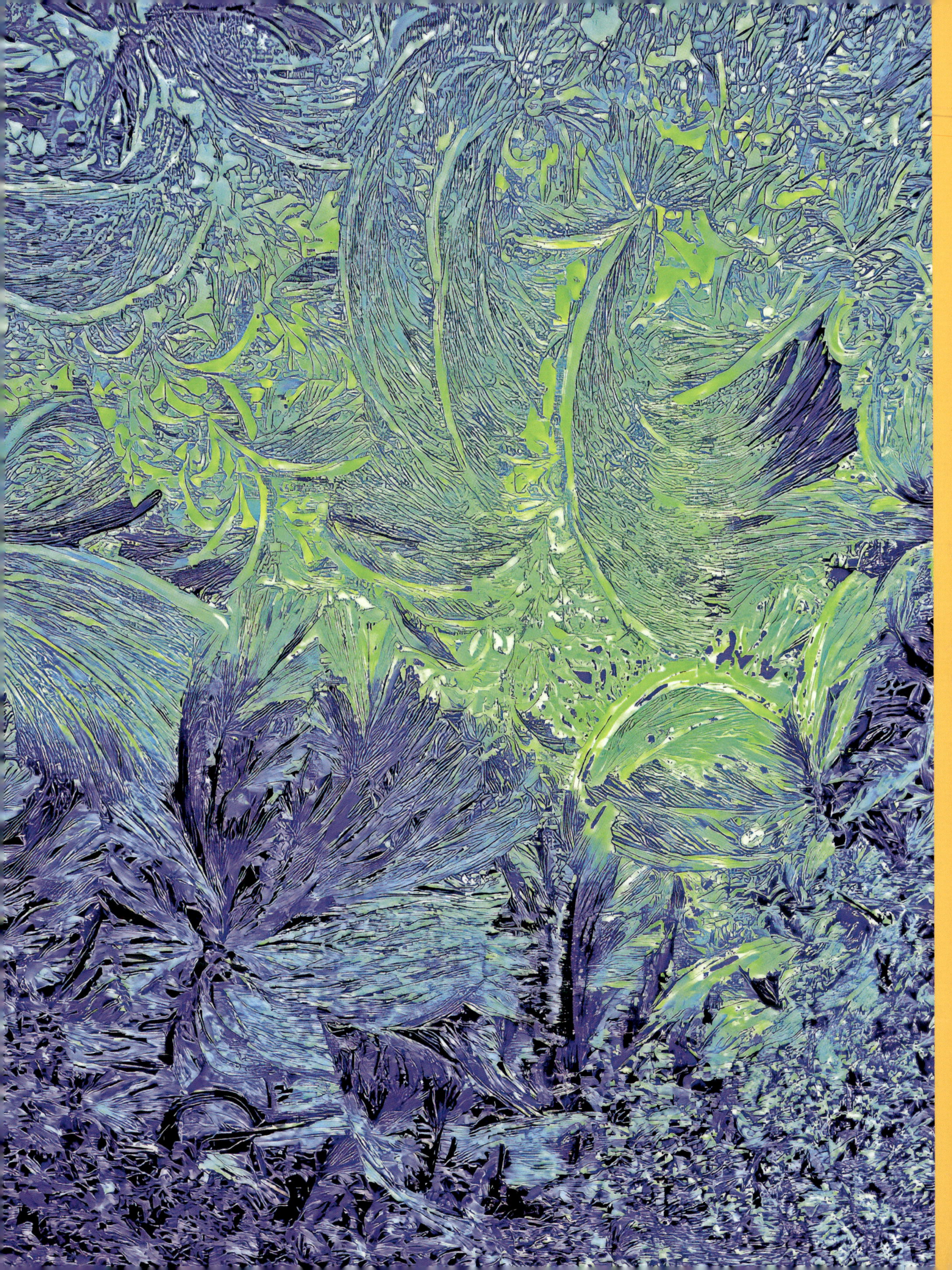

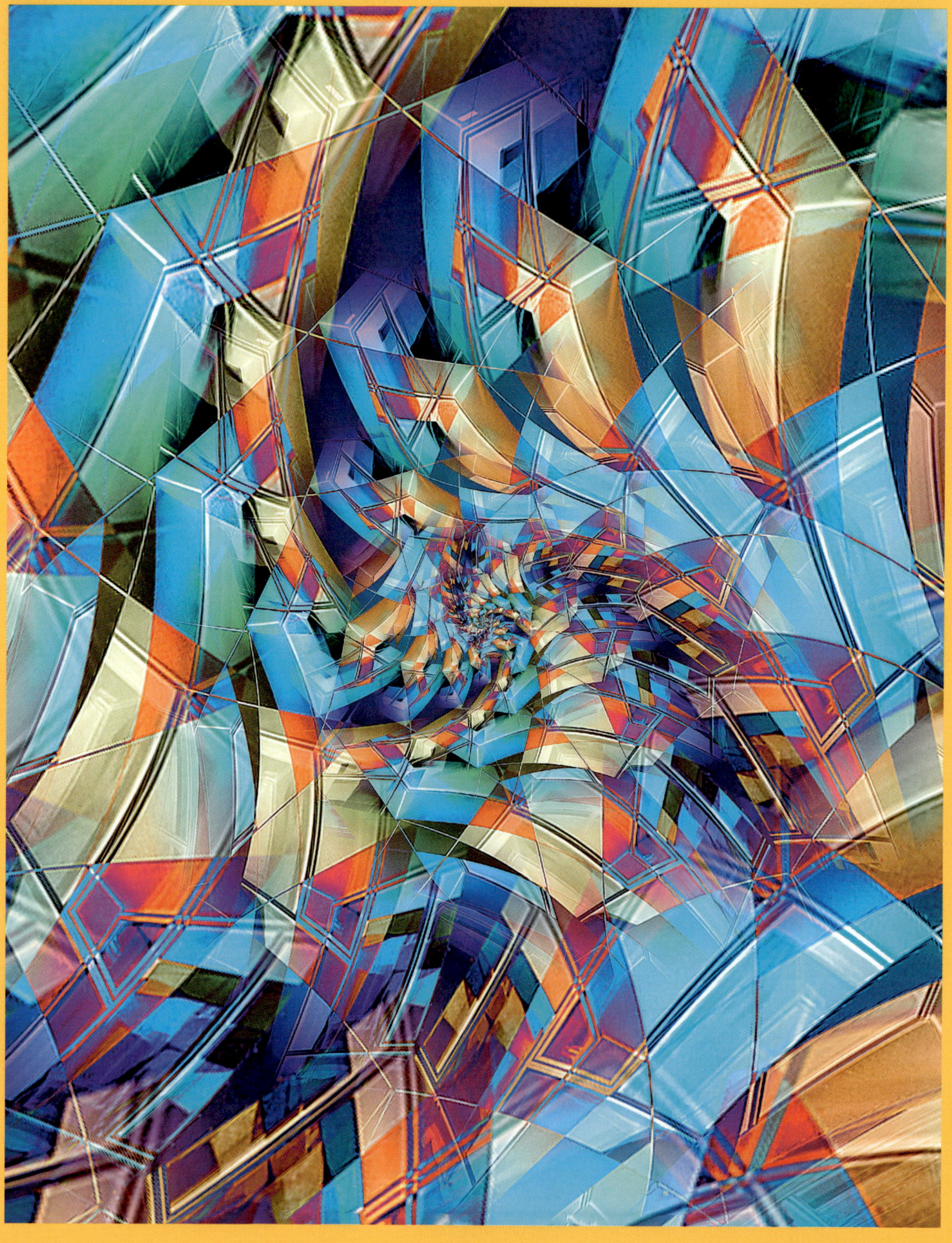

Fig. 14.1 **A picture of windows, split toned as described in Lesson 2, with the spiralling Droste effect applied using PhotoSpiralysis software.**

LESSON 14
SHRINKING

Intriguing pictures can be produced by making copies of an image and repeatedly shrinking the copies into the original. In art this is known as *mise en abyme*, a term from heraldry meaning 'placed into abyss', in which a picture recursively appears within itself. This results in a loop which in theory could go on forever, mathematically described as a 'fractal'. The technique was used by the Italian painter Giotto in the fourteenth century, and extensively by the Dutch artist Escher in the twentieth century. Recursive images are striking because they have a sense of infinity and depth; they draw the viewer into the picture. This Lesson looks at methods of adopting this style for use in photography.

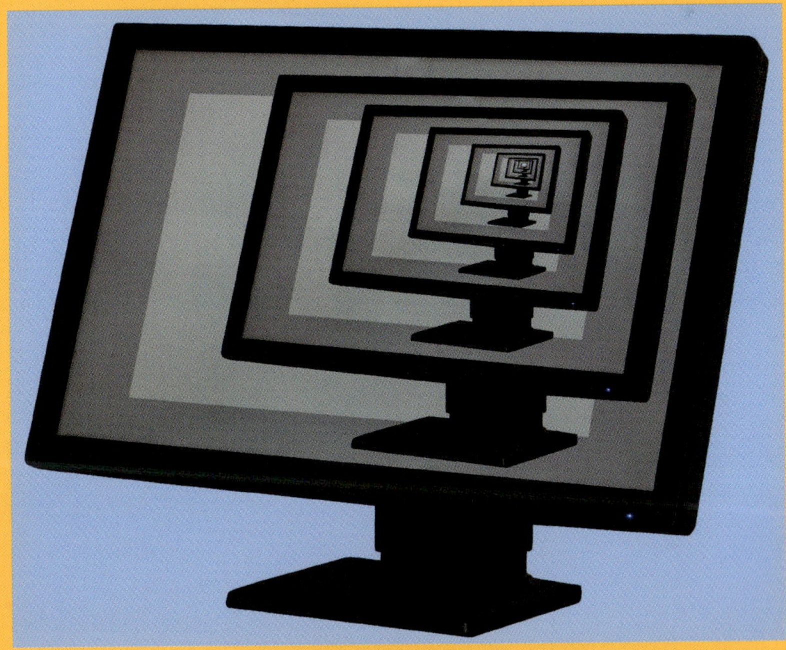

Fig. 14.2 **A recursive picture of a computer monitor created by selecting and copying the monitor, reducing image size and pasting onto the original. This is repeated until the final reduced image is too small to view.**

THE DROSTE EFFECT

The recursive presentation of images within themselves is often referred to as the Droste effect. This is named after a brand of Dutch cocoa. In 1904 it was packaged in a tin portraying a nurse holding a tray, on which was the same tin. This was designed by the commercial artist Jan Misset and is still used today, though on cartons rather than tins.

SHRINKING IN PHOTOSHOP

Early versions of Photoshop included a plug-in filter set called Pixel Bender, which enabled the shrinking process to be automated. This has long since been discontinued, so the shrinking of images in Photoshop must now be undertaken manually. A stand-alone alternative to Pixel Bender is described later but, in practice, the manual route often gives the greatest control. The basic steps are as follows:

1. Open an image.
2. Duplicate and paste the image on a new layer (Layer > Duplicate Layer, or drag the layer onto the new-layer icon at the bottom of the Layers panel).
3. Make the Move tool active and drag the image corners to scale the duplicate image down to size.
4. Drag the rescaled image into the desired position.
5. For repeated shrinking, repeat steps 2 to 4 continually until the desired result is achieved, or until the resolution of the reduced image is too small for further treatment.

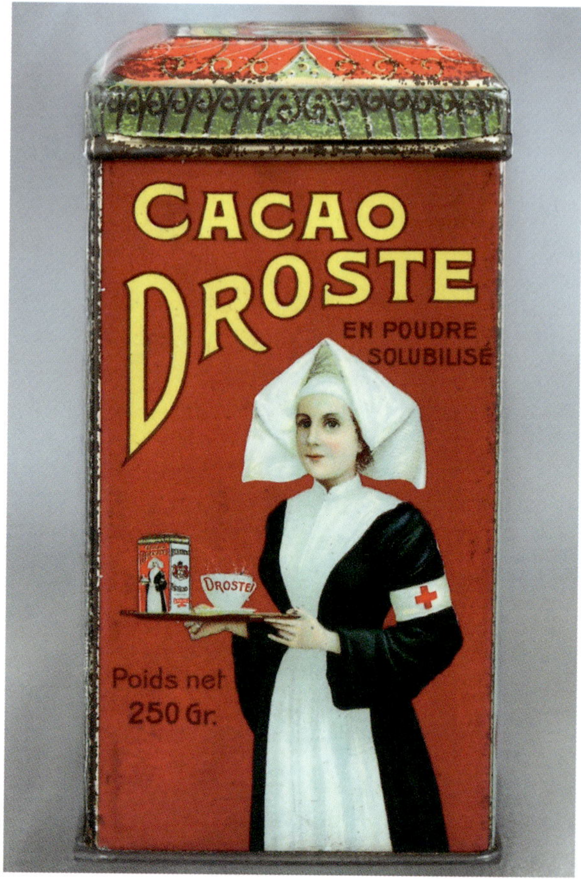

Fig. 14.3 **The original cocoa tin, designed in 1904, showing a nurse holding a tray on which is the same tin. The cocoa brand Droste gave its name to the artistic treatment of reproducing an image within itself.**

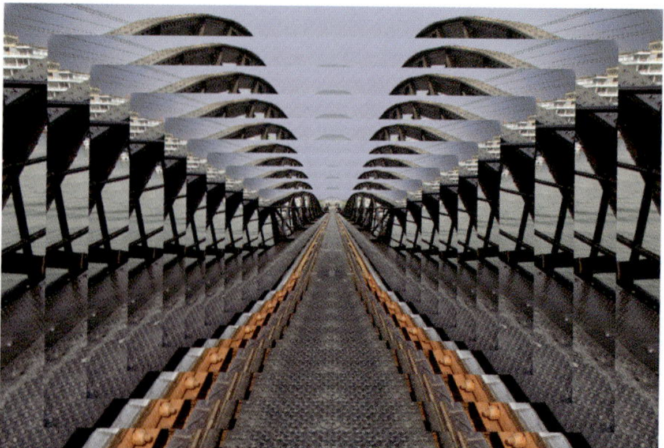

Fig. 14.4 **A railway bridge horizontally mirrored as described in Lesson 11 and repeatedly shrunk into itself. In this case, the size reductions were made in Photoshop on new layers. Each layer was centred over the original image.**

Adjusting

If the desired effect is to be, for example, the illusion of infinite recession then the sharp edges of the starting picture might intrude and give the game away. In this case, some adjustment of the image edges will be called for. Make the reduced-size layer active by clicking on it (it will probably be the top layer) and apply a layer mask (Layer > Layer Mask > Reveal All). Then paint on the layer mask with a black brush to remove the unwanted areas. It will usually help if the brush hardness is reduced (the setting at the top of the screen when the Brush tool is selected). This will prevent the appearance of a hard edge around the new layer.

In some circumstances, just a section of the original picture can be copied, shrunk and repeatedly pasted. This can add depth to a chosen section of the picture or, as in Figure 14.6, extend the reach of a spiral staircase.

There is further scope for creative adjustment by modifying the appearance of each layer as it recedes. For example, by progressively reducing the saturation of the diminishing layers, or adding increasing levels of blur as the layers appear to recede into the distance.

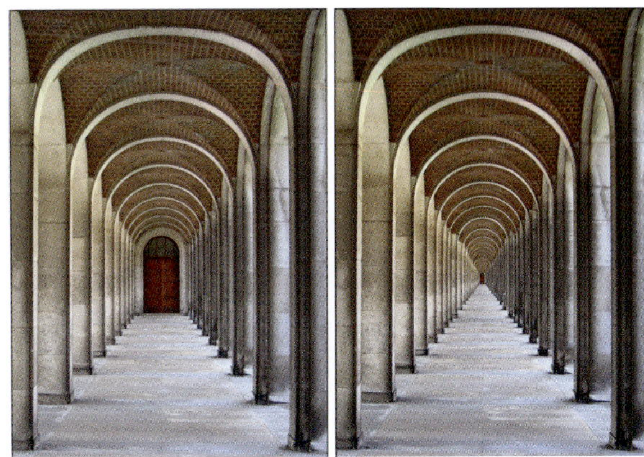

Fig. 14.5 **A walkway in Hertford County Hall extended by copying and pasting shrunken pictures of the starting picture across the original door. To prevent the hard edges of the copied pictures appearing in the result, a layer mask was used to brush out unwanted sections.**

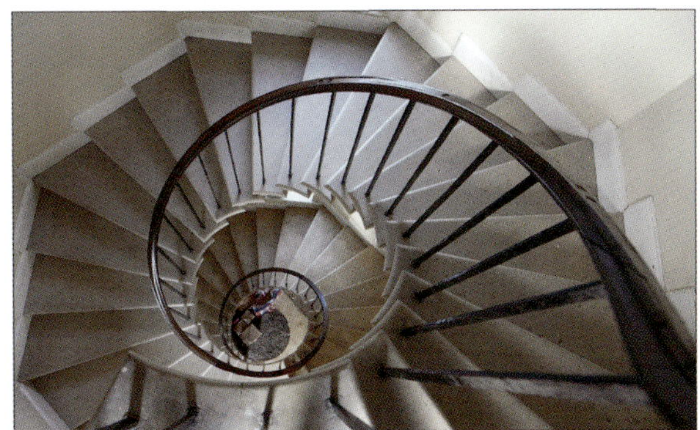

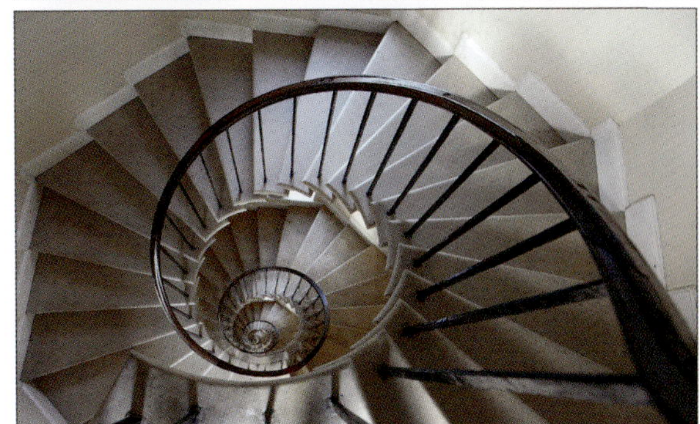

Fig. 14.6 **A circular section from the picture of a spiral staircase was copied and pasted onto the original. This has the merit of extending the spiral as well as hiding the decorative bunting on the floor.**

Surreal Effects

Recursion is often used in surrealist art and can be a rewarding area for photographic creativity. An example in painting is René Magritte's picture *The Human Condition*, which features an easel with a canvas that appears to continue the landscape behind it. Photographic examples can include portraits of people holding their own portrait or, as in Figure 14.7, a gallery displaying pictures of itself.

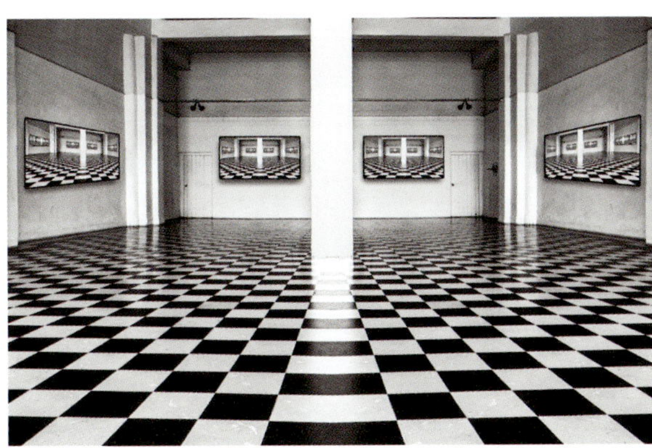

Fig. 14.7 **A surreal representation of an art gallery achieved by pasting the original picture onto the gallery walls. The outer pictures were distorted using the Photoshop Distort tool (Edit > Transform > Distort) so that they matched the perspective of the gallery walls.**

ROTATION

A frequent variation in the application of the Droste effect is to slightly rotate each of the diminished images. If each of a succession of repeated images is similarly rotated, the effect is of an infinitely receding spiral. This can be achieved in Photoshop during the sequence described earlier, by holding the cursor outside the reduced-size image until it is represented as a curved arrow. This allows rotation, with the degree of rotation displayed in the panel at the top of the screen. The rotation can then be fixed by clicking the tick or pressing Enter, but the new image can still be moved around on top of the starting picture. This can be repeated, using the same angle of rotation each time, until the reduced images are too small to view.

Fig. 14.8 **A picture of oil and water on a coloured background, repeatedly copied, reduced in size, pasted and rotated to create the spiralling Droste effect.**

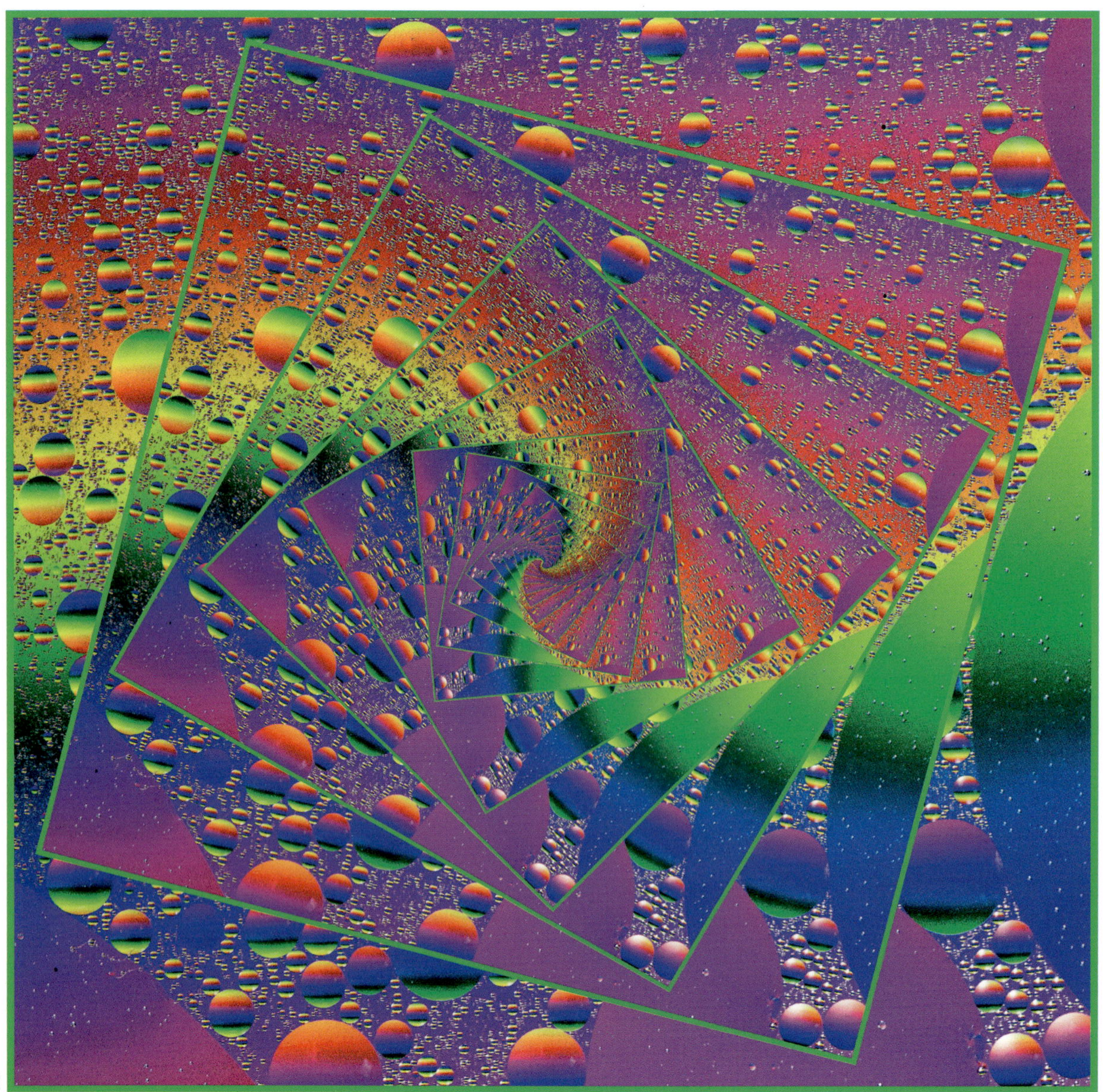

Alternative Software

Whilst Photoshop and equivalent imaging software can deliver Droste-type results, the process can be laborious if the intention is to produce complex spiralling pictures. However, alternative software can deliver rapid results and create a wider range of artistic effects. For precise mathematical control, the MathMap plugin for the graphics editor GIMP can be used, but a simpler stand-alone program specifically designed for the Droste effect is PhotoSpiralysis.

Like all photo software, PhotoSpiralysis can look daunting at first. The control sliders are different from those in photo-editing programs and are used to control the magnitude, quantity and position of the spiralling images. Once the starting picture is loaded, the effects of the variables can be viewed and adjusted to suit before saving.

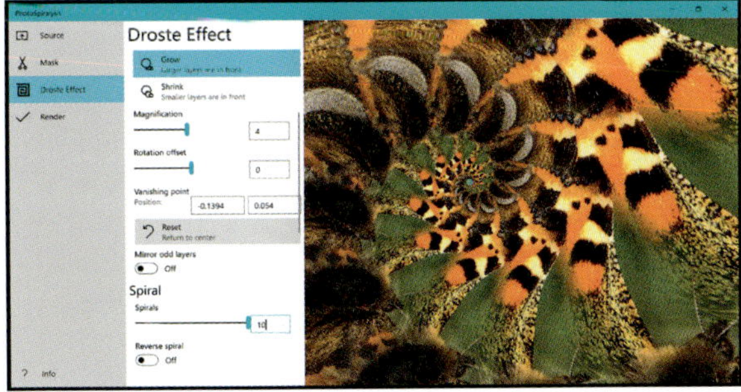

Fig. 14.9 **The control page for PhotoSpiralysis software. The image being distorted is a picture of a butterfly. The effect of the settings and the sliders can be viewed in real time before rendering and saving.**

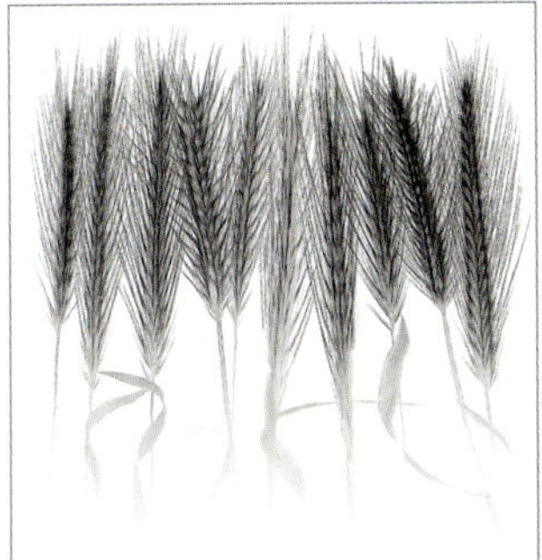

Fig. 14.10 **Ears of grass converted to black and white, alongside the image after application of the Droste effect in PhotoSpiralysis.**

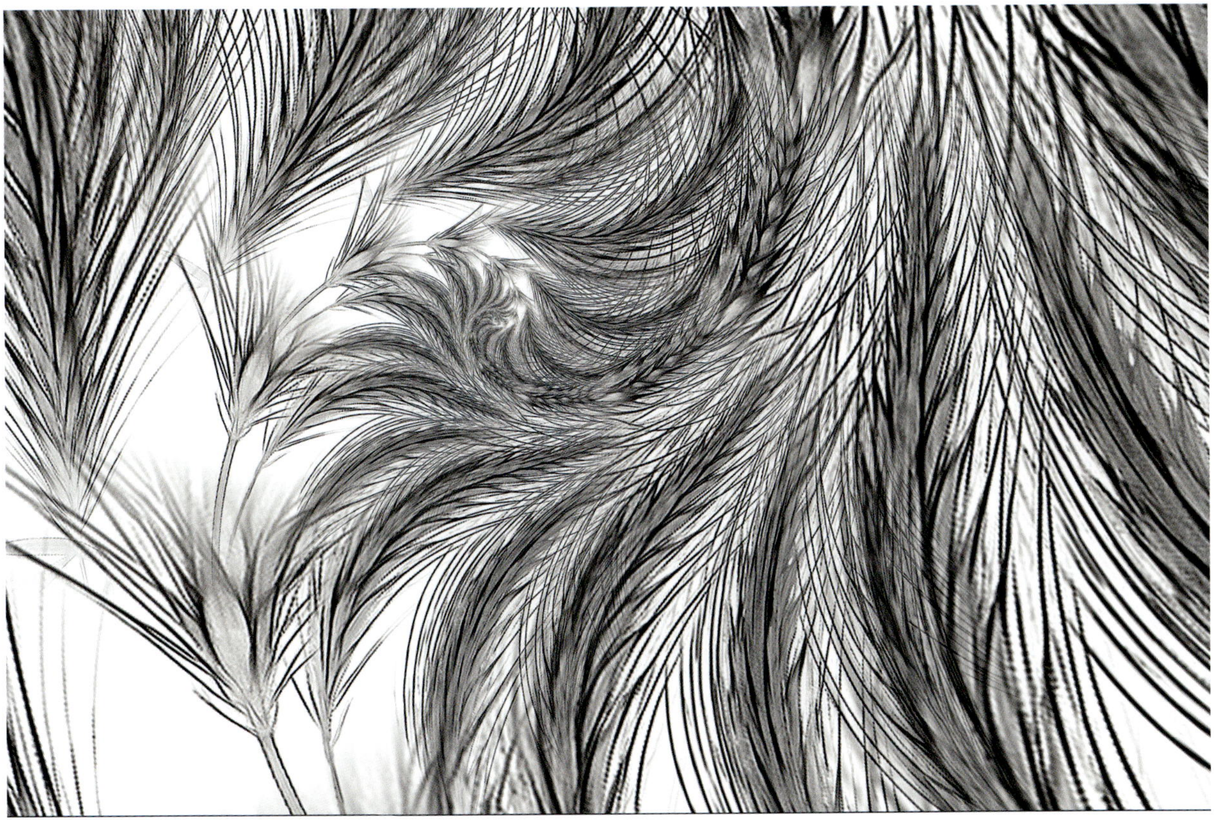

The key steps for Droste treatments in PhotoSpiralysis are as follows:

1. Open PhotoSpiralysis, www.photospiralysis.com.
2. Upload an image using Source > File.
3. Click Droste Effect and adjust the variables with the sliders and options on the interface. These are the key settings:
   Magnification controls how much the image zooms in with each recursive loop. Higher levels have a more dramatic recursion effect.
   Rotation offset adjusts the angle of the recursion to create spirals or twists.
   Position X/Y moves the focal point of the spiral to different parts of the image and shifts the centre of the Droste effect.
   Spiral sets the number of spirals in the effect.
   Other settings adjust the position of the image, with the preview updating in real time as the sliders are moved. This allows the effect to be fine-tuned. It is worth experimenting with different zoom and rotation values.
4. Click Render to process the image and chose the format and size of the result.
5. Export the result by clicking Save, choosing the format (JPEG or PNG) before saving.

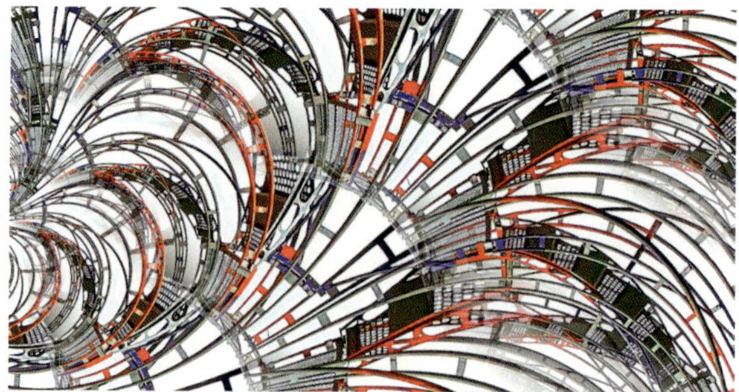

Fig. 14.11 **The PhotoSpiralysis Droste treatment applied to the mirrored picture of scaffolding in Figure 11.1.**

An interesting photographic challenge is to photograph repeating images without the use of software. These can be found when mirrors reflect in each other, as is sometimes found in elevators, or a fairground 'house of mirrors'. The so-called infinity mirror has two parallel mirrors, one of which is only partially reflective so that the full infinite sequence can be viewed. The photographic challenge is to prevent the photographer appearing in the picture. Or, of course, to include them for pictorial enhancement!

SHRINKING – KEYS

THE technique in which a picture is reduced in size and repeatedly copied into itself has been widely used in artistic compositions.

THE treatment is known as the Droste effect and can be replicated in imaging software by progressively copying, shrinking and pasting the starting picture.

THE results can be surreal in appearance, or create extended depth, for example to corridors or spiral staircases.

ARTISTIC application of the effect often involves slight rotation of each repeated image, creating a continuous spiralling loop.

SPECIALIST software is available that produces Droste images without the need for laborious repeated copying.

FACING PAGE
Fig. 14.12 **A section of a tulip with the continuous spiralling effect of the Droste treatment. The central point of the spiral was moved off centre to give a more satisfying composition.**

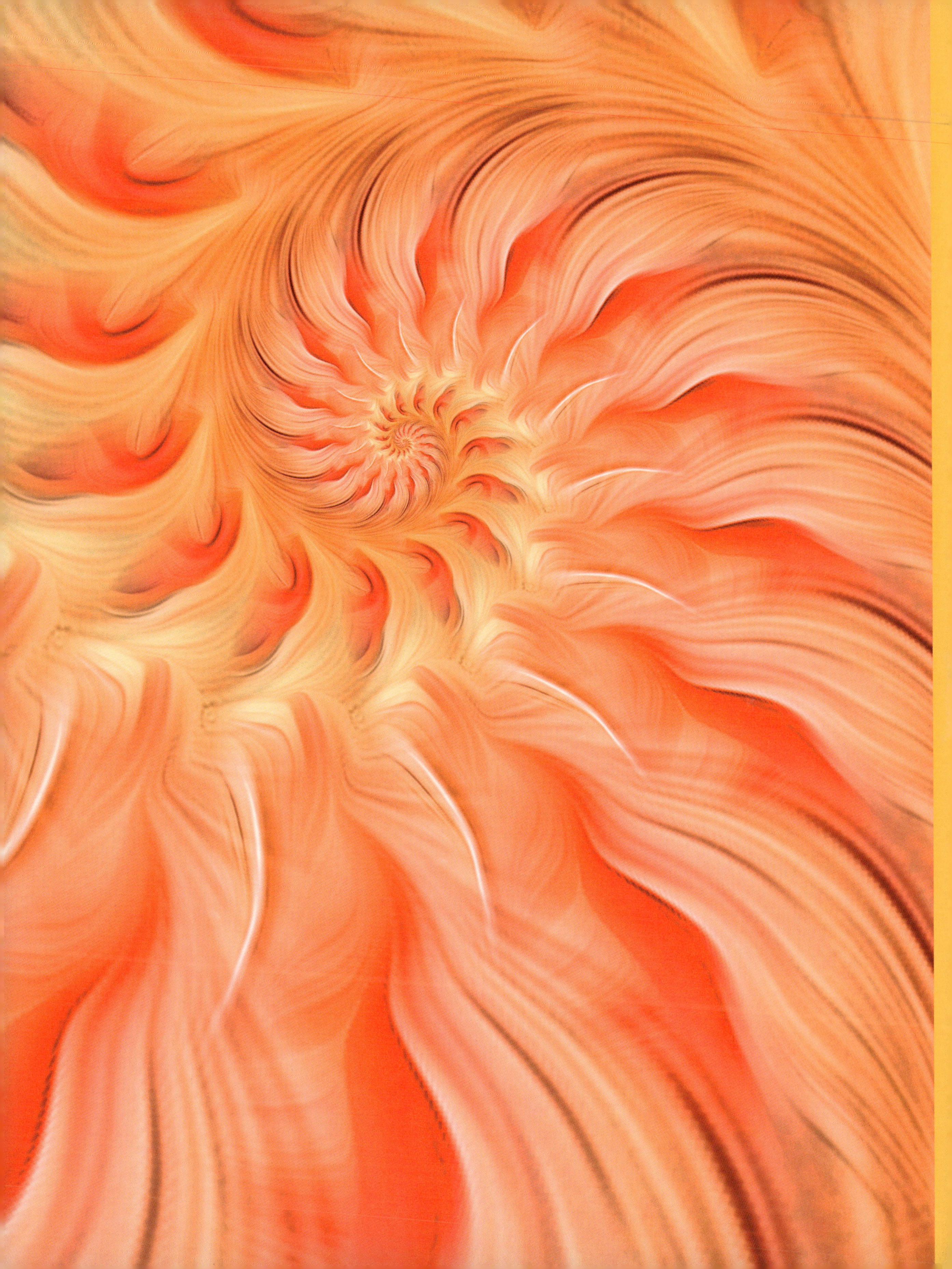

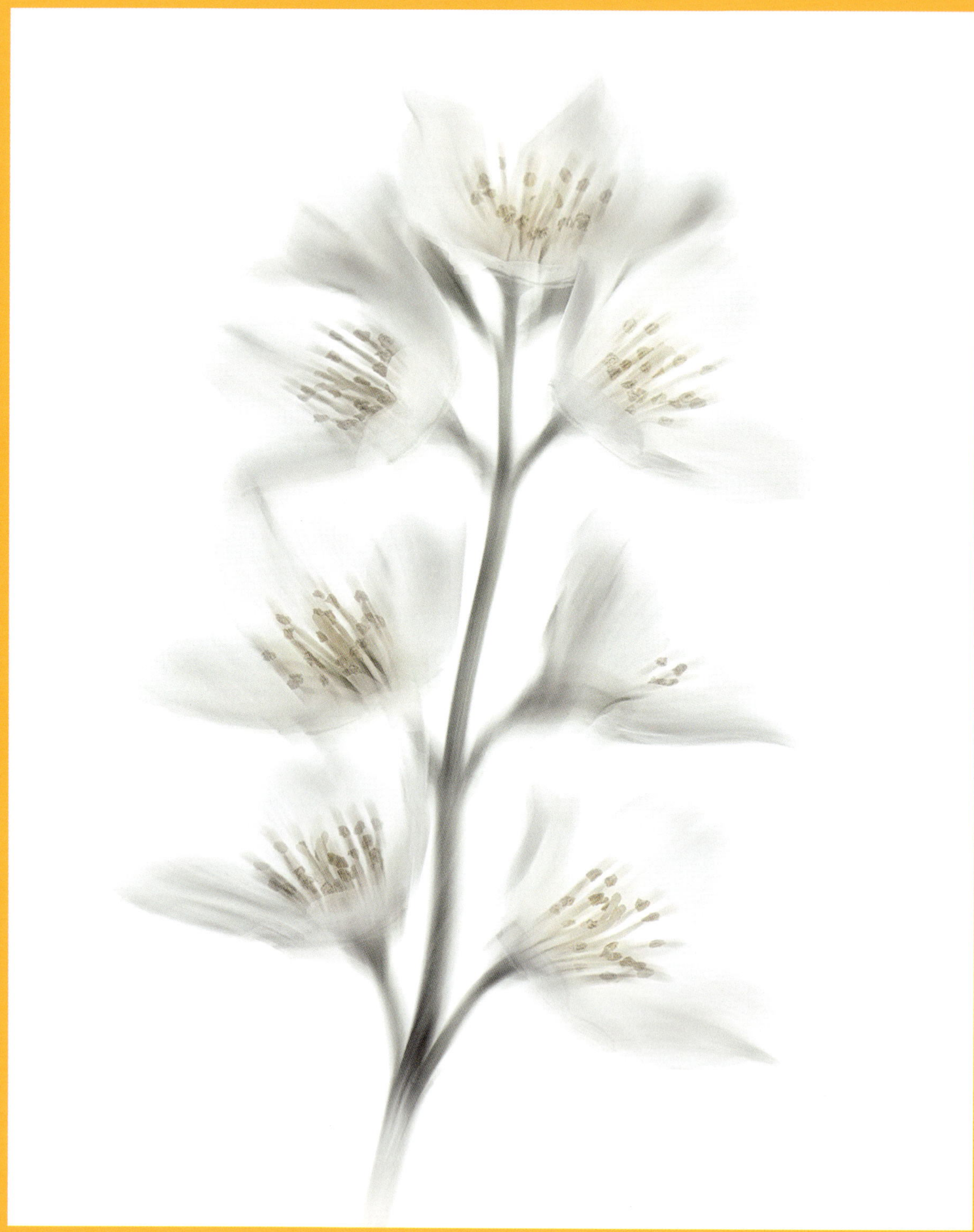

INDEX

FACING PAGE
A picture of blossom with path blur applied to the individual flowers. The image is converted to black and white and a layer mask used to reintroduce colour to the flower centres.

First published in 2025 by
The Crowood Press Ltd
Ramsbury, Marlborough
Wiltshire SN8 2HR

enquiries@crowood.com
www.crowood.com

British Library Cataloguing-in-Publication Data
A catalogue record for this book is available from the British Library.

For product safety-related questions, contact:
productsafety@crowood.com

ISBN 978 0 7198 4573 4

See more of the author's images on his website
www.johnhumphrey.co.uk

Frontispiece: Fig. 0.1 A close-up of reflections on the surface of a soap film. The image was cropped and resized using methods from Lesson 13, and recoloured and saturated using the techniques in Lesson 7.
Facing Contents: Fig 0.2 Detail of a London cityscape, isolated as discussed in Lesson 13 to present as an 'intimate landscape'.

Typeset by maru studio G.K.
Cover design by Sergey Tsvetkov
Printed and bound in India by Parksons Graphics